# AN AMERICAN PROCESSION
## 1855-1914

*Leslie's Weekly*

THE GREAT CHICAGO FIRE OF 1871

# AN AMERICAN PROCESSION

## 1855–1914

## A PERSONAL CHRONICLE OF FAMOUS MEN

*By*

## WILLIAM A. CROFFUT

*With reproductions of woodcuts from
Frank Leslie's Weekly*

BOSTON
LITTLE, BROWN, AND COMPANY
1931

5044

# INTRODUCTION

LIBRARIANS tell us that hardly anything in literature is so persistently demanded as trustworthy biographies of men who have served the public long and well; yet hardly anything is so difficult to obtain. It is lamentable that distinguished men have been so reluctant to leave behind them a record of their personal careers, coupled with some chronicle of the sayings and doings of their illustrious acquaintances. In the absence of such portraiture it will be difficult for the next generation of Americans, even with the aid of photography and moving pictures, to form an accurate mental image of the eminent men who were at the front of the stage during the last generation of the nineteenth century. As most of those whose personal annals would have enriched such a history are now gone, it remains for their surviving acquaintances to snatch from oblivion some memories of their lives for the instruction and entertainment of posterity.

In undertaking such a record, partial and fragmentary as it must be, this reporter is conscious of possessing some unusual advantages and qualifications; for, in following the chosen occupation of his life, he has met and conversed with every President of the United States from Millard Fillmore to Woodrow Wilson, and, with few exceptions in that span, with every American famous as author, artist, inventor, explorer, statesman, editor, or warrior. Some of the meetings here recorded were merely casual and fortuitous, but all that have been deemed worthy of mention, it is believed, will be seen to have some important significance in their bearing upon both personal and general history. If some of the episodes be deemed trivial, let it not be forgotten that even the most conspicuous life is largely made up of trivialities, and that some occurrences, quite unimportant in themselves and in their immediate relations, assume historic proportions when seen through the mist of years and magnified by distance.

In the presentation of this chronicle the reporter feels a keen sense of his responsibility. If errors have crept into the page, they are trifling errors. Many of the persons who were parties to the interviews are still living, and most of the residue had an opportunity to read the conversations attributed to them while they could revise them.

In repeating and arranging these conversations, it has often been found necessary, at the risk of the charge of egotism, to speak in the first person singular, in order to give some symmetry and coherence to a narrative the desultory character of which precludes logical sequence and chronological arrangement.

In one respect this volume may be regarded as a distinct novelty. It is a collection of personal interviews with famous people, most of them recorded on the same day they occurred, and the remainder recalled by a very retentive verbal memory. Whether the snatcher-up of unconsidered trifles has done a work of supererogation, and whether the reminiscences, stories, and conversations are worth recall — well, that is to be seen.

W. A. C.

# CONTENTS

# ILLUSTRATIONS

AN AMERICAN PROCESSION

WILLIAM A. CROFFUT enjoyed a long and eminent career in American journalism. From 1855, when, a boy in his teens, he took down in shorthand a speech by Daniel Webster, until his retirement at the beginning of the Wilson administration, Mr. Croffut was closely identified with the Washington scene. He knew every President from Millard Fillmore to Wilson. He was on terms of familiarity, often of intimacy, with almost every American of consequence in his time, and as an editor in chief of Eastern and Mid-Western dailies he was in a position to record with singular insight the formation of events which are now American history. His memoirs, which are published posthumously, paint a very human picture of the men who shaped our destinies for more than half a century.

THE EDITORS

# I

## A CUB REPORTER IN NEW YORK

IT IS not conceivable that the reader of this page cares whether the writer of it was born or when; but the event itself is of some consequence, for if it had not occurred he would not now be called on to occupy the office of *raconteur* and reporter-in-ordinary to some of the most famous men and women that America has produced. To save unnecessary embarrassment and loss of time as the narrative proceeds, the scribe will be permitted briefly and unceremoniously to introduce himself here.

I was born in the ancient town of Redding, Connecticut, just before I can remember; I conceived an early aversion to the stony pastures and bleak hills of the locality, and did not appreciate the great honor of first beholding daylight in the same town that had given to the world Joel Barlow, poet, diplomat, and friend of Washington, and that had furnished headquarters to General Putnam in the times that tried men's souls. Nor did I foresee the interesting fact that if I tarried permanently there I should have Mark Twain's company in curling up and spending my second childhood in this sequestered nest. Not comprehending my patriotic inheritance or my illustrious environment, I was probably delighted when my father resolved to try a change and moved the family to Orange, near the learned town of New Haven.

For the first year or two I was educated at home, and my favorite aunt often assured me that if I would be good and tried hard, I could get to be President of the United States. Very likely I could have been, but having a lot of other things to do, and early learning how much worry the office involves, I have never sought the nomination.

My life before the age of fifteen seems to have been rather purposeless and colorless. While visiting at my ambitious aunt's in Birmingham, I was fond of playing with the bright children next door. There I first saw phonography. A sedate and scholarly but ingenious and enterprising man their father was — Mr. George Kellogg. He took a most kindly interest in the curiosity which the strange characters excited and told me what they were for. He even lent me an English book of phonography, one of Isaac Pitman's earliest, and, though a busy man, he gave me some suggestions and practical hints which I afterwards made useful. His pretty little daughter Clara Louise, whom I played with, became America's great prima donna, and her father is still remembered through Connecticut as an inventor of much useful machinery and one of the most intelligent of phonographic teachers and authors.

About this time one Thomas Ranney began a desolating campaign of pothooks and trammels in Connecticut. My father encouraged all my vagaries; phonography to him was always a wonder and delight. He arranged that I should enlist under the Ranney banner, and I walked to Derby, four miles, and back three times a week to attend the evening classes. He used Andrews and Boyle's class book and reader. They were of the sixteenth edition and had just come out. The days took on a serious hue. I went around the house analyzing orally all the words I could think of and got the reputation of talking to myself. I made a feeble effort to report the sermons of our bucolic parson; but, as I did not wholly conceal my machinery, I excited his jealousy by attracting more attention than he did. Then I laid aside my pencil and followed the skeletons of words on my knee. Some of the spectators thought I was crazy, but my schoolmates considered me inspired. I persistently followed this habit of spectral phonography, if I may so call it, and it greatly assisted me in mastering the art, which I pursued with avidity and which I early determined to practise for a living.

My next impulse took the form of a desire "to get a job." I was quite incompetent for any reporting position, but of this I was unconscious and I thought I saw light ahead. In an adjoining town a good uncle of mine solaced his conscience and shriveled his pocketbook by keeping a temperance hotel. For the comfort of his guests he took a daily New York newspaper, and when they laid it down, his nephew cribbed its substance eagerly. One day I found an advertisement stating that for one dollar a lesson Mr. Theron C. Leland, "professor of phonography," would in eight lessons prepare any young man for an amanuensis and would "guarantee him a position." From the dictionary I learned what an "amanuensis" was. My father immediately arranged to have me "polished off," as he called it, and I was not long in hunting up and finding Mr. Leland in the great city. He was an alert, slender, handsome man, and he wrote the most beautiful phonography I have ever seen. He was an ideal teacher, for he was not only a graceful writer of shorthand, but a scholar withal, who knew what he was writing about and was quite capable of correcting the rhetorical or historical inaccuracies of the speaker and doing all those things which an accomplished reporter is expected to do.

My training began at once, and it was severe. The difficulties were diminished by the presence and friendly encouragement of two brilliant boys in the class: Ned Underhill, who soon got to be reporter of the Surrogate Court in New

York City, with a salary of $10,000 a year, which went as fast as it came; and Theodore Tilton, a long-legged, lank youth with blue eyes and sunny hair, a forehead like an acclivity, delicate sensibilities, quick-witted, talented, and generous, whose career I thenceforward followed with fraternal interest. He became in a few years the versatile and accomplished editor of the Independent and other important periodicals, a widely known poet, and one of the most popular lecturers on the American platform.

Mr. Leland gave his lessons in the editorial rooms of the Herald of the Union — a pro-slavery weekly newspaper, especially devoted to the interests of Daniel Webster. He received the editor's articles from dictation while his pupils looked admiringly on and followed with their tardy pencils. As the dictations were given in what was virtually a public room, the organ of the great Expounder could hardly be said to have a secret policy. This building was where the tall Western Union towers have since risen on lower Broadway, and the distinguished editor was accessible only after a climb of four flights of stairs. This gentleman was C. Edwards Lester, author of several popular books — *My Consulship, The Glory and Shame of England, History of the Bonapartes,* and so forth. He also officiated at this time as the American correspondent of the London Times.

One morning I got there before any of the office staff, and was busily writing when I heard the clump of heavy boots coming up the stairs, for in those days everybody wore top boots who could afford them. The owner of the boots paused on the upper landing, balanced himself a moment at the newel post, looked around through the empty rooms, and said, "What! Mr. Leland abed yet?" I answered that he would probably arrive very soon and pushed an armchair towards the visitor. He was a portly man, with thin hair, a lean, wrinkled face in need of the razor, beetling brows, and unfathomable gray eyes. He seemed weary. Conspicuous articles of his apparel were a very tall silk hat, a blue coat with flat brass buttons, nankeen vest, and a high inflexible stock that looked like a ring of cast iron around his neck.

"No," he said, "I will not wait. Tell him that I called — that Mr. Webster called. And I want to see him at once."

Mr. Leland came in shortly and said: "Ah, yes; Mr. Webster is in town, then. I must go over to Number Eleven. Don't you want to come along?"

It was Mr. Leland's generous and amiable custom to invite his pupils to accompany him when he called to report, and of course I went with him gladly. The Number Eleven he had mentioned was a large parlor on the second floor of the Astor House which the Expounder of the Constitution occupied whenever he was in the city. And there we presently found him. He walked leisurely up and down the room as he spoke. The dictation seemed the outline of a law speech which he was about to deliver, — perhaps the last he ever did deliver; I have forgotten where or in whose interest, — but, as he mentioned "dollars" frequently, I have since fancied that it perhaps had something to do with the tariff, then a foremost topic of discussion. Mr. Webster folded his hands behind him as he walked, and between his sentences emitted a slight buzzing or humming sound from his lips — a peculiarity which I have never seen referred to. I had my notebook and was very much astonished at the extreme slowness of the orator's dictation. He spoke on that occasion not more than fifty or sixty words a minute, and it could not have been difficult to follow him in longhand. The "mighty Daniel" looked the sick man that he was, and his various infirmities were emphasized by the deep disgust that had taken possession of him when General Taylor was nominated over him at

Philadelphia in 1848 and when General Scott was given similar precedence in the nominating convention at Baltimore in 1852. To have two "ignorant frontier colonels" preferred to him was more than his proud soul could endure.

I remember a phonographic feat of my teacher's which would still be considered very remarkable — indeed I do not think it has ever been repeated or paralleled. Mr. Leland announced a lecture on the novelty, Phonography, and during his address Mr. Lester appeared on the platform and said: "It is well enough known that I am the American correspondent of the London Times. Mr. Leland is my amanuensis. I will now dictate to him, in your presence, my regular weekly letter. He will take it down as fast as I utter it, put his phonographic notes in an envelope, without reading over, seal it in your presence, and post it to-night, and it will go to England by the morning steamer and be set up by a typesetter in the London Times office who understands phonography, and it will be printed exactly as you hear it spoken." The programme was followed out and Lester's letter appeared in the Thunderer without being revised or read over either by the author or by the reporter. This extraordinary triumph of a mysterious art gave my teacher great prestige, and his classes were at once reënforced by pupils who caught his own enthusiasm. He was one of the most industrious, faithful, humane, and earnest of men.

At the end of my prescribed course Mr. Leland promptly said, "Very well, sir, your term is ended. What next?"

"Work," I said, "if I can." His question seemed to lack positiveness. I inferred that he was quite as doubtful about my competency as I was myself, but he added, "There's nothing like trying, is there? I have spoken to a man named Pray who sometimes has work for a phonographer, and I will give you a note to him."

He wrote a few hasty lines, enclosed them, and handed them to me.   I was not long in finding the handsome residence of Isaac C. Pray, No. 23 Irving Place, close to the great Academy of Music.   It was a bashful and awkward boy who rang the door bell and handed in an improvised card, and the note.   Bridget reappeared presently and briefly said, "Folly me!"

I did.   My disqualifications seemed mountainous as I walked through the hall and presented myself to Mr. Pray, who wheeled in his cushioned chair as I went in, looked surprised, and exclaimed, "Dear me!   A mere stripling!"

This was discouraging, but in lieu of something more sensible I said, "I have grown quite a little this last year, sir." He laughed, took me by the hand, and said, "However, young man, it is n't age that always tells, is it?"

Not thinking of anything better to say, I answered, "No, sir, it is n't.   I am older than I look."   Thinking it over afterwards, it occurred to me that this was malapropos, but he laughed again, as if I had said a very bright thing.

"Can you report?" he suddenly asked.

I have admired myself ever since, because I had the self-possession and mendacity to look him straight in the eye and answer, "Yes, sir."

"How many words a minute?" And I ventured audaciously, "A hundred or a hundred and fifty."   I ought to have said fifty or seventy-five.

I must have turned scarlet, for I felt myself a guilty thing whose sins were about to be exposed.

"Let's try it," he said, and motioned me to a table.   He spoke five or six minutes perhaps, and then stopped to take breath.   "Now read it," he said.

How I ever got through it I cannot now conceive, but he remarked approvingly, — or reprovingly, — "Ah! you remembered it, you rascal!"

I felt now that my doom was just as good as sealed. He had guessed right, for at least half of the paragraph was attributable to a good memory. I was greatly relieved when he continued, "Perhaps you 'll do. Can you earn eight dollars a week? Suppose you begin by running errands!"

"Yes, sir," I answered. "It will give me pleasure to be of use to you."

"You will board with me," he resumed; "breakfast, eight; dinner, six — be punctual! Meanwhile you can take this down to the Herald office and deliver it to Mr. Bennett in person. In person. Be sure and leave it!" And he handed me a large sealed envelope from his desk. I took it, bowed myself out, and in a few minutes found my way to the den where the elder Bennett forged his thunderbolts. It was at the top of a building adjoining the American Museum at the junction of Broadway and Park Row, and Underhill had pointed it out to me as a fearsome cavern where ambitious reporters were tortured. I trembled as I handed the great man the parcel.

The Scotch editor who terrorized New York at that time was, as I recall him, rough-hewn and bony, six feet high, with a harsh and strident voice, a crescent of white whiskers under his chin, and so terribly cross-eyed that when he looked at me with one eye, he looked out at the City Hall with the other.

"Who from?" he bluntly asked, without taking the document.

"Mr. Isaac C. Pray," I answered.

"Nothing to do with Mr. Isaac C. Pray! Nothing to do with Mr. Isaac C. Pray!" he exclaimed angrily. But he took the parcel and tore off the envelope, disclosing a quantity of printed matter. With a savage gesture he flung it out the door into the hall, fixed me with one good eye, and shouted, "I don't want it! I won't have it! Carry it back and tell

him to keep his stuff!" And he turned his back on me. I
went out at once and collected the matter before it could blow
away, but not before I had discovered it to consist of galley
proofs. Notwithstanding the order "Be sure and leave it," I
made my way up town again with it, bewildered and amazed
at the reception, and wondering if my job depended on the
singular performances and ungovernable temper of the master
of the Herald. I was reassured by my reception at Irving
Place, where the author pleasantly accepted the package,
merely exclaiming, "Yet that fool once got his living as a
proofreader!"

Without more mystery or concealment Mr. Pray now took
me into his confidence.

"You must say nothing at any time to any person of anything you may hear in this house," he said quietly. "Or of
my business." He added, "I have undertaken to write a
life of Mr. Bennett, rather against his protest. He does n't
like the idea wholly and gets angry about it. He is odd, but
will come round all right. These are some of the early
proof sheets, and I wanted to give him a chance to revise them
and correct any errors. Bennett does not want his life written
at all, and declares he will not contribute a word." Here-
upon the author handed me the rejected proofs to read, saying
I had "better get the hang of it."

It was still a riddle to me, as week after week I went on
making copy from his dictation, and the riddle was not wholly
solved when the handsome finished book issued, the next
year, from the press of Stringer and Townsend. In the introduction as there printed will be found the following illu-
minating paragraph: —

The author of these pages has sought no person's counsel upon
his theme or its mode of treatment. Neither Mr. Bennett nor any

one connected with him has been consulted either directly or indirectly, with respect to the writing or publication of these memoirs. It would have been easy, had circumstances permitted and he been willing, for Mr. Bennett himself to supply some points in his career which he alone can justly elucidate; but the desire of the author has been to be free from influences which might arise from personal inquiry.

It is obvious that Mr. Pray had imposed upon himself a terribly difficult task: to write a friendly biography of an unfriendly man without the active assistance or even the passive sympathy and acquiescence of the subject of it, and even under his prohibition. The reader who desires to know how that herculean labor was accomplished is referred to the volume itself — *Memoirs of James Gordon Bennett and His Times.*

As a manuscript maker I managed to give satisfaction, for Mr. Pray was fortunately very amiable and not very exacting, and he had many callers to occupy his time. I was repelled once more in a second visit to the Herald, but I always suspected, though I never knew, that while the volume was in course of preparation, Mr. Bennett's wrath subsided without being placated.

There were eight persons, if I remember correctly, around the dinner table the first night of my employment. I talked as little as possible, for I immediately discovered that silence was my rôle. It was far the most brilliant company I had ever met. The conversation ran on the latest books, the latest plays, the latest songs, the new magazines, and, generally, what was going on in Bohemia. The second or third day Mr. Pray pushed across the table to me a little brown envelope containing two tickets to hear the great Forrest, asking me, "Have you heard him?"

"No, sir," I said, delighted, "I have never been to the theatre but once — that was to hear Mr. Burton the other night as Toodles."

"Good thing! Good thing!" he exclaimed; "and you'll be delighted with Forrest in *Macbeth*. He is having wonderful success at the Broadway, you know."

I did n't know, but I kept that to myself.

By this time I had come to harbor a respectful curiosity concerning the people with whom I was breaking daily bread and to whom I had been barely presented. So I asked Ned Underhill who they were.

"Well," he answered, "they are lots of things. They are literary 'fellows.' They are theatre sharps. I have done some work for Pray, myself."

"He gave me some tickets to Forrest the other night," I said.

"Well he might!" he exclaimed. "He has the entrée of all the greenrooms in the city. He used to edit the *Journal of Commerce* and, later, the *Ladies' Companion*. Now he writes for the Sunday News. He was manager of the Park Theatre for years. And, bless your soul! He's a highly successful actor himself. Before 1850 he played Hamlet, Othello, Sir Giles Overreach, and Shylock at the Queen's Theatre in London. Did n't you know he wrote the farce entitled *Here She Goes and There She Goes,* also several serious plays like *The Hermit of Malta?* Oh, he's a great boy! And don't you know that it is his sister, Miss Malvina Pray, who has made such a hit at the Broadway?"

I was astonished. I felt that my genial friend had pumped me full of information, and I sat up late that night receiving dictation, the better to qualify myself for my work. Mr. Pray himself later expanded this information by telling me that in 1850 and '51 he was the musical and dramatic editor of the Herald, and that he resigned that position to become manager of the National Theatre. I drew some inferences and kept still.

It now seemed to me as if I had struck a permanent job, as it certainly was an agreeable one.

The front parlor was the workshop. It was small and frequently crowded. When my presence for any reason was undesirable, Mr. Pray would toss a bit of blank paper to me across the table, saying, "Take that to Harris." He had reminded me that this was the authority of Mrs. Gamp. "And," said he, "this is a Dickens household and these were Dickens's headquarters. He went from here to the banquet in 1842 on Washington Irving's arm. And there probably never was so much embarrassment round a dinner table as when Irving, the chairman, broke down in his presentation speech."

Mr. Pray sometimes kept me up late by dictating dramatic reviews for the city newspapers after a play, and I soon learned that he was not only a regular critic, but was considered an authority on actors and acting. He often gave me a ticket to some theatre, and thus I heard Junius Brutus Booth as Richard III.

One morning the great American tragedian, Edwin Forrest, stepped in. I recognized him immediately without the masquerading make-up of Macbeth. He had now attained not only distinction but, unfortunately, notoriety, for he had fomented the Astor Place riots on account of jealousy of the great Englishman Macready then acting in New York, which resulted in the death of twenty-two exasperated citizens and the wounding of a hundred more, and Mrs. Forrest had sought and obtained her divorce after a long contest.

All his life Forrest longed to be a comedian, though he had the very face of Melpomene, the frame of Virginius, and a voice of thunder. No man was ever more obviously fitted to his rôle and his environment. Capable of great tenderness

and genuine emotion, he was turbulent and aggressive in expression and a giant in stature.    I saw him many times during
those months and sometimes, at Mr. Pray's request, received
from him the dictation of a letter.    But his quarrel with Macready had soured him and he was already past the meridian
of his powers.

Forrest had cavernous eyes and a magnificent head, topped
with a wealth of dark, tousled hair.    He was a very handsome
man.    I recall hearing a prolonged conversation, or rather a
monologue, about his Congressional ambitions.    "You can
and you shall go to the Senate," exclaimed Pray.    "See what
incredible idiots this state has sent there!"    "Thank you —
thank you — for the classification!" said the actor, and they
both laughed heartily.

The subject was a favorite one and was often resumed.
Pray used to excite Forrest's pride and ambition by painting
in rosy colors the career of a statesman and forecasting the
day when "America's greatest orator" should fashion legislation and in thunder tones advocate great causes under the
central dome at Washington.    The actor was fascinated by
the picture, although he had often played Claude Melnotte
and was now asked to essay the rôle of Pauline.    He really
wanted to go to Congress, for he felt that only there could there
be a proper recognition of his eloquence.    He said one day
to a bevy of his admirers, "What is an actor's fame?    'T is
nothing — nothing!    'T is here, 't is gone!    Its breath evapor-
ates in the cheers that make the rafters ring."    This sounded
like poetry, and I never knew whether it was a quotation or
impromptu from the habit acquired in a life of blank verse.
I have since read of Mrs. Siddons apostrophizing the careless
waiter in tragic tones that made him tremble.    "You 've
brought me water, boy!    I asked for beer!"    Forrest was
lionized by the masses and a local committee waited on him

and submitted a plan of the campaign for Congress. But his hard life had told upon him. Symptoms of paralysis appeared which put an end to all his forensic ambitions.

I often saw Forrest afterwards. As I summon up a picture of him through the intervening years he seems to have been a Farnesian Hercules in a dress coat. He was tall — a human mastodon. Such colossal calves! Such biceps! The author of the *Gladiator* obviously knew for whom he was writing. Every Macduff found Forrest's Macbeth a tough customer to tackle, and sometimes created amusement by the way in which he used to shy at Forrest's onsets. Forrest did not like Hamlet or any quiet part, but preferred the characters cast for his own legs and larynx, like Metamora, Jack Cade, William Tell, Spartacus, and Tecumseh.

Another of the royal line of monarchs of the American stage I met about this time. One evening came a violent and aggressive *rub-a-dub* in the Pray vestibule, like a volley of musketry. When the door was opened it admitted a grotesque inebriate who staggered to the sideboard and grabbed the decanter. His coat was much too small for him, his necktie was erected under his left ear, and he spoke with an inimitable stutter as he clutched the empty air above his smashed white hat and took up the rôle which he had rendered so familiar. Yes, it was verily the same old "Toodles," in which he had appeared more than seven hundred times. Miss Malvina ran into the hall; in fact, the whole household appeared and shouted a welcome. We were in the presence of the leader of the dramatic profession of the United States. Burton reversed the preference of Forrest. He always wanted to be a tragedian, and insisted that he should have made an unparalleled success, while his whimsical face was a perfect mask of Momus and he was one of the drollest creatures that ever lived. In private he was sometimes phlegmatic and saturnine, but when he stepped over the footlights, he was the vivacious impersonation of fun.  A heavy jowl, a twisted nose, a lopsided face, thin and wandering hair, a mouth like Colley Cibber's, twinkling eyes, a laugh-provoking, strident, stammering voice — this was Burton.  He was the king of low comedy.  He had made his own such characters as Bob Acres, Sir Toby Belch, Falstaff, and Aminadab Sleek, and he had literally created the stage Micawber, Sam Weller, Captain Cuttle, Mark Tapley, Bunsby, and twenty others of the splendid Dickens galaxy.  It is needless to say that the man who could present to his audiences both Sam Weller and Caleb Plummer must have possessed an immense fund of humor underlaid with a tender pathos.

This remarkably productive genius not only gathered about him a company including Lester Wallack, Joseph Jefferson, Laura Keene, Billy Florence, Miss Malvina Pray, the accomplished dancer whom Florence presently married, and the talented wives of A. H. Davenport, Edwin Booth, and John Brougham, but he had written a play, *Ellen Wareham,* which had the unprecedented distinction of being acted at five theatres in London at the same time.  I learned all this from dinner-table conversations.

I was of course immensely interested in the personnel of my temporary domicile.  It was unique.  One evening the partition of the dining room slid noiselessly aside like a piece of stage scenery, and the table was drawn out to seat twenty persons instead of eight.  It was a theatre party.  I was not invited, but I had met several people who were there.  Voices that penetrated my room proclaimed a convivial evening and a jolly assembly of the devotees of the sock and buskin.

I was not long in discovering that well-defined hostilities still existed between Mr. Bennett and his biographer.  In the "Moral War" which had been waged for years against the

Herald by almost all the newspapers of New York, the object of which was its suppression and annihilation, Mr. Pray had defended Mr. Bennett, but not in that exclusive and whole-hearted manner which the editor claimed as a right.  Pray, a highly educated and refined man, insisted that the assailants, whom he called "assassins of character," were indeed a disgrace to journalism and to the city, but he also insisted that in the battle of invective and vituperation Mr. Bennett had placed himself upon their level.  This is a sufficient explanation of his repudiation of the volunteer biographer.  But Mr. Pray did not shrink from his self-imposed task.  He said in the book: —

While censuring the indiscriminate attacks made upon Mr. Bennett, where the most indecorous treatment was used towards those connected with him without regard to sex or to those chivalrous restraints which subdue passion and malignity even in their most fiery moods, be it not understood that any recriminations by the Herald are justified.  They are just as censurable as the assaults of which complaint is made.  All such personalities are disgraceful, spring whence they may, and provoked by whatever injustice and wrong.  No mind cultivated by taste and education can view them with anything less than loathing and contempt.

As a specimen of the prolonged battle of indecency, a hand grenade from the enemy, with only a portion of its powder remaining, may show that vile combustibles were used by the "moral" editors: —

Stigma on the city — obscenity and profanity — vicious and depraved — corrupting influence — vice and vulgar licentiousness — hypocrisy, ignorance, and bloated conceit — most diabolical and execrable — double apostate and traitor — liar and poltroon — political Iago — half crazy, uneducated wretch — slipshod, ribald style — profligate ridicule and impious jests — immoral and blas-

THE INTRODUCTION OF GREELEY AND BENNETT AT THE EVERETT HOUSE,
NEW YORK CITY

phemous monstrosity — a vagabond who fled his country — wretch
— pest — villain — forger — blackmailer, etc.

To such a broadside of envy, hatred, and malice Mr. Bennett
laconically replies: —

These blockheads are determined to make me the greatest man
of the age.  Newspaper abuse made Mr. Van Buren chief magistrate of this republic, and newspaper abuse will make me the chief
editor of this country.  Well, — be it so.  I can't help it.

The first years of the Herald had been years of desperate
poverty, disappointment, and failure.  Mr. Bennett made
the paper inoffensive and even prudish.  He was without
money and without friends.  Frequently he could not pay for
paper for the next edition.  But he was determined to succeed
and at last found that he could do it only by constantly
piquing curiosity and exciting alarm.  He tried and adopted
a decent and dignified course at first, and pursued it until it
was obvious that if he persisted in it the paper could not exist
for a single month.  He then became the father of sensational
journalism — the "yellow" product of the times.  He assailed
the character and impugned the motives of distinguished
citizens, with a result that might have been foreseen, and
perhaps was.  He was assaulted upon the street with clubs
and knocked down three times in as many weeks.  After
one of these assaults he made a humorous report of it, saying,
"My damage is a mere scratch," and adding: —

As to intimidating me, or changing my course, the thing cannot
be done.  I tell the honest truth in my paper and leave the consequences to God.  I may be attacked, I may be murdered, but I
never will succumb.  I never will abandon the cause of truth,
morals and virtue.  To me, these attacks, lies, are as the idle wind.

They do not ruffle my temper. Conscious of virtue, integrity and the purest principles, I can easily smile at the assassins and defy their daggers. My life has been one invariable series of efforts, useful to the world and honorable to myself, to create an honorable reputation during life, and to leave something at my death for which posterity may honor my memory. I am building up a newspaper that will take the lead of all others that ever appeared in the world, in virtue, in morals, in science, in knowledge, in industry, in taste, in power and influence. My whole private life has been one of virtue, integrity, and honorable effort in every relation of society. I mean to make the Herald the great organ of social life, the prime element of civilization. I shall mix commerce and business, pure religion and morals, literature and poetry, the drama and dramatic purity, till the Herald shall outstrip everything in the conception of man.

The other newspapers shake their sides with ribald laughter at this exhibition of egotism and effrontery. The braggart is set upon by Tray, Blanche, and Sweetheart, but they have serious moments, too — these scoffing editors. They wish they could guess the riddle of this Sphinx of journalism. He calls upon God, Christ, and the Virgin Mary so often that they hail him blasphemer; he protests his own personal virtue with an earnestness that is very comical, and they call him hypocrite. But above the racket of their railing is heard a complacent voice venturing to prophesy that the Herald will be the champion of truth, honesty, and virtue after they are all dead, and they know not what to think. They had seen this magician establish the Herald with less than five hundred dollars in his pocket. They had seen him repeatedly knocked down and rise from the prostration as if refreshed, merely remarking the next day, "The Herald is producing as complete a revolution in the intellectual habits of daily life as steam power is in the material. If a splendid fortune shall result for myself, that may be a matter of complacency, but it is a matter of course."

To this magnificent forecast the unanimous press of the city would belch forth its volley of abuse. It called the offensive editor virago, vixen, Xantippe, public scold. One of them erected a gallows to hang him on, and another prepared a ducking stool at the Battery. The hostility of the large and rich papers to this impudent intruder knew no bounds.

He gave his enemies as good as they sent, "and worse," as Sir Boyle Roche might say. Bennett was not a gifted writer, but his columns bristled with exclamations, interrogations, sneers, lampoons, reprimands, sardonic grins. They flung at each other Billingsgate and the argot of thieves, till all the combatants were in danger of being suffocated in the reek and effluvium of their unsavory battlefield. The Herald was small and lively. The big papers were chagrined and maddened past endurance to see its jocose, scandalous, and quizzing paragraphs sought for and laughed over while their own brilliant essays were ignored. His motto was, "Never be more than a day ahead of the people, and never an hour behind."

I, an unsophisticated youth in my teens, and quite unacquainted with the great world's way, had but a vague comprehension of the dreadful tumult, and only a shadowy conception of the singular character of Mr. Bennett and his relation to the public. It was only when I absorbed the spirit of the book by a reperusal that I became thoroughly acquainted with the curious controversy.

While condemning Mr. Bennett for the Herald's bad manners, Mr. Pray could not help adding in extenuation: —

The dark character of journalism was necessary to educate the people into the enjoyment of a higher style of art, just as negro minstrelsy was necessary.  Persons of fashionable habits and wishing to be esteemed patrons of the arts and admirers of literature, would not support Mr. Bennett while the Herald was in its infancy, modest, prudish, and daintily fashioned.  He tried them, and they sorely tried him.  He could not prosper.  In other words, he could not attract public attention till he caricatured himself physically and morally, mentally and editorially, and became, to all outward appearance, that which he had never been.  He must be a mountebank.  He must blacken his face, or the public would not look at him.  Mr. Bennett might have written in prose or verse, with the force and elevated fervor of a Milton, yet, in the city of New York, he would not have sold newspapers enough in the year, to furnish him with shilling dinners, provided he honestly paid, as was ever his wont, his printers and paper-makers.

When Mr. Bennett married and returned from his honeymoon with his bride, the newspapers of New York leagued together to compel the manager of the Astor House to refuse to entertain them on the ground that they were immoral persons!  He did not resent the dastardly conduct except to say: —

Praise and dispraise — abuse and condemnation — are equally thrown away on me.  Born in the midst of the strictest morality, educated in the principles of the highest integrity, inclined, from the first impulses to existence, to be a believer in human virtue, I have grown up holding with a death grasp to the original elements of my soul, while every new discovery has but revealed a deeper depravity in every form both in this country and Europe.  I have seen human depravity to the core.  I proclaim each morning the deep guilt that is encrusting society.  What is my reward?  I am called a scoundrel — a depraved wretch — a vile calumniator — a miserable poltroon — these anonymous assassins of character are leagued and stimulated by the worst men in society — by speculators — by pickpockets — by sixpenny editors — by miserable hypocrites, whose crimes and immoralities I have exposed, and shall continue to expose as long as the God of Heaven gives me a soul to think and a hand to execute. Slanders the most vile and dastardly that blackness of heart can conceive are circulated against the Herald and my personal character — a character that has never yet been stained either in the old world or the new.

When forecasting the destiny of the Herald its master speaks like an inspired prophet on some mountain of vision. The Herald before 1840 is full of these marvelous predictions. For instance: —

When I started on my own hook last Spring I could not, to save my soul, get credit from friend or foe for five dollars. With industry, talent, and reputation acknowledged on all hands, I was cried down by some secret influence, attempted to be trampled on, and even audaciously assailed in the open street by the very persons I had spent years in supporting and raising in the scale of society. I never quailed — I never feared — I never saw the man I dreaded to meet face to face, or the obstacle I would not attempt to surmount.

I go for hard work, just principles, an independent mind, a name that will last for ages after my death, and a place in the glorious hereafter, side by side with the greatest master spirit and the purest benefactor of the human race.

My ambition is to make the newspaper press the great organ and pivot of government, society, commerce, finance, religion, and all human civilization. I want to leave behind me no castles, no monuments of marble, no statues of bronze, no pyramids of brick — simply a name. The name of James Gordon Bennett as one of the benefactors of the human race will satisfy every desire and every hope.

I mean to link my life, character, fortune, faith, all with the Herald. If I live, I know I shall succeed in my purpose, for I never yet set my heart upon a thing that I did not accomplish it.

To the obloquy and reviling of the current newspaper press resounding through the country, Mr. Bennett calmly answered: —

I have been a wayward, self dependent, resolute, free-thinking being from my earliest days. Yet there were implanted in my burning soul those lofty principles of morals, honor, philosophy and religion, that the contumely of the world cannot shake or all the editors or bankers in Christendom intimidate. I feel myself, in this land, engaged in a great cause — the cause of truth, public faith, and science, against falsehood, fraud, and ignorance. I would not abandon it even to reach the glittering coronet of the extinct title of the Duke of Gordon.

I bear a charmed existence. Neither fire nor sword nor steel nor competition nor hate nor abuse nor falsehood nor slander nor indictment nor persecution in a thousand forms can quench my spirit or impede my movements. I do sincerely believe that some superior power watches over me.

How gentlemen of taste, refinement, and education could carry on so absurd a warfare for ephemeral notoriety is indeed surprising. But it went on and on till every vestige of character seemed to be lost by every belligerent. The afflicted public appears to have regarded the combatants only as tragedians who die on the stage at night and come to vigorous life in the morning. And so the campaign of swashbucklers persisted, the garrulous scolds persuading themselves that they were dealing with brother bandits and that the safety of society required that they should be deemed bestial and despicable.

It is not necessary to call attention to the tremendous improvement in editorial courtesy since the days of the elder Bennett. If editors of the New York newspapers of the present day should conduct themselves towards each other as did Weed, Bennett, Greeley, Raymond, Webb, and their contemporaries, they would not survive the derision with which they would be greeted.

While in New York I had seen the poet N. P. Willis a good many times. I had been delighted with his *Letters from Under a Bridge* and, boylike, sought every opportunity to get a glimpse of the brilliant author. There was a bookstore in Union Square which I had heard he was in the habit of visiting, and thither I went and lay in wait for him. About the third morning I saw him and shadowed him — followed him quietly around till I heard the proprietor address him by name. Then I was happy. I stole to his side and clandestinely inspected him. A pair of bright eyes, I remember, a graying reddish beard, long hair flowing almost in ringlets, a soft "Kossuth" hat, with broad wayward brim and crown irregularly indented, a vest of yellow cut velvet, and a large black brigandish cloak drawn around his trim figure. I feasted on him. I gloated over the privilege with youthful enthusiasm. He went away. I moved along and stood exactly where he had stood. He vanished. I followed him. To the sidewalk. To the corner. To an omnibus — I thought his hands the handsomest man's hands I had ever seen. I was ashamed to follow him further, but I went away radiant, and said to myself, "I have seen another great man." And so I had — one of the most remarkable of his kind. At a later day I learned that the critics declared Willis's style artificial and affected. It always seemed to me exceedingly natural. It was not simple; it was complex and fantastic, but it was natural — to him. But I have always wondered how "Absalom's Lament" and other religious poems which I had wept over at school could ever have been written by such a dilettante, exquisite, and leader of fashion as this man became.

Willis was cordially loved, not only by his own family, in which he was a model husband and father, but by his employees and by everybody who came into intimate relations with him. He had a warm, buoyant, happy nature, which reflected its colors on all.

Like most of the men who gave their lives to journalism two generations ago, N. P. Willis is forgotten now. Indeed, it does not appear that he ever aspired to permanent fame. He wrote chiefly on evanescent topics, but he produced some good poetry, and I think he would have made a great editor if he had had laid upon his shoulders the responsibilities of a daily newspaper. His delicate and refined letters descriptive of rustic life and manners were very dainty and a constant protest against the coarse and brutal journalism then prevalent. His pen dealt mostly with dress and fashion, parties, dances, coquetries, and all sorts of trivialities. If he had gone earnestly to work to extend his horizon he might have rivaled Washington Irving. He was a gifted and manly Turveydrop, a little airy maybe, a trifle egotistical maybe, but his tastes were those of a scholar and a gentleman, and he knew exactly what people liked to read.

The reader can hardly guess how disappointed and distressed I was when my services as an amanuensis on Irving Place came to a sudden end. This was announced in a letter from my mother, "We have concluded that it is best for you to come home and go to school." The summons was a great shock. In vain I pleaded that I was "now at school" — the best school that any boy was likely to have, where I was being taught the mysteries of bookmaking and the methods of accurate composition, "besides having important lessons every day in American history." This was strictly true. I did not go into details, but it seems that information had already reached my home that I had been inadvertently thrown into the company and under the influence of "play actors" and that I was somehow involved in the immoral "Moral War" on the strange and incomprehensible editor of the Herald.    In after years I discovered that it was the fear that I might drift to the stage that made my recall peremptory. The apprehension was entirely unfounded.    I was interested in the curious life of the actors whom I saw, but not attracted to share it — partly, perhaps, because I never possessed the smallest dramatic talent.

## II

## THE APPROACH OF THE CIVIL WAR

A NEWSPAPER life always attracted me strongly, and when I went home from the great city I multiplied my contributions to the local press. I had become possessed of that impetuous yearning for expression which results in assailing the ear of the world with so much adolescent wisdom. In pursuance of this tendency I secured an engagement to write editorials for a Waterbury newspaper. From the point of view of self-support this excursion into polemics was hardly worth while, for the proprietor had a constitutional disinclination to part with money and never paid me any of the meagre stipend that was promised. That was not all. I had not only written for nothing, but I had earnestly, if feebly, supported a party which I believed to be in the wrong. I now looked upon the loss of my wage as a just retribution and solemnly resolved that I would never again hire myself to advocate principles or measures in which I did not believe. I cannot affirm that I have adhered to this resolution without any exceptions, but I hope the diversions have been few and trivial. I may add that this concession to the moral sense has enabled me to do the best work of which I was capable and has been an advantage to me at every step in my life.

After leaving New York and making the Waterbury fiasco, I was sent to the Methodist Seminary at Charlotteville, New York, where there were eight hundred pupils. My father had a large and growing family, and, in spite of all that could be done, I was on a short allowance.   On arriving at my destination I went straight to the principal, Dr. Alonzo Flack, and told him that I could pay wholly for my tuition and partly for my board, and I asked him if he would permit me to make it up by teaching.   I was then seventeen, and as I look back it seems to me to have been an audacious request to make.   He looked down at me and smiled as he said: "Teach?   What in the world can you teach?"

"Grammar," I answered promptly, "and phonography."

"We have a teacher of grammar," he said, "but the other — what's that?   Oh, shorthand, is it?   We do not teach shorthand."

"I can make the class pay for it," I said, "and then I can pay you."

"What do you know about shorthand?" he asked.

"I can write pretty fast," I replied.   "Nearly as fast as you can talk."

The "Whew!" he uttered seemed a signal that he was impressed.   "Very well," said the generous and enterprising educator, — I think of him at this moment with gratitude, — "we'll try it to-morrow morning at the chapel assembly.   I will tell them what you say you can do, and you can try to report the proceedings."

I gave a gulp of joy, which was speedily turned into great apprehension when I remembered that there were eight hundred young strangers to face.   It gives me satisfaction even now to remember that I did not shirk even if I shrank. I was there.   Dr. Flack was there.   Eight hundred students were there.   He told them of my offer at the very beginning and added that I would report the exercises.   My hand and heart trembled, but I felt as if life depended on it, and scribbled as fast as I could, jotting down the opening remarks, the paternal advice to the school, and even the hymn and prayer.

Then Dr. Flack sat down and quietly said, "Now we will have a report of what we have been doing." The announcement startled me, and for a moment almost paralyzed me. But I stood up, disentangled my notes as well as I could, and secured pretty nearly a duplication of the proceedings. My report made a deep impression. Those who were present say that in repeating the prayer I unconsciously fell into the singsong intonations of the Methodist parson, combined with the obvious and special nasal twang of the principal himself. At any rate, the repetition of the prayer in lugubrious tones was an immense success, for it brought down the house with both applause and laughter. In conclusion, the principal announced that all who wished to study shorthand and become reporters would meet me at Classroom Number Four at eleven o'clock. At the appointed time the room was full. I felt as if I was mobbed. When I definitely undertook to make up a class, however, I found that they were attracted by curiosity as the chief motive. But out of a hundred some forty joined the class at once, and about twenty followed its fortunes through the term. The fault of having a small class was largely my own. I was not a very skillful teacher, and never possessed the enviable gift of imparting knowledge to others. Of those who persisted in spite of all obstacles, a few became successful reporters.

At the Seminary I listened to voluble and fervent prayers and incidentally studied geometry, algebra, Latin, and Greek. I have never ceased to regret the hours thus wasted, for I have never ascertained that I derived a particle of good from those studies which I could not have obtained much more easily in other ways. I studied Latin, Greek, and algebra when I ought to have been studying French and German, and more rhetoric, English literature, and biology, and I read Virgil, Livy, and the *Anabasis* when I ought to have been reading

Gibbon, Macaulay, Hume, Goethe, Fénelon's *Télémaque,* Paine's *Rights of Man,* Madison's *Federalist,* and Washington's letters. I am sure that the time spent on the dead languages was almost absolutely wasted, and that my days of antique study ought to have been devoted to getting information concerning live branches of knowledge, of which I was deplorably ignorant. My teachers knew no better, and are not to be censured; but without doubt the time will soon come when schools of all grades will find their chief service in giving instruction in the lines of knowledge which the student is most seriously to need in a practical career.

Of course my school days were not to be greatly prolonged. I had had a glimpse of real life — a taste of the vital interests of the world. I had seen some of the giants who wielded its forces, — the makers of public opinion, — Bennett, Edwards Lester, Pray, N. P. Willis, Greeley, Bayard Taylor, Bryant, Beecher, Webster, Forrest, Burton, Booth, Charlotte Cushman. Could I again become a contented recluse of the classroom? Not easily.

Suddenly Derby became very much excited by the announcement that the great Horace Greeley, prophet and expounder of the New Republicanism, was coming from New York to lecture to Naugatuck Valley on "Reforms and Reformers." When he came I presented myself to him and made a very full report, occupying three columns in the Derby Journal. The lecturer wrote me a note of thanks the next week, and, in reply to an application I had made, mentioned that there was a "very small position" vacant on the Leader, which he and his brother-in-law, John F. Cleveland, printed in the back part of the Tribune building. He said he thought I might like the place. I jumped at the chance, and two days later found me on hand at the office.

I was a good-sized and lively boy and I mailed the paper I

had never heard of before, wrote wrappers, read proof, and kept the books of the concern after an original fashion of my own. I was occasionally summoned by Mr. Greeley to go and report some small meeting for the Tribune. In addition to the above functions, I was sometimes called news editor, though what I did to earn the title I never found out. In recent years I have imagined it was used ironically. The Leader was a weekly, — spelt both ways; it was never a leader and is now quite forgotten. It was owned — so far as there was anything to own — by John F. Cleveland and Horace Greeley, whose sister, Esther, Cleveland married. The editor was Augustus F. Boyle, the famous promoter of Pitman's phonography, and an enterprising and accomplished Bohemian. The book reviewer was Thomas Dunn English, author of "Ben Bolt," whose "sweet Alice" was then a musical favorite with everybody.

Greeley used to shuffle in almost every noon and go to lunch with Cleveland. One day when he climbed the stairs English wheeled round on his stool with some loose sheets in his hand, and said, "Hold on, Greeley, I want to give you a valuable hint about lunch." He was tall and lithe, graceful, distinguished-looking, quite tawny, with long black hair, piercing eyes, and a pleasant voice. He read aloud what he had just finished, and this is it, for he let me copy it, and I found it in an old trunk thirty years later: —

AN ODE TO LAMB

Hind quarters of the type of innocence!
Whether with peas and mint I must dispense,
Or go the twain, blaspheming the expense,
And thus enjoy thee in the fullest sense,
        That is the Question.

*Leslie's Weekly*

HORACE GREELEY IN HIS PRIME

Rear section of young mutton! — tender food,
Just in the dawn of grass-fed juicyhood,
Dainties like thee should not be served up nude,
But graced with all the trimmings understood
    To help digestion.

Then boil the peas, the fragrant mint prepare;
Be thou, prime joint, not overdone or rare;
Concoct the gravy with exceeding care,
When all is ready, serve — I shall be there —
    I always am.

Incipient sheep's meat: When on thee I dine,
Hot be the plate and icy cold the wine,
Three slices midway of the leg be mine,
Then put the rest away, for very fine
    Is cold roast lamb.

It was unanimously voted brilliant, and Mr. Greeley laughingly remarked that it was both "rare and well done."  And he added, "Now come with us, English, and get your cold roast lamb."  It was by no means Greeley's ideal lunch, for he preferred bread and milk or crackers and cheese or some such dairy nutriment, but his challenge was joyfully accepted, — for the author of "Ben Bolt" was impecunious, — and so they shuffled down the stairs together.

Greeley was very much disgusted with the treatment "sweet Alice" received from her lover, and English lived to go to Congress from New Jersey at the beginning of the succeeding century.

It must be confessed that the Leader did not fill "a long-felt want."  It was earnestly, even enthusiastically, devoted to classical literature, poetry, art, music, phonography, and various other accomplishments of which the American public knew little and cared less.  Therefore it withered.  It was not for this world.  After three or four short months it uttered a plaintive obituary, drew its last breath, and turned up its toes to the daisies.  It was a thing of beauty while it lived, but one carriage would have held the mourners.

Home I went again.  My father was proud of my accomplishments — proud also, I imagine, of the instability and versatility which his son exhibited in occupying so many places in so short a time.  He was one of the most industrious and hardest working of men, but without hesitation he drew upon his meagre means and bought for me a half interest in the Derby Journal.  This small paper I conducted for about a year — probably to the greater satisfaction of the editor than of the community.  Then I changed my purposes anew and made an excursion into the journalism of the far-off territory of Minnesota, accepting an offer which took me first to St. Paul, where I edited the Times, and later to the frontier village of Minneapolis, just struggling into life as St. Anthony's Falls, as editor of the Falls Evening News, and then of the state Atlas.  I had a "career" to be remembered if not emulated, and during several interesting and fleeting years I harvested a large and valuable crop of experiences.

During the last year of that decade of stormy politics I returned East and established a weekly newspaper, the Jeffersonian, in Danbury, in my native state.  While thus engaged I visited Washington and found some friends there involved in a menacing controversy.  Among them was Colonel William S. King, owner of the state Atlas above mentioned.  He was a strenuous and aggressive Republican and one of the bravest men that ever lived.  He thought and vociferously declared that the slave power had cracked its whip with impunity long enough.  Passionate discussion and fiery speech were the order of the day in Congress.  Pennington was chosen Speaker of the House.  Sumner delivered his great speech, "The Barbarism of Slavery." Lincoln was elected President. It was more than could be endured. For some years Northern Congressmen had been intimidated by those of the South, the latter being generally expert swordsmen or pistol shots, and the former unfamiliar with either weapon and brought up to regard duelling with abhorrence. Several Northerners had been insulted, browbeaten, and "posted," and there was a growing feeling among Mr. Lincoln's friends that it was necessary for some "Yankee" to fight. The word was passed around, "We will be bullied no longer," and half a dozen Republicans announced that they would fight if challenged.

Mr. Roger A. Pryor, of South Carolina, rose to a question of privilege one morning, saying that at the Congressional Globe office he had discovered that Mr. Potter of Wisconsin had inserted at the end of his, Potter's, speech on the death of Elijah P. Lovejoy the words: "The Republicans will be heard, in this House, let the consequences be what they may." No such words, Mr. Pryor alleged, had been uttered in the debate.

Mr. Potter hotly contradicted this assertion and declared that he had used the words referred to and that Pryor had erased them from the Record, and added, "He had no right to do it. It was none of the gentleman's business. I stand by what I said."

The words are not properly challengeable, perhaps, but those were hot times, and Pryor sent a challenge and escaped to Virginia to avoid arrest. Potter also concealed himself and answered through his friend, Colonel F. W. Lander, that he would fight with bowie knives, each party to have two friends present who should be armed with navy revolvers to see fair play. "Distance, four feet at commencement of engagement. Knives of equal weight and length of blade. Fight to begin at the word 'Three.'" It was added, "These terms alone are such as will enable my principal, who is unacquainted with the usual weapons of duelists, to meet your friend on equal terms."

Mr. Chisman, whom Pryor had left in the Capital to represent him, consulted with several of his principal's friends — Keitt, Brooks, Yancey, and others — concerning the strange acceptance. They all agreed that the weapon named was inadmissible, and that Potter, instead of being fought "like a gentleman," should be denounced as a barbarian. So Mr. Chisman answered that "not recognizing this vulgar, barbarous and inhuman mode of settling difficulties," he could not allow Pryor to engage him.

The next day Pryor returned from hiding in Virginia, and, seeing what a mistake his seconds had made, straightway repudiated them and asked that the matter might be reopened, announcing his willingness to accept the terms and fight with bowie knives. His seconds declared a reopening impracticable. Colonel Lander offered himself in Potter's place "without restrictions," but nobody had any quarrel with him. King was also ready to respond at the drop of the hat. Pryor sent word to Potter that he would attack him at sight, and a few hours afterwards Potter was arrested by the police and put under bonds to keep the peace.

Potter was the hero of the hour, for pluck was just then at a premium. Pryor suffered from the outcome mainly because, in the heat of passion, it was generally believed that he had refused to fight with bowie knives and had rather ignominiously backed out. If the fight had taken place, one or both would certainly have been killed, and it might have done something to abolish the savage and preposterous custom of duelling.

I had a talk with Mr. Potter about this affair a year afterwards. "I always confide wholly in my wife," he said, "and even in this strange dilemma I went to her the first thing. I showed her just how we stood; that I had done no wrong; that the North sorely needed a champion and that our cause was depressed because we were called cowards and no man would fight; and then I asked her what to do. She had a 'good crying spell,' as the women call it, but she said my duty was clear — I must fight him. She stood by me pluckily straight through. I got such hints and instructions in the use of the bowie knife as I could, and practised for an hour every day. I am very strong and very quick. If we had fought, I should certainly have slain Mr. Pryor. It is better as it is."

After Pryor had threatened to kill him at sight, Potter's friends, somewhat against his will, hedged him about with their vigilance, accompanying him in his walks to and fro. One of the most constant of these was Colonel King, who was quick as a cat and strong as a tiger. Whenever Potter started from his seat to leave the House, King rose at his side like an apparition.

The temporary absence of the duelists from their seats was made the subject of a ghastly joke. When Potter's name was called, Pryor's colleague exclaimed, "He has a Pryor engagement!" and when Pryor's name was called, a Republican shouted, "Gone to be made into Potter's clay!"

At last accounts Pryor was Justice of the Supreme Court of New York and Potter was a comfortable and quiet farmer in Wisconsin.

Before this time Colonel King had acquired a wide local distinction in Minneapolis for being an abolitionist of the aggressive and militant type. Slaveholders were accustomed to go to Minnesota with their colored property to spend the summer. Antislavery people took good care to inform the

Negroes that they were free, and many of them left their masters. Proslavery merchants wanted the Southern trade and threatened to mob those who interfered with the "rights" of the planters. Riots, mobs, and violence resulted. At last a suit was brought against a Missourian for holding slaves in Minnesota, and the case was tried at the Minneapolis court-house. King was never quarrelsome and never carried arms, but it was generally understood that he was a bad man to tackle. When the verdict was announced declaring the slaves free, and their importers tried by bulldozing to hold them, King was very much in evidence. He was there. Standing upon the courthouse steps, he made the colored visitors understand that they were free men and women, to the great rage of their masters. Then he took the gentlemen themselves in hand and gave them a "dressing down," in language very far from polite or pious. Technically it was profanity, but it seemed a sort of vociferous invocation, so uninterrupted and picturesque that many who heard it declared that it sounded like a poem or a psalm, and when the planters hastily retired, leaving their "chattels" behind, an old and devout Presbyterian deacon edged his way up the steps, slapped King on the shoulder, and exclaimed, "Thank you, Bill! Thank you! I couldn't have done it better myself!"

When the slaveholders became still more angry and menacing and the cotton states went through the forms of seceding from the Union during the first month of 1861, it began to look as if the fountains of the great deep were broken up, and I revisited my old home in New England to await results and take my bearings anew. While tarrying here I suddenly and to my great surprise found myself in the middle of the current.

On February 11 I was in the depot at Springfield, Massachusetts, awaiting the train from the North.   An immense crowd had assembled which increased every moment and seemed to be waiting for the same train.   Inquiry brought the information that Senator Hannibal Hamlin, Vice President elect on the ticket with Mr. Lincoln, was about to pass through the city on his way to Washington.   It occurred to me at once that this was an occasion when phonography was likely to be valuable, and when the train from Maine arrived and halted amid the tumult, I jumped upon the step where a solidly-built, large-sized, earnest-looking man appeared and responded to the frantic cheers of the crowd.   To report the short speech at the moment I used the flyleaves of a book I had brought with me to read on the train (Lowell's *Fable for Critics*) and I sacrificed the virgin pages to this useful purpose all the way to New York.

A member of Mr. Hamlin's party told me that on leaving Bangor a procession of sleighs a mile long, decorated with flags, escorted the illustrious citizen from his residence to the station, to salute him and bid him Godspeed.   Mr. Hamlin was very kind to me and looked over and corrected my manuscript as I wrote out my notes on the way to New York.   It seemed that I was the only reporter aboard, the Boston papers having missed their opportunity, and the distinguished passenger was greatly interested in having the report correct.

The train made only five or six stops on the way to New York.   There was an excited crowd wherever it paused, generally patriotic and vociferous, but sometimes ugly and insolent.   At Hartford there was a clamorous multitude.   In response to the mayor's salutation Mr. Hamlin spoke briefly.   One of the crowd, obviously a foreigner, jumped up on a truck and continually and impudently interrupted him.   "And yet this is the land of the free!" shouted Mr. Hamlin to

the interrupter; "still this is the refuge of the oppressed!"
At this point the Irishman interrupted again with, "It's you
Black Republicans that's breaking up the Union for the sake
of the damn nagers!" Mr. Hamlin continued: "Still we
welcome all the poor and helpless who take refuge on our
shores — from the famine-stricken homes of Germany, from
the lazar houses of Spain, yes, and from the miserable hovels of
Ireland [great applause], only demanding of the immigrant
that he shall obey the laws when he comes, and behave himself decently in the presence of his neighbors!" At this the
cheers were deafening, and the man on the truck disappeared.
"That man's neighbors seem to know him," said Mr. Hamlin
on recovering his seat. "I must have hit him on the raw."

At Meriden Mr. Hamlin spoke from the baggage car, and
the bouquets which the ladies brought were tossed up to him
and fell about his feet. At New Haven he made a very
earnest and eloquent speech for an undivided country, and
the enormous crowd insisted on shaking hands with him one
by one, while he was talking. He reached out both his hands
and said, "If I had as many arms as that ancient fellow, what's
his name, — Briareus? — they say he had a hundred —"
At this very moment he was pulled off the car by his frenzied
admirers and the train started for New York, leaving him
submerged in the too demonstrative crowd. Mrs. Hamlin,
a refined and reticent lady, was left on the train somewhat
alarmed. Of course the error was immediately discovered
and the train was pushed back to the platform, giving the
orator just time to round off his speech. Some newspapers
voiced the suspicion that he was pulled off intentionally by
some muscular Democrat, but Mr. Hamlin himself was
not of this impression.

I accompanied the Vice President elect and his retinue
to the Astor House, then the centre of intelligence in the City

of New York, and there committed my report to paper. Putting the substance in triplicate, I sold it to the Tribune, Sun, and Times, who were glad to pay a good price for it — my first phonographic harvest. The next week I went to Washington and remained during the inauguration. These were eventful days, filled with threats and turmoil. Washington was virtually a secession city — a camp of treason. Buchanan declared that secession was unconstitutional, but that he had no power to prevent it by coercing a state. His Cabinet was busy dispersing the navy, dismantling the forts, and allowing the treasury of the country to be plundered in the interest of rebellion.

When March 4 arrived it was found that some preparations had been made to preserve the life of the nation. Salient points on the line of march to the Capitol were defended. Up Pennsylvania Avenue from Willard's Hotel to Capitol Hill, President Buchanan rode in the White House carriage, Abraham Lincoln by his side. Ward Lamon was on horseback within ten feet of his great friend, and the procession was flanked by a strong military guard. The housetops along the avenue bristled with riflemen. The Capitol building was in possession of the army and a battery of flying artillery was stationed at the northern entrance to the plaza at Delaware Avenue and B Street, for the protection of the platform reared over the steps upon the east front. The dome was half built at this time, and the bronze goddess intended for the summit stood undraped upon the pavement facing the steps at a distance of a hundred feet, where Greenough's Washington afterwards stood and shivered. Never before was such a multitude present at an inauguration as that which faced and surrounded the President elect when he took the oath of office, and Stephen A. Douglas received and held his tall hat during the remainder of the ceremony. It was estimated that two thirds of the audience were secessionists, and their sympathies were indicated by the frequent interruptions, sometimes quite drowning the voice of the speaker.

During the first two minutes it became obvious that Mr. Lincoln possessed a voice of great carrying power and that his words would be conveyed to the auditors who were most remote. He was calm and unperturbed and his tall form overtopped the distinguished assembly. The stories current about him served to excite an extraordinary interest in his unique personality, in addition to the extraordinary significance of the occasion.

Some of the exclamations heard during the delivery of the address, uttered in so loud a tone as to be a serious annoyance, were: "That won't do!" "Never! Never!" "Worse than I expected." "Too late!" "We defy your threats!" — this when the President avowed his intention to preserve the authority of the government and retain possession of its property. The last five minutes of the address was listened to in hushed expectancy, and there was warm applause at the pathetic close: —

Such of you as are now dissatisfied still have the old Constitution unimpaired, and, on the sensitive point, the laws of your own framing under it; while the new administration will have no immediate power, if it would, to change either. If it be admitted that you who are dissatisfied hold the right side in the dispute, there is still no single reason for precipitate action. Intelligence, patriotism, Christianity, and a firm reliance on Him who has never yet forsaken this favored land, are still competent to adjust, in the best way, all present difficulties.

In your hands, my dissatisfied fellow countrymen, and not in mine, is the momentous issue of civil war. The government will not assail you. You can have no conflict without being yourselves the aggressors. You have no oath registered in heaven to destroy the government, while I have the most solemn one to "preserve, protect and defend it."

I am loath to close.  We are not enemies, but friends.  We must not be enemies.  Though passion may have strained, it must not break our bonds of affection.  The mystic chords of memory stretching from every battlefield and patriot grave, to every living heart and hearthstone over all this broad land, will yet swell the chorus of the Union, when again touched, as they surely will be, by the better angels of our nature.

Among the auditors was the famous statesman and wit, James W. Nye, who held no office but was perhaps the most eloquent orator of the Republican party.  He stood upon a slight mound, and when hisses and yells interrupted Mr. Lincoln he led the applause which drowned them.  At the close of the exercises hisses and denunciations were renewed, when Nye, raising himself to his full height, and shaking his fist at the noisiest band of secessionists near by, shouted, "Now you've heard the truth for once in your lives, you damned traitors!  That's the best speech that's been delivered since Christ's Sermon on the Mount."

It was an audacious utterance likely to be remembered by the thousands who heard it.  Within a month Nye was appointed Governor of Nevada, later to come thence as United States Senator.

Two days after the inauguration I accompanied the Ohio delegation in a call upon General Scott.  The tall and stalwart old hero hobbled to the porch with evident effort.  He was "framed in the prodigality of nature."  None who saw him that morning will ever forget his appearance or the pathos of the occasion.  He was grim and grizzled, with his face drawn with pain and deep-set with wrinkles.  On being introduced, he laid his hand on the railing for support and exclaimed with much emotion, "God bless Ohio!  God bless

all the loyal states!  God bless the Union forever!  Some of
our people are in rebellion; some states we may have lost for a
short time, but the good God willing, we shall win them back.
We shall reclaim them [enthusiastic cheers] and enfold them
— all of them [the General here exhibited increased emotion]
— within the arms of that Union that has given us so much
prosperity, so much happiness, so much honor, and so much
glory!"  As the speaker paused he was greeted with tremendous cheering from the audience which half filled the street,
lasting some minutes.  "But whether they return to us
brothers or remain aloof as strangers, we have still left to us
a great and glorious Union [cheers]."

One of the crowd here shouted, "You must lead us, General
— lead us to the front!"  This was received with frantic
cheering, and the General continued, "You have all of me
there is, fellow citizens, hand and heart, experience and
patriotic love, but I am no longer young enough to be a leader.
Seek some younger man and I will follow as I may.  I have
been faithful to my country, and there is now no reward remaining for me but the love and confidence of its people."

Here the General's voice again broke and he was unable to
proceed.  When it was seen that he was in tears, the emotion
became indescribable.  Some wept.  Others crowded more
closely around the old man and up the steps, and the air
was filled with cheers, sobs, and ejaculations.  It was impossible for the General to shake hands with everybody, and
he was presently sustained through the doorway and into the
privacy of his parlor.

I called again in the evening to get a pass to the front
in Virginia.  The General had quite recovered his serenity
and referred me to one of his aides, Captain Drake DeKay.
Him I speedily found.  He seemed a vivacious schoolboy —
a prim, smooth-combed, and beardless youth, who looked

over the soldiers old and young who presented themselves and speedily disposed of them.  He gave me a pass attesting my loyalty written on a full sheet of letter paper with his name in letters two inches long — so large that a sentinel could read it as the bearer held it up and rode by on a gallop.

During 1861 Washington was virtually a military camp, and to escape the turmoil and turbulence I returned to Minnesota, to take up again the work of journalism.  It was not to be.  The voice of treason had penetrated to the remotest village in the land, and when the cannonading of Fort Sumter became the tocsin of war, I was mustered into the First Minnesota Regiment at Fort Snelling for three months.

# III

## WASHINGTON IN '61

But even now I greatly preferred writing to either shooting others or being shot, and at my muster out I found service on the Potomac as correspondent of the New York Tribune. On July 20, just before the battle of Bull Run, I pushed into Virginia to ascertain for the Tribune if anything was likely to happen. That paper was shouting "On to Richmond!" with an enthusiasm that was shortly proved to be premature. I found General McDowell surrounded by his showy staff, sitting upon a grassy bank in the shade, with large maps spread out upon the ground. As I rode towards the group I was met by a Captain, evidently one of the staff officers, but he would tell me nothing except that a severe skirmish had occurred at Blackburn's Ford of Bull Run. Towards that ford I headed.

It was afternoon as I made my way through a picturesque company of Zouaves encamped upon a dreary-looking hillside. Suddenly, as I was urging my melancholy beast forward, and seeking somebody of whom I could ask questions, a soldier stepped out and took him by the bridle. He was a German, and neither of us understood the other. Being arrayed in a linen coat, I was at once arrested as a spy and put in "the guardhouse," as they called a small plot of ground fenced in with rails and defended by riflemen at the corners. I now conjectured that I was a guest of the famous Zouaves, organized and commanded by that Colonel Corcoran, who, the year before, had defied a court-martial by refusing to order out his regiment in honor of the visit to New York of the Prince of Wales, afterwards King Edward VII.   My guess proved to be correct.

I was detained in the "guardhouse" with some other hard-looking cases more than two hours, perspiring and protesting, when at last the bit of paper which I had sent to the command-ing officer procured my release.   I was taken to the captain of the company, who proved to be Thomas Francis Meagher, the eloquent Irish patriot who had been sentenced to death as a traitor to Great Britain and had escaped via Van Diemen's Land to America.   I happened to know something of his personal history and felt greatly relieved at being his prisoner.

He was sitting on a rail laid on the ground, broiling a bit of chicken over the camp fire.   He apologized for the Dutch regiment, said they had sent my horse off where it could not be got for a few minutes, and insisted on my taking a soldier's lunch with him.

"I never saw any meat quite as savory as these Virginia chickens," said the captain, sucking a wing.

"Not even the chickens on Waterford mountains?" I asked.

He looked up quickly.   "Sure, you are not an Irishman," he said questioningly.

"No," I said.   "Oh no, but I happen to recall your old home."

"Chickens!" he resumed.   "We did not forage there.   I do not remember seeing a fowl of any sort during those few exciting days.   But I remember being hungry there the first time in my life."

"It seems to us a strange bit of futility — that Irish war," I said.

"Futility, yes; insanity, no!" he answered with a serious look and tone.   "We had a cause, — a splendid cause, — and if we could have made a successful stand then and there, and called to us the army that was ready to come, matters would be better on the old sod to-day."

I asked how they happened to rise in rebellion just at that time.

"The smell of blood was in the air. When 'Young Ireland' gathered around Smith O'Brien you were fighting Mexico. There were two or three rebellions in South America. Mazzini led the revolution in Italy, and was elected triumvir of Rome that very year. That summer, too, Kossuth was in revolt in Austria and Carl Schurz and his friends in Germany. The French republicans were at the barricades in February and drove the king from the throne. Everybody was fighting. Why shouldn't we?"

"Well," I said, "we Americans are glad that you do not abhor and stigmatize the sword."

"No! And I never did," he cried passionately. "I was greatly misunderstood about that, and even misrepresented."

It occurred to me to surprise my entertainer, and to his great astonishment I exclaimed: "Nor do I conceive it profane to say that the King of Heaven, the Lord of Hosts, bestows his benediction on those who unsheathe the sword in the hour of a nation's peril. Be it in defense of a people, or in the assertion of their liberties, I hail the sword as a sacred weapon; and if, my lord, it has sometimes reddened the shroud of the oppressor with too deep a dye — "

"Good God!" he broke out. "What are you saying? Where did you get that?"

I explained that when a schoolboy I had learned and recited a part of his celebrated "Sword speech" at the district school in Connecticut.

He was evidently amused and pleased to know that an emotional declamation made in Dublin when he was twenty-two years old should be remembered across the sea, especially when I continued: "Stigmatize the sword? No, my lord, for at its blow a giant nation started from the waters of the Atlantic, and by its redeeming magic and in the quivering of its crimson light, the crippled colonies sprang into the attitude of a proud republic — prosperous, limitless, invincible!" As this climax was reached, he laughed and spatted his palms together in approving pantomime.

We then turned to discuss our chicken and the immediate surroundings, and just as I was about to lead the young captain's speech back to '48, an orderly led my horse back to me and, after exchanging some conjectures with the captain as to what would happen on the morrow, I galloped off, glad to have had even a few words with the plucky visionary — one of that gallant band of fanatics who had risen in arms (twenty muskets) to overthrow Great Britain and had been captured by the deputy sheriff before their guns went off.

The next day Meagher's horse was shot under him in battle. I never saw him again. After the war, in which he rose to the rank of Brigadier General, he practised law successfully and married Miss Townsend, a lady of wealth and beauty. He was appointed governor of Montana, but on the steamer going up "the Big Muddy" he spent too pleasant an evening with his cronies in the cabin and, at one of the stopping places, accidentally walked off the gangplank into the Missouri River. His body was never recovered.

Without difficulty I found my regiment bivouacked at Centerville and took a fragmentary supper with my old comrades of Company E. Then, it being announced that we must leave early, I lay down with them under the trees to sleep. In the darkness of night we woke and took a hasty cup of coffee at three o'clock, and started on the long and circuitous march for Bull Run, said to be four miles away. We marched a couple of hours in the darkness, then three or four hours more through the thickest of dust and under the hottest of summer suns.

When we were pretty nearly exhausted we halted in a narrow lane. Presently I was glad to see another civilian come walking across the field, apparently from a carriage which I saw hitched beyond the hill. It was Henry Wilson of Massachusetts, Chairman of the Military Committee of the Senate, and he inspected the splendid array of troops with evident satisfaction and asked Colonel Gorman what they were going north for. He was informed that we were marching to Sudley's Ford, on the right, to outflank the right wing of the rebel army. Shortly another civilian came up and joined us. Like myself, he wore a long linen duster, and strapped on his shoulders was a box as large as a beehive. I asked him if he was the Commissary.

"No," he laughed; "I am a photographer, and I am going to take pictures of the battle."

I asked him if he could get the fellows who were fighting to stand still and look pleasant. With a very serious face he said he supposed not, but he could probably get some scenes that would be worth while. His name was Brady, he added, and the protuberance on his back was a camera. It was N. B. Brady — not Nota Bene, but Napoleon Bonaparte. I saw him afterwards dodging shells on the battlefield. He was in motion, but his machine did not seem effective, and when about two o'clock a runaway team of horses came dashing wildly past us, dragging a gun carriage bottom side up, I saw Brady again and shouted, "Now's your time!" But I failed to stir him. I have often wondered how many pictures he took that day and whether he got out of the battle on our side or the other. I know that he was in a good many battles after that and he sold his pictures to the government for $60,000 when Grant was President.

*Leslie's Weekly*

THE BATTLE OF BULL RUN

The Minnesota First was greatly fatigued with the long march under the hot sun and heavy accoutrements, but at last we slaked our thirst and bathed our faces in the run at Sudley's, then climbed trees on commanding knolls to locate the enemy, and started at a double-quick for his works, from which shells were by this time pouring.

I felt considerably in danger and asked Colonel Gorman for a musket, but he declined to give me one, saying that as I was in citizens' clothes, covered by a duster, I was very likely to be hung as a spy if captured in arms. Before noon I had no need of weapons, for I was engaged in carrying our wounded back to the hospital which Dr. Stewart of the First Minnesota had improvised in the old Sudley Church. There was a sickening spectacle. The pulpit had put on the appearance of a drug store, and the communion table had become the horrible amputation table, while the floor was covered so thickly with wounded and dying that it was difficult to get across it by stepping carefully. For hours we made rapid trips between the battlefield and the hospital, and still the carnage went on. By the middle of the afternoon fugitives began to go to the rear. But there was very little panic visible even when darkness fell. There was a pause that seemed almost a truce, for hours of fighting had terribly fatigued all who were engaged. The fact is that both armies were fairly defeated, and whichever had held its ground, the other would have run. General Joseph E. Johnston, in command on the other side, repeatedly said, "The Confederate troops were more disorganized than the Federal." Not till two hours after the battle closed were there any serious signs of disorder among the Union troops on the right. Then came all sorts of rumors about "the Black Horse Cavalry" being in close pursuit, which resulted in a hasty retreat through the darkened woods. This midnight experience seems a wild phantasmagoria as I recall it. I did not leave Dr. Stewart's hospital till it was quite dark, when he said to me, "You had better go. It might be dangerous to be captured in citizens' clothes and you probably cannot be of much more assistance." I found a horse astray and rode him into Centerville, overtaking the First Minnesota on the way, and sleeping again with Company E.

We cannot dictate to the Parcæ. I was not destined to be a soldier, or, exclusively, a war correspondent. The art which I had been studying and practising in New York suggested a different occupation. At the outbreak of the war so many clerks fled from the departments at Washington to their Southern homes, and so many resigned and joined the Northern armies, that every administrative bureau besought Congress for more help. Among those that remained there were hardly any efficient phonographers — not half a dozen in the whole city. One day Governor Ramsey said to me, "See here! It just occurs to me. You're a shorthand writer, ain't you? Well, Chase wants you." At this he straightway took me to the Treasury Department and introduced me to its chief. My examination consisted merely of the question, "What state are you from?" I was appointed with the understanding that I might continue my newspaper work. Now my service for the Tribune intermitted with my service for the government, the latter being mostly rendered in the rooms of the distinguished Secretary of the Treasury, whom hosts of Americans hailed as the ablest member of Mr. Lincoln's cabinet.

It will not be deemed a breach of confidence if I reveal at this late day the inordinate ambition of the masterful financier who was steering the country through the seething rapids of Hell Gate. Senator Pomeroy of Kansas came in one morning and spoke to the Secretary as if resuming a previous conversation. "I can speak more emphatically this morning than I did yesterday: the office is certainly within your reach. I have talked with our friends, and there is practically a unanimous feeling."

"Oh, yes, among our friends," exclaimed the Secretary; "but our friends alone can't elect a President." He rose from his chair and walked up and down the room as he added bitterly, "No! It is exactly as I told my father, years ago. I did n't want to be a lawyer; I wanted to go to West Point to be a soldier. And I called Father's attention to the fact that the popular heroes are always soldiers, and that a mere lawyer could get to be President only by accident. I saw it when I was a boy as plainly as I do now, Senator! My father's three brothers were all lawyers, and that 's all the good it did them."

The gentleman from Kansas shortly bowed himself out with, "You 'll see I 'm right next year, Mr. Secretary."

It occurred to one auditor who was not supposed to be hearing anything whatever that little Salmon must have possessed extraordinary prescience and self-confidence to look so far ahead when he was wandering through the woods of New Hampshire and to forecast so accurately a far-off time when he should be dissatisfied with his lot, though Abraham Lincoln's chief adviser and the dictator of the fiscal policy of millions of people.

During these strenuous days of war and tumult, when all able-bodied men were peremptorily summoned to the front, the government departments at Washington were always short-handed. Impelled by patriotism and the public need, some divisions began work at eight o'clock in the morning, and almost all continued till five o'clock, or later, and even then desks were left loaded with reports and documents imperatively requiring attention. To meet the exigency clerks were shifted around from bureau to bureau, for temporary service where the demand was sharpest. The Treasury Department was one of the severest sufferers, for it had to audit the accounts of a rapidly increasing army and furnish the money to support that army in the field.

Gold was already at a premium and rapidly rising. Congress had passed a law providing for a large issue of "demand notes," so-called because they were redeemable in gold on demand. These at first were attested by General F. E. Spinner, whom Secretary Chase had appointed to the office of Treasurer. He went at the work with great energy. But he was handicapped. No other public man in America produced such an entangled and illegible autograph as his — not even Bloss of the Cincinnati Enquirer or Greeley himself. When Mr. Lincoln saw the first demand note, bearing the Treasurer's preposterous labyrinth at the bottom, he exclaimed, "Well, boys, I defy the devil to counterfeit that." It is not known that he ever did, but the General had underestimated his job. When he had perspired through the whole of one August day, signing the new notes, and discovered that he had not produced enough to pay off a single regiment, he uttered one of those rough Saxon expletives which decorated his conversation and declared that he "never could make money" and would n't try any longer.

So it happened that forty or fifty clerks were transferred from various divisions as they could be spared, and assembled around tables in a spacious room to sign demand notes. I was usually detailed from the Secretary's room when the morning's mail had been disposed of. The notes were in sheets of ten and were for five, ten, twenty, and fifty dollars. Some clerks could sign their names 3500 times in ten hours, but 2500 signatures constituted a good day's work. Each clerk signed his own name — certificate and voucher for the name of "S. P. Chase."

I found that I issued the tremendous amount of $30,000

some days, and the whimsical notion entered my head that I could be held responsible for nearly $200,000 a week. I asked the Secretary about this one day. He smiled and said, "Possibly — don't be alarmed."

The city of Washington during the war was a desolation. The Capitol's unfinished dome and wings looked like a Roman ruin. Secretary Seward and his clerks were cooped in a small and dingy brick building where the north end of the Treasury pushes its superb classic colonnade, and Secretary Stanton with his small department filled an insignificant building where now is the forelawn of the White House. Along the north edge of the Mall slowly crept and soaked through the city a fetid bayou called "The Canal," by courtesy, floating dead cats and all kinds of putridity and reeking with pestilential odors. Cattle, swine, goats, sheep, and geese ran at large everywhere. There were only two short sewers in the entire city and these were so choked as to backset the contents into cellars and stores on Pennsylvania Avenue. Happy hogs wallowed in the gutters. At night the city was in darkness, scarcely ameliorated by a faint glim on remote corners, and the rustic lantern was by no means unknown.

Few of the streets had any pretense of pavement. Some were paved with cobblestones so unstable as to be worse than none at all. On wet days Pennsylvania Avenue was a river of mud and filth in which carts and even light buggies were often mired so deep as to be extricated with great difficulty. The sidewalks were filled with Union soldiers on parole or absent without leave, and many of the houses concealed members of Mosby's guerillas acting as spies and waiting to dodge back across the river. There were forty-eight forts around the city and within the circumvallation were eighteen vast hospitals, sheltering thousands of sick and wounded. To make the round of these was a melancholy task indeed.

# IV

## ANTISLAVERY MEETINGS

For nearly three years I served as one of Mr. Chase's phonographic corps, but at least once a week I ran over into Virginia and picked up the broken thread of correspondence for my paper.

It was in the fall of 1861 that our activities were suddenly increased. The battle of Bull Run was over; McClellan was slowly reorganizing the Army of the Potomac; masterly inactivity prevailed, and life in Washington was rather a sleepy affair. Opportunely a happy idea presented itself and moved me to insert in the morning paper of the city, the National Republican, this paragraph: —

Notice. — Young men in Washington who desire to have a course of lectures during the winter similar to those of northern cities are invited to meet this evening at ———.

Responsive to the invitation, several young men, mostly strangers to each other, met at my rooms. A comparison of views revealed the fact that they were all heartily in favor of the abolition of slavery, and one, Lewis Clephane, manager of the National Era, which had a year before been the victim of a proslavery mob for publishing Mrs. Stowe's *Uncle Tom's Cabin,* had just been appointed postmaster of the city by President Lincoln. We took counsel together and an adjourned meeting was held at Clephane's residence the next week.

On that occasion at least twenty young men were present, and much interest was manifested. About nine o'clock there was a knock at the door and it was opened to admit a venerable man with long flowing white hair and beard like Raphael's Saint Jerome, a quick, nervous manner, a glowing pink face, and vivacious and merry blue eyes. He paused, leaned against the door, and said, "Gentlemen, I saw an advertisement summoning young men to come here to consult to-night, and here I am!"

The little speech was greeted with a welcome of applause and laughter, and Mr. John R. French, of the Treasury Department, rose and introduced the newcomer as the Reverend John Pierpont. We knew that the poet and apostle of temperance had come down as chaplain of a Massachusetts regiment at the age of seventy-six, and that Charles Sumner had rescued him from the swamps of Virginia and induced him to accept a clerkship under Mr. Chase. Without much discussion, or even consideration, we elected this "young man" to be our president, organizing as the Washington Lecture Association.

In our advertisement authorized by that meeting it was announced that "desiring to aid in placing the community of which they form a part on a higher plane in regard to literature, loyalty, and liberty, one hundred citizens of Washington have united in an organization with the present design of a course of lectures by men who have earned a reputation for the highest culture and the most earnest patriotism." And we named the men already on our list — Wendell Phillips, Henry Ward Beecher, Horace Greeley, Edward Everett, Orestes A. Brownson, Daniel S. Dickinson, Bayard Taylor, James Russell Lowell, George B. Cheever, Charles G. Ames, Moncure D. Conway, George William Curtis, John Jay, William Goodell, Gerrit Smith, Frederick

Douglass, Samuel J. May, Joseph Holt, Anna E. Dickinson, Richard S. Storrs, William Lloyd Garrison, Ralph Waldo Emerson, and George Thompson, the great English abolitionist. Not one of them had ever spoken south of Mason and Dixon's line, and several of them enjoyed the exalted honor of having a perpetual bounty offered for their heads. As secretary of the Association I was directed to "engage these lecturers and obtain a suitable hall." The former duty involved a voluminous correspondence, but was comparatively easy, and, in fact, all of them except Everett, Garrison, Beecher, Lowell, and Miss Dickinson, appeared in the course.

The second duty assigned to me was much more easily defined than performed. There was no public hall in Washington that would seat a thousand people, but we wanted to seat two or three thousand. The churches were all closed to us. In this dilemma I made a bold and what seems to me at this distance an audacious request for the House of Representatives, but Speaker Grow instantly and peremptorily vetoed the suggestion. I have an impression that he spoke sharply and severely about it, but do not remember exactly what he said. He probably remarked that I was crazy to imagine that such a preposterous thing was possible.

At any rate, I gave it up, replenished my courage, and immediately went and asked Professor Joseph Henry to give us the large amphitheatre of the Smithsonian. This was apparently worse yet. He was struck with horror at the sacrilegious suggestion and froze me out with harsh words which made me almost wish that I had been burdened with less responsibility. Heavy-hearted, I took all these troubles to the Honorable Owen Lovejoy, with whom I had the privilege of such acquaintance as a zealous young recruit might enjoy with a kind-hearted veteran, and he valiantly entered the lists. "Henry's an old traitor!" he exclaimed hotly. "We 'll bring him to terms. Come with me." And he led the way to the rooms of the Honorable Schuyler Colfax. Here, too, was a sympathetic listener. "I am a regent of the Smithsonian," Mr. Colfax said, "and Hamlin is another. I 'll see him to-day about it. Call at my residence to-morrow morning at ten o'clock and bring John Pierpont, and we 'll do something."

Lovejoy's severe arraignment exaggerated the current local distrust of the illustrious savant and discoverer who had anticipated Morse in telegraphic possibilities, and who was brilliantly executing Smithson's splendid bequest; but it must be admitted that Professor Henry was by some suspected of sympathy with the Rebellion. It was about this time that the official who had been put in charge of the confiscated Arlington estate of General Lee across the Potomac appeared before Mr. Lincoln and said: "Mr. President, I bring to you this morning the proofs of what I told you a month ago — that Professor Henry is a rebel. He is right in with them. Last night at midnight he flashed red lights from the top of his building, signaling to the Secesh who flock on the hills back of us. I saw them myself."

Mr. Lincoln — so the story goes — turned a whimsical smile upon a beetle-browed man who sat contemplative in a corner of his room, and said, "Now you 're caught! What have you to say, Professor Henry, why sentence of death should not immediately be pronounced upon you?"

All three, it is said, had a laugh together when it was explained that new army signals were being tried in the tower of the Smithsonian, and that the President himself had climbed up there the night before, with Henry, Totten, Bache, and Rhees, to exchange messages with the surrounding heights. Professor Henry had no sympathy with the Rebellion, but he was neither a soldier nor a partisan. He did not comprehend the uproar, and he wished to keep the Smithsonian Institution entirely out of it.

Dr. Pierpont and I were at Mr. Colfax's door promptly next morning, and were delighted to find the Vice President there waiting. They had arranged for an assault on the fortress of science without delay, and had sent word to Professor Henry and made an appointment. When he had crossed the broad but unkempt Mall and reached the red sandstone pile of Norman towers and turrets constituting the handsomest public building in Washington, its distinguished master was armed with arguments and protests and ready to receive us.

"How can such lectures as you contemplate be permitted here," he asked, "when this institution, like science, is nonpartisan and peaceful, and when we do not allow a lecturer to speak even on chemistry without knowing in advance whether his theories are sound? Besides, you would be sure to offend some of the regents."

This gave Vice President Hamlin the chance for a leading question.

"Which ones?"

"Gentlemen from the South," replied the Professor.

"They are getting scarce," said Mr. Hamlin. "Jefferson Davis has gone and is not likely to return at present," he added, remembering, no doubt, how active Mr. Davis had been as a friend of the Smithsonian and how intimate his family had been with Professor Henry's family.

"Senator Mason is a regent yet," suggested Mr. Colfax, "but he has fled from Washington and will not come back to plague you."

"And the Mayor of Washington has resigned and gone to Richmond," pursued Hamlin. "Then look at this," he added, taking up a list of the new regents President Lincoln had selected, but had not yet appointed, and sticking a pen through it to punctuate the names, "Fessenden, Trumbull, McPherson, W. B. Astor, W. L. Dayton — none of them will object, and as for Badger, of North Carolina, he has gone home, and is in very bad company; I guess he will not trouble you. If he does, Colfax and I will stand by you. Lincoln will." (A year later Mr. Badger was expelled from the Board of Regents on motion of Mr. Hamlin.)

For a fortnight, while lecturers were being engaged, the siege of the Smithsonian was carried on. Gradually Professor Henry weakened and prepared to surrender. Lincoln took a hand. It was finally agreed that the dreadful innovation should be tried, but he stipulated that it must be published that it was against his remonstrance, and that the presiding officer should make it distinctly understood at every lecture that the Smithsonian Institution was in no way responsible for the sentiments avowed.

So when John Pierpont, the venerable poet, came forward to introduce the first lecturer, Orestes A. Brownson, the distinguished Catholic of Protean creed, he said: —

"Ladies and Gentlemen: I am requested by Professor Henry to announce that the Smithsonian Institution is not in any way responsible for this course of lectures. I do so with pleasure, and desire to add that the Washington Lecture Association is in no way responsible for the Smithsonian Institution."

This announcement was received with much merriment and applause. Thereafter every week throughout the winter Mr. Pierpont gravely repeated the declaration with some modifications, just before each lecture; and the audience soon got to expecting it, and when he would rise and begin, "Ladies and Gentlemen," two thousand people would break into cheers and laughter.

And so the course began.  Even the first lecture was heard by an audience that crowded the large hall in every part, and it was noticeable that the most radical utterances concerning slavery received the warmest applause.  Dr. Brownson became an abolitionist during the next few months, for his two sons had perished in the war.

The course was a success from the beginning.  Brownson was followed by Daniel S. Dickinson, George William Curtis, and Bayard Taylor.  For months the audiences increased, both in enthusiasm and numbers, so far as a full hall could become fuller, till it was necessary to go very early to get a seat of any sort.  There were always scores of Senators and Representatives in the hall.  Cabinet officers often lent their approval by occupying seats on the platform; but when Wendell Phillips lectured, as he did three times, I think they avoided conspicuousness by taking seats in the body of the hall.

This period was marked by that outpouring of anonymous letters which often accompanies great excitement.  Most of the lecturers experienced the sensation of having their lives threatened while they were in Washington.  Mr. Pierpont was menaced both through the post office and orally, and even the unobtrusive secretary had his share of this unpleasant attention in letters bearing mysterious suggestions and a great variety of badly drawn skulls and amorphous coffins.

In response to the invitation to come, Horace Greeley replied, "Yes: I was intending to come down there to talk, anyway; and I am glad to have this chance — especially as I have already earned the reputation of being the poorest public speaker in America."  When he arrived he asked me if Lincoln would be present.  I did not know, but at his suggestion I went at once to the White House and asked the President if he would attend.

"Yes, I will," he said.  "I can get away, can't I, Hay?  I

never heard Greeley, and I want to hear him. In print every one of his words seems to weigh about a ton; I want to see what he has to say about us."

So the President came, and consented to be perched on the high platform immediately at the great editor's right. Near him were Secretaries Gideon Welles and Edward Bates, and at Greeley's left sat the chief of the Treasury, Salmon P. Chase, glowing with pleasure at the significance of the occasion. Before introducing the speaker, President Pierpont began, as usual, "It is my duty and pleasure to announce to you, ladies and gentlemen, that the Smithsonian Insti —" The rest of the reminder, which had become amusingly familiar, was drowned in a great roar of laughter. Mr. Lincoln turned, with a puzzled smile, and asked the nearest officer of the Association what it meant. When it was briefly explained as the proclamation required by the Smithsonian at the beginning of each lecture, he joined in the laugh heartily, though a trifle behindhand. The object of it — Professor Henry — was within ten feet, concealed from the audience behind the little door that opened on the platform from the rear. Here, after the first lecture, he was generally found listening to the dangerous utterances, but in his next report to Congress he complained that the experiment had raised up enemies for the Smithsonian and ought not to be repeated.

When Mr. Greeley turned and addressed himself personally to Mr. Lincoln, who sat almost within arm's length, appealing to him to cease trying to make peace with the Mammon of Unrighteousness, but to free the blacks and arm them, proving equal to his high responsibility, in the crisis of the nation's fate, the audience, which had already listened to the same injunction more than once, rose and uttered a wild and prolonged cheer and cry of joy. A more dramatic scene has seldom been witnessed by any popular assembly.

After the lecture Mr. Greeley and the President, with Secretary Chase and others, had an animated conversation in the anteroom, in which Mr. Lincoln remarked to the professor, "The laugh was rather on you, Henry."

In Rice's *Reminiscences of Lincoln,* the Honorable George W. Julian says of this evening: —

"Mr. Lincoln used to attend the rousing anti-slavery meetings that were held in the Smithsonian Institution in the winter of 1861–62, which were addressed by the leading orators of abolitionism.  At one of these meetings Horace Greeley delivered a written address, which Mr. Lincoln listened to and very greatly admired. I sat by his side, and at its conclusion he said to me, 'That lecture is full of good thoughts and I would like to take the manuscript home with me and read it over carefully some Sunday.'"

It will be noticed that four of our most distinguished orators did not appear in this course — Edward Everett, Anna Dickinson, William Lloyd Garrison, and Henry Ward Beecher.

Mr. Everett curtly replied to the secretary, "I thank you, but I cannot come. There has been too much talking already."  It will be remembered that he had been defeated the year before for Vice President.

Miss Dickinson had peremptory engagements — her card was full.  But she came two years later and delivered her "Joan of Arc" in the Senate Chamber to a record audience, the Vice President in the chair.

Mr. Garrison was not invited.  Over him there was what might be called a quarrel in the executive committee of the Association.  It was about evenly divided on the subject, part of the members insisting that he was the best representative of the principles which the government was contending for, and the other half insisting that a man who pronounced the

Constitution of the United States "a covenant with death and a league with hell" would not be likely to strengthen the war for the Union. The contest over him went on week after week without settlement, while he sat in the *Liberator* office at Boston, wondering why he did not hear from Washington.

Getting a negative from Mr. Beecher, I went to Brooklyn to make a personal appeal to him. When I called at the house on the Heights after dinner, he had already left to lecture in Patterson, but was expected home at eleven. Mrs. Beecher kindly urged me to wait and see him. "Perhaps you may get him," she said. "I want him to go to Washington, and will add my appeal to yours. I want him to go though I see so little of him. I do not complain of his absence, for a woman who marries a popular favorite must be ready to divide him with the public. It keeps getting worse, though, every year. When I married him I merely had to share him with the congregation, but since then," she added with a pathetic smile, "he has married the Platform and the Press and the Goddess of Liberty, and I miss him a good deal. However, I want him to go to Washington to speak, and I think it is a thing he ought to do."

I waited. At last Mr. Beecher returned, and, leaving in the front parlor someone who had accompanied him, he came through into the family sitting room. Well remembered is the breezy gesture with which he flung off his overcoat, as who should say, "Here's vitality for you."

Being presented, I told my errand, outlined our purpose, and offered him two hundred dollars for a lecture — the highest price then paid anywhere. "Don't decide hastily, Henry," said Mrs. Beecher. "I think you ought to go. Mr. Lincoln will perhaps attend. You can do good there. It seems to me the occasion calls for you."

He walked up and down the room a few times, talking

about Washington city and asking questions about our course, and then he said, "No, I can't think of going. I've got just all I can carry. I'd like to speak in Washington very much and especially to see Lincoln, but I can't get away. I can fix you out, though. We have here the most brilliant and eloquent young man I have ever known. Take him!" And he put his head out through the folding door and said, "Come here, Theodore!"

A tall and handsome youth entered and I was presented to him. We exclaimed that we had seen each other before. It was Theodore Tilton.

"He's just the man you want on these questions," persisted the great preacher. "An original thinker, and a fervent and electric speaker — and he's one of my chickens!" added Mr. Beecher. As Mr. Tilton blushed a little and disclaimed the compliment of eloquence, I recalled that my commission did not include the engagement of any substitute, but I thanked them for the chance presented and agreed to lay the suggestion before the board on returning to Washington. This was done, but the conclusion was unanimous that we would not hear from Plymouth Church vicariously. A few years later I sat through the fearful trial of Mr. Beecher in the suit brought by his "chicken" for $100,000 damages for the destruction of his family.

I wrote to John G. Whittier and asked him if he would address such an audience as ours. He answered, "I do not talk in public. I wish that great good may come of thy work. But thy way is not my way."

One or two other episodes of these lectures may be worth recalling. Emerson spoke on "American Civilization," in February, 1862, and Mr. Lincoln sat upon the platform. The lecturer declared, "Emancipation is the demand of civilization. That is a principle; everything else is intrigue.

*Leslie's Weekly*

HENRY WARD BEECHER

What is so foolish as the assertion that the blacks will be made furious and revengeful by being given freedom and wages?" Like Thurlow Weed and many other publicists, he favored paying for the slaves, and he and Secretary Seward had a long talk with the President the next day upon the subject. It was in this lecture of Mr. Emerson that the fine epigram was first heard: "Let's hitch our wagon to a star."

When Wendell Phillips came to Washington I waited upon him to complete the business arrangements.

"What sort of audience is it?" he asked. I told him as well as I could.

"I feel afraid and embarrassed," he said. When I expressed astonishment at hearing he was ever afraid of any audience, he said, "I am always afraid. It is a tremendous responsibility, to try to interest a crowd of intelligent, perhaps learned persons, whom you don't know and never saw before. Why, I sometimes have stood paralyzed in front of an audience with the audacity of it — tongue-tied and not knowing what to say next."

Phillips had a musical voice which rang out like a trumpet when his deep feeling was enlisted. His handsome face covered a volcanic and emotional nature and the pleasant lips easily broke into invective. He said to me on leaving for Boston, "A great enterprise this of yours, but tell your Association for me that it will leave its good work half done if it fails to secure Garrison."

Just before Phillips died Schuyler Colfax received from him this letter: —

Boston, June 4, 1883

MY DEAR SIRS: I was glad that anything brought us again into communication, for among the pleasantest recollections of that visit to Washington (my first) is your kindness to me. It was in March, 1862, I spoke on the War, Friday, the fourteenth; "Lost Arts," Saturday, the fifteenth; "Toussaint l'Ouverture," Tuesday, the eighteenth.   How freshly it brings back those days to get behind the scenes and see how difficult it was for the friends to get us a hearing.   It makes a fine background for that Cincinnati mob that choked me off the next week, Monday, the twenty-fourth.   Do you remember the exceedingly happy terms in which Pierpont introduced me that evening — graceful and happy — no flattery or nonsense, but apt, witty, and so appropriate.   I envied him.

Cordially yours,

WENDELL PHILLIPS

In sending me this letter Mrs. Colfax reminded me that Mr. Lincoln and three of his Cabinet were on the Platform at the last of Phillips's lectures.   I had forgotten it.   It certainly showed a most forgiving disposition for the President to go from the White House to listen to a lecture by the orator who had often stigmatized him in public as "the slave-hound of Illinois."   There was a very large minority in our board opposed to hearing Mr. Phillips at all, and their hostility prevented it until very late in the season, as it had already vetoed an invitation to Garrison.   The next week after his Washington lectures Phillips was assailed in Cincinnati by a mob which repeatedly struck him with clubs and missiles.

Yet from Cincinnati Phillips wrote to Ann Phillips in Boston: "Assure Garrison that Washington is as safe for him as New York is.   I think he ought to go there and lecture. He knows not the enthusiasm with which he will be received or the good he will do."   Garrison replied to this, "One reason why I do not go to Washington is that I have not been invited."   He then disposed of the objections that had been made to him by saying, "I am in the position of Benedick in the play.   When I said I would not support the Constitution because it was a covenant with death and a league with hell, I had no idea that I should live to see death and hell secede from the Constitution." Garrison visited Washington later and had a pleasant interview with Mr. Lincoln. The President alluded to his guest's experience in having been mobbed and put in jail in Baltimore in 1830, and, being told that the old jail was torn down he added, "Then you could n't get out of jail, eh? and now you can't get in."

John Jay lectured in full evening dress and wore white kid gloves which he quietly slipped off as he proceeded. After his lecture I called on him at Willard's to see if he had been paid and had received proper attention. I asked if our treasurer had called.

"No, I think not; have n't seen him," he answered. And then after a pause, he added, "I hope he 'll call soon."

His anxiety seemed a trifle odd, but I reassured him, and said that such a visit would not be forgotten or long postponed, intending to remind and hasten the treasurer as soon as I went out. As I rose to go, Mr. Jay said with much earnestness, "I am afraid your treasurer will neglect to call. Can't you and I fix it?"

Embarrassed at the suggestion that I should pay him one hundred dollars and somewhat confused by the impossibility of doing so, I merely murmured, "I am not prepared just now."

"How much do you need in all?" he inquired.

I told him his question was not understood.

"How much does your Association need?" he repeated.

The significance of his mistake struck me so humorously that I sat down and laughed, quite speechless. On recovering words I explained.

"You meant to hire me?" he gasped with astonishment. "Well, that beats all I ever heard of! This lecture course actually pays? And in Washington! Now I have hope of the country!"

So his fee was left in the treasury and on inquiry we found that he was a millionaire. The subject of his lecture was "The Great Conspiracy and England's Neutrality." We cleared two thousand dollars that winter and when summer came we divided it up and made personal distribution of food, medicines, and various luxuries among the soldiers, who were already clustered by the ten thousand in the hospitals on the hillsides above Washington.

The most dramatic incident of our course was the lecture of George Thompson. Mr. Greeley had written to me from New York, "Be sure and get Thompson." Thompson was an English reformer. With Clarkson and Wilberforce he had been a potent influence in securing the abolition of slavery in the West Indies. He then transferred his philanthropic work to this country — before it was ready for it. He was fined and mobbed in Indiana and Illinois, spent some months in jail in St. Louis, and had a narrow escape with his life from Kentucky. He organized over one hundred and fifty antislavery societies, was frequently mobbed, and finally in Boston, in 1835, he escaped death only by fleeing in a small rowboat to an English vessel. President Jackson denounced him by name in a message to Congress as a dangerous incendiary.

In 1861 he visited our shores again. He received in Washington the greatest ovation ever extended to a private individual in the city. Twenty-four Senators and twenty-two Representatives signed a paper inviting him to lecture; the hall of the House of Representatives (at last!) was offered to him for the purpose; the Vice President of the United States presided; and the man who had fled from state to state a generation before as a felon and an outlaw addressed the

American people surrounded by the President and his Cabinet.

It is not too much to say that these lectures helped to change the moral atmosphere of Washington. From being fanatically proslavery, the capital city became neutral; to intolerance succeeded tolerance; to treason, loyalty; to sectionalism, nationalism; and even the army felt itself less a trespasser on the soil and rights of others after Greeley, Phillips, and Douglass had faced friends and enemies in the spacious semicircle of seats in the Smithsonian. Both Cabinet and Congress acknowledged the support which these courageous addresses gave, and it will never be known how much influence they had in the enactment of that law which six months later decreed the abolition of slavery in the District of Columbia.

Of all the lecturers of this remarkable course only one is alive as I write — Ames, preaching in Boston. He replies thus to a note asking for a paragraph of his recollections of that visit to Washington: —

I wonder if your memory of my lecture at the Smithsonian on the evening of February 18th, 1863, can be half so vivid as mine! A heavy rain was falling into a deep snow, and I had traveled six or seven hundred miles to speak to eighty people. John Pierpont presided, Owen Lovejoy, George W. Julian, and William Henry Channing loomed large on the platform. I saluted the scanty audience as "a company of particularly selected friends" as their presence on such an inclement evening proved; for in such a downpour I would hardly go two squares even to hear myself. A prompt burst of applause: and we were all on the best of terms.

Mr. Channing made up for my slim audience by giving me a church full on the Sunday afternoon following; and Kate Chase had me meet her father that evening with Gen. McDowell and Senator Harris, which led to a breakfast invitation when the Secretary honored me with a private interview.

The burning issue of the hour was the probable policy of the administration in respect to slavery — a subject which had been dealt with by me both in lecture and sermon. I had had the audacity to say in the pulpit, "If in the course of military events there comes a moment when the President shall have the clear power and right to proclaim emancipation and he shall fail to exercise that power and right, such failure will leave him the only slave-holder in America." How strenuous we were!

When Secretary Chase inquired about Western opinion and asked whom I meant by the reactionaries, I answered, "Those who insist on restoring the original condition of the patient, disease and all!" This seemed to please him. As I expressed concern over the report of divided cabinet councils, he told me that the members were unanimous in the conviction that the war could not be terminated without the removal of slavery as its cause, but that they were not agreed as to the time and manner of striking the blow. I ventured to repeat this and it went far to quiet the fears of many loyal men. The "masterly inactivity" of McClellan had also its depressing effect; but

> "The war that for a space did fail,
> Now trebly thundering swelled the gale."

You ask for "a paragraph." Well, let me see you get it out of this long story. All of us who lived through the horror and glory of those days grow either silent or garrulous.

Four years before, Moncure D. Conway had been dismissed as pastor from the "Liberal" Unitarian church in Washington: now he preached in the Senate Chamber before two thousand people! The next day he spoke in the lecture course, his topic being "The Golden Hour," and his first sentence, or rather exclamation, "Lost: yesterday, between sunrise and sunset, one golden hour set with sixty diamond minutes," the meaning of which was that the Administration was losing the opportunity to save the Union by abolishing slavery.

Conway had denounced the President's removal of Frémont, and the next day Senator Wilson took him to call at the White House. Mr. Lincoln said to him: "Frémont is in a hurry. Slavery is going downhill. We may be better able to do something towards emancipation by and by than now." Conway answered, "Dear Mr. President, our fathers compromised with slavery because they said it was going downhill; hence, war to-day. Slavery is the commissary of the southern army."

To Mr. Phillips the President pleaded, "Defeat in the field makes everything seem wrong. Almost everybody wants to run the government." Phillips replied, "Let the administration honestly seek to destroy slavery, Mr. President, and you will have no enemies left, and no rebellion left."

These lectures were attended by more distinguished men than any others ever delivered in this country. Half of Congress was frequently present. General and Mrs. Frémont occupied seats at Greeley's lecture, and their presence created such a furore of welcome that Schuyler Colfax and George W. Julian went and induced them to go upon the platform. Their reception by Mr. Greeley was the signal for another prolonged outburst. This meant a criticism of the President. After the battle of Wilson's Creek in Missouri (August 10, 1861) Frémont arrested active Secessionists and announced that he would emancipate the slaves of all men who were in arms against the United States. President Lincoln wrote to him, asking him to withdraw the emancipation clause. Frémont, declined to do so and the President annulled it himself in a public order. The Smithsonian audience was vociferously upon the side of Frémont.

Shortly afterwards the General and his incomparable "Jessie" gave an immense reception at the hotel. Of his difference with the President he spoke modestly and quietly, only wishing that the correspondence might be published, and saying confidently that the people could be of but one opinion when the whole truth was out.   Mrs. Frémont, witty, graceful, and brilliant, was less reticent and forbearing.   I recollect seeing her stand in the centre of a group leading an animated conversation concerning the indignities to which she thought her husband subjected.   She spoke warmly and even defiantly, with the sharp emphasis of outraged honesty, as any loving woman might speak of her husband in peril, and her eyes flashed as she exclaimed: "Justice! Justice! Justice!   Why may not Mr. Frémont have some kind of a public trial before these bewildered millions who do not know the facts?"   For the General's friends believed and asserted that he was the victim of a proslavery conspiracy, with the Blair family at its head.

After the close of the course I conceived a scheme for emphasizing its lessons by publishing the lectures in a volume, and I made arrangements with a publisher to that end. Almost all of the lecturers agreed to coöperate, and several of them sent me their manuscripts.   Mr. Greeley's was found to be quite illegible in places, for, although it had been originally dictated by him, and copied in an elegant hand by somebody, it had been so scratched out, interlined, and turned topsy-turvy, that whole pages here and there were as if inky spiders had executed a dance over the paper.   In this dilemma I went to New York to get the author to interpret it.

It was in April 1862 that I climbed up the back stairs to the Tribune office, seeking its editor.   The principal room was crowded with editors and reporters, and was very dirty and noisy, recalling the soldiers' barracks I had recently occupied at Bristow Station.   Charles A. Dana was still at the post of managing editor, and he gave me the address of his chief. Up to the indicated residence I went — on Nineteenth Street,

I believe. There I rang long and repeatedly, and knocked ditto, ditto, and at last a lady came to the door with sleeves tucked briskly up her arms and hair twisted to a knot on top of her head.

The following conversation took place: —

"Is Mr. Greeley in?"

"He is not."

"Can you kindly direct me to him?"

"I can not."

"You do not know where he is?"

"I do not. He is not living here now."

"Can I see Mrs. Greeley, then?"

"You do. I am Mrs. Greeley."

"Do — was — does Mr. Greeley come here sometimes?"

"Occasionally. He has not been here this week."

"May I inquire — do you know where he is stopping?"

"I do not. He stopped at the Everett House last week."

I walked down to that hotel and inquired. No, they said, but they thought he was at the New York Hotel. I shortly found him there, on the third floor, raging up and down the room like a wild man and storming over a pile of dispatches on the table. I seemed very much *de trop,* and in some alarm inquired what was the matter.

"Matter?" he repeated in his high falsetto voice. "Enough matter, I should think! Quite enough, I should think! In the battle yesterday at Pittsburg Landing the rebels whipped us, of course. Licked us like hell, apparently. And our soldiers are being driven into the Tennessee to-day — right now, perhaps! Not their fault, either. Fault of our damned incompetent generals! Both generals drunk! Oh dear!" he said, over and over as he walked up and down the room. "Such a sacrifice! Buell ought to be shot and Grant ought to be hung!"

After a while the old man quieted down sufficiently to enable me to leave the book with him for revision, and take my leave. Before night better news came, that Buell had hurried up and crossed the river to Grant's support, that Lew Wallace had at last made his appearance on the right, that Johnston, the rebel general, was killed, and that the whole rebel army was in retreat for Corinth, after incredible losses. This probably brought hope again to the bosom of the despondent editor who lived to be defeated for the Presidency by the soldier whom he had doomed to the gallows.

December 1862 was a melancholy month in this country, and at this time, when the hope of the loyal millions had almost given way to despair, President Lincoln sent out a circular letter asking the governors of the free states to meet in conference in Washington and Altoona, Pennsylvania. Most of them made their appearance ready to offer the President carte blanche and any number of men he needed to put down rebellion. I saw Governor Buckingham of Connecticut as soon as he arrived in the city, and outlined in my correspondence the definite purpose of the gathering. He said it was to reassure Mr. Lincoln and each other. On the morning of the meeting the governor said to me, "Why don't you come up to the White House with us? I am sure there will be no objection."

I went to the White House and asked Mr. Lincoln if I could properly be present.

"Certainly," he said, cheerily; "you can, as far as I am concerned."

I hesitated, but the occasion was a very important one and I resolved to go as far as the door of the conference room, at any rate. There were assembling Governors Curtin of Pennsylvania; Kirkwood of Iowa; Ramsey of Minnesota; Sprague of Rhode Island; Gregory Smith of Vermont; Stanford of

General Pemberton Surrenders to General Grant at Vicksburg

California; Dennison of Ohio, and others. In all, sixteen states were represented either in Washington or Altoona.

The doorkeeper knew me very well and merely nodded to me as we filed in. It was the room off the corridor on the second floor, then and since usually occupied by Cabinet meetings. Mr. Lincoln was standing with his back to the south window, but he immediately advanced, smiling and shaking hands with the visitors as he came down the room.

I felt a little out of place, so, not to be disguised, or seeming to be present under false pretenses, I took out my notebook, prepared for business. Mr. Lincoln asked that all be seated, then spoke a few words of welcome to the Capital, and of congratulation over the victory of Antietam, and announced that he would be glad to advise with the officials present as to the situation. Governor Curtin of Pennsylvania rose first in response to the invitation. He had spoken but a few words concerning the grave errand that had convened them when Governor Yates of Illinois arose and, looking directly at me, asked if all were state executives.

"I am an exception," I said, and was about to beat a hasty retreat when Governor Buckingham laid his hand on my shoulder, mentioned my name, and said that I was present at his invitation, as he could not conceive of anything requiring a secret session. I wanted to get out, but Mr. Lincoln remarked that I had applied to him in the morning and was present with his sanction. "We shall not say or do anything today that is secret, in any sense," he added, "and our only chance is to take the American people frankly into our confidence. However, it is for you gentlemen to say." This with a whimsical smile of acquiescence, but the position had become intolerable to me, and I bolted. Those who know what executive sessions are need not be told that I secured a full report of the conference without difficulty. No confidential business was considered.

During my service with Secretary Chase I became quite expert as a shorthand writer according to the standards of that day, and when I had been in his service for a few agreeable months he said to me one morning, "I may have to detail you for other work. How would you like to go over to the War Department?"

The question surprised me unpleasantly, but I hope that I did not reveal the fact too distinctly as I answered that I liked my present position more than I could tell, but I should be glad to go wherever it was thought I could be most useful. I had heard from every quarter that Mr. Stanton was a harsh and unreasonable chief and I knew that Mr. Chase was one of the most considerate and lovable of men.

"Well," he added, "Mr. Stanton has organized the Freedmen's Inquiry Commission of three members, and they have a lot of shorthand work to do in preparing their report. The assignment may be short, though, and then you can come back." He told me that I had been appointed secretary to the commission, gave me a note of introduction, and asked me to join the headquarters in parlors on the third floor of Willard's Hotel.

Thither I went and found myself in the presence of the gentlemen appointed to assist the President in solving the difficult problems which had arisen when slavery's existence was threatened and myriads of fugitives sought safety in the track of our advancing armies.

The gentlemen whom I was to serve were well known and even distinguished. The chairman was Robert Dale Owen, the famous socialist, who had been twice a member of Congress and who had framed the beneficent law under which the

Smithsonian Institution was organized.   He had written and spoken incessantly against slavery, and Secretary Chase declared that "his letter on that subject had more effect in deciding Mr. Lincoln to issue his proclamation of emancipation than all other causes combined."

The second member of the commission, Dr. Samuel G. Howe, of Boston, was equally distinguished as a philanthropist.   He had served as an officer by the side of Lord Byron in the Greek revolution, but was even better known for his persistence and ingenuity in the education of the blind, notably Laura Bridgman.   His wife, Julia Ward Howe, was famous as the author of the ringing "Battle Hymn of the Republic," which she wrote while on this visit to the Washington camps.

The third member was Colonel J. McKayes, associated with Frederick Douglass in the work of receiving and directing to places of safety the frightened fugitives.   The chief function of the commission was to establish clearly the relation of the government to the Negroes, free and slave, and to ascertain and define the conditions under which they should be enlisted in the Union armies.   The three commissioners, with Douglass, were called to frequent conferences at the White House, for they were unanimously in favor of the immediate emancipation of slaves and their enrollment as soldiers, while Mr. Lincoln feared that they were in danger of being superserviceable.   He was more conservative, and said to them one day, "See here!   If I don't look out you 'll run away from me."

They preserved their consistency to the last, insisting that the war could not end until it had guarded against the restoration of slavery in any form, secured to the freedmen the means of making a living, and given them a fair chance. Mr. Lincoln agreed that if, like whites, they must be self-supporting, they must not be compelled to labor with their hands bound.

The commission was appointed in March 1863, and it made its preliminary report on June 30.

Much of the discussion of the board was academic rather than practical, and it covered not only slavery but many cognate subjects. Dr. Howe was deeply interested in the work of the Sanitary Commission and, in the intervals of advocating various phases of prison reform, was at this time preparing to bear supplies to the Cretans in their struggle with the Turks.

Robert Dale Owen, who had settled the Northwestern Boundary question with the calm prescience and wisdom of a true statesman, and ought to have learned something from the disastrous experiment of New Harmony, was very fond of lecturing his associates on the noble work of his esteemed father and Fourier and of insisting that the millennium would be hastened and the happiness of the human race promoted by an equal distribution of all the property of all the thrifty.

The secretary has hesitated to consider it within the lines of his duty to record here the fact that the sessions of the commission were mostly occupied with conversation — high-toned conversation too, but not generally relevant to the purposes of the meetings. This was inevitable, for the temptation was irresistible. Rarely has such an extraordinarily brilliant audience been assembled. Abstruse and recondite topics were always in order, for these scholars had drunk deep at the fountains of the Sagas and Vedas, the Zend-Avesta and the Bhagavad-Gita. Not only were they at home with Confucius and Plato and the ancient philosophers, but they were students of Kant, Hegel, Spinoza, Comte, and Fichte. Every member spoke fluently several languages, which seemed somewhat superfluous in dealing with the runaway Negroes from Virginia. Such eloquent conversationalists have seldom got together since Coleridge explained to his friends the merits of the Pantisocracy.

Colonel McKayes was a plain, practical, efficient soldier, who took very little interest in this theorizing, but busied himself in bringing order from chaos along the extensive frontier. Douglass used playfully to allude to himself as "the fifth wheel of the coach," but during the life of the commission he was active in season and out of season in rescuing slaves from their bondage, and he raised two regiments of colored troops among the fugitives and sent them into the field, receiving the thanks of Mr. Lincoln for the success of his efforts.

The outcome of the deliberations and discussions of the Freedmen's Commission cannot be said to have been very fruitful of results. Its published reports consisted of a series of humane essays on the wrong of slavery, the blessings of freedom, and the future of the African race, and had very little practical effect on the termination of the great conflict.

# V

## PEGGY O'NEILL AND GENERAL JACKSON [1]

WHEN I was writing letters from Secretary Chase's dictation in 1863, an old lady was seen walking the streets of Washington every day, whose unique personality excited much interest and curiosity. Her good-natured face, full of wrinkles and smiles, was surrounded by an aureole of white curls on which was perched an ancient poke bonnet of bygone style. And by the side of her wasted cheek flamed a great rose as large as a peony. Accompanied or alone, she coursed hither and yon through the streets, nodding familiarly to everyone she met. And everyone she met returned the attention and wheeled around to look at her when she had passed. She had an air of authority, and carried with her a suggestion of youthful grace, vivacity, and beauty. The people of Washington knew Peggy O'Neill better than they did President Lincoln, and they knew of her sore trials and wonderful triumphs as a leader in society and politics. They knew, too, whose protégée she had been, and they did not hesitate to handle her reputation freely. I should have spoken to the distinguished old lady and recalled her radiant youth, but I felt that it might seem intrusive, and contented myself with completing a knowledge of her history.

When the popular idol of the West, Andrew Jackson, was a member of the United States Senate, he boarded in Washington at the spacious tavern at I and Twentieth streets kept

[1] From *Putnam's Magazine,* September 1908.

by an Irishman named William O'Neill.  He had taken a special liking, years before, to Mrs. O'Neill, the efficient landlady, and he kept the acquaintance warm and bright.  Major John H. Eaton, the other Senator from Tennessee, boarded at the same place, and together they petted and surfeited with candy the daughter of the O'Neills — Peggy, a girl of twelve or fifteen, who grew during the years of their presence into an uncommonly handsome, intelligent, and lively young lady. It was about the worst possible place to bring up a girl in. Clay and Randolph were continuous guests.  Growing up in the environment of an average inn, with all the familiarity which such a position implies, Peggy lacked refinement and delicacy, but she had, besides the inevitable *chic* and cheek, the flippancy of speech and the voluptuous beauty which characterize so many of the maidens of the North of Ireland.

Peggy was thoroughly unconventional and defiant of proprieties, and soon became willful and reckless.  She flirted in a way that she considered harmless, had a nodding acquaintance with most of the good-looking travelers, arranged twice to elope, and finally, about 1822, suddenly married Purser John B. Timberlake of the United States Navy.  But she disliked the sea and preferred to remain in Washington among her old associates.  Three handsome children were born to her during the next five years.  In 1828, the very year of Old Hickory's election to the Presidency, Purser Timberlake, then on duty in the Mediterranean, jumped into the sea after cutting his throat in a fit of melancholy, and left a most attractive and fascinating widow to mourn her loss.

She was not wholly inconsolable.  Her grace and beauty had taken Washington by storm.  She had a thousand admirers — more than enough to spoil her.  When Madison was President, his popular wife had publicly crowned Peggy at a ball as the prettiest girl in Washington.  She was brilliant and superficial, courageous and capricious, vain and vacillating, affectionate, generous, and quick-tempered. She was now at the zenith of her loveliness — one of those examples of Irish beauty which suggest both the Greek and the Spaniard, yet at times present a combination which transcends both. Her form, of medium height, straight and lissome, was of perfect proportions. Her skin was of that delicate white, tinged with red, which one often sees among even the poorer inhabitants of the Green Isle. Her dark hair, very abundant, clustered in curls about her broad forehead. Her perfect nose, of Grecian proportions, and her finely curved mouth, with a firm, round chin, completed a profile of faultless outlines. Such a girl was sure to have a great variety of experiences. To her Edward Coate Pinkney at a public banquet addressed his famous poem, "A Health," beginning: —

I fill this cup to one made up
    Of loveliness alone,
A woman, of her gentle sex
    The seeming paragon;
To whom the better elements
    And kindly stars have given
A form so fair that, like the air
    'T is less of earth than heaven.

As soon as the sad news of Timberlake's death could make its way home, Senator Eaton said to Jackson: "General, I 've a good mind to marry Peggy myself."

"Do, by all means, Senator, if you love her and she 'll have you," was the reply. "It will restore Peggy's good name, and she will make you a good wife."

So merrily rang the bells, and they were wed. This was in January 1829. And there was a great time in Washington that week. The bride was proud and ambitious, and she made the most of the occasion.   Jackson, Clay, Benton, Van Buren, Calhoun, and half the Senate and many members of the House, and scores of army and navy officers were present at the wedding.   But the ladies of Washington tabooed the ceremony, on the ground that the bride was too well known.

In the tavern she had lost the first bloom of her reputation. In the select homes of Washington she was voted "impossible" and left to her own inevitable preferences.   Men flattered and talked about the handsome Peggy, but women pointedly ignored her.   Mrs. Jackson fervently disliked her and declined to speak to her; and when she and the Senator went home to Tennessee, she rejoiced publicly and opposed his election to the Presidency by every means in her power. "Andrew," she pleaded pathetically, "I don't want to go back to Washington on any acount."

In spite of the prayers and tears and gentle opposition of his Rachel, the hero of New Orleans was elected at sixty to be President of the United States, and when he hurried back to her with the news, she exclaimed: "It is not as I wished it!   It is not as I wished it!   Andrew, I cannot go to Washington again."   Two weeks after the victory was known at the Hermitage, she died suddenly of heart disease.

Jackson mourned his wife sincerely, and proclaimed her, as she no doubt was, chiefly a martyr to the partisan aspersions of her character on account of her having lived with him as his wife some years before their marriage, erroneously supposing herself divorced from her former husband.   For alluding to this circumstance Jackson had already fought a duel with Governor Sevier, and had killed Charles Dickinson.

When he came back to Washington as President, he at once called his friend, Senator Eaton, into the Cabinet as Secretary of War.   Then there was a breeze!   The other ladies of the Cabinet circle refused to associate with Mrs. Eaton officially or to recognize her personally. The virtue of the whole United States was stirred up, and a committee of clergymen was sent to the White House to lay the scandal before President Jackson, supposed to be entirely ignorant of it. They assured him that they had come only in his behalf; that Peggy had been careless of her reputation from girlhood; that she had told her servants to call her two children Eaton and not Timberlake, as Eaton was their proper name; and that she and Senator Eaton had traveled together on several occasions.

Jackson angrily repelled his visitors and called them slanderers. A correspondence of months resulted — on his part long, vehement, and bitter. The whole mass of this confidential controversy, mostly in the handwriting of General Jackson himself, is still extant, and would fill many pages of a magazine — not less than two hundred letters in all. He brought to Peggy's defense all the energy that had made him such an Indian fighter.

But he was fighting women now, instead of mere Indians, and they defied him and cut Peggy dead.

Among those who were "terribly shocked" by the President's championship of the wife of his Secretary of War were two eminent clergymen, the Reverend Mr. Ely of Philadelphia and the Reverend Mr. Campbell of Washington, the latter being the pastor of the church which General and Mrs. Jackson had habitually attended. Mr. and Mrs. Campbell felt moved to visit the President and remonstrate upon his conduct. They did call at the White House. It is to be regretted that only a very brief epitome of the interview has come down to us.

"The last time I beheld your face, Mr. President," said the reverend caller, "you and the dear partner of your bosom sat beneath my ministrations. She was a most exemplary and virtuous female." The General trembled at such a coarse and intrusive allusion to one whom he so dearly loved and revered, but he said nothing, and the garrulous caller went on: "That beloved partner of your life, Mr. President, has been called from among us, she has departed hence. Whom the Lord loveth He chasteneth. We cannot be too grateful for the privilege of having known so beautiful a character, whose conduct should be an example to us all. Let us pray."

He suddenly dropped upon his knees and poured forth a fervent if fragmentary supplication that they might all be "defended from the wiles and assaults of the devil." On resuming his seat he told the President that he had something important on his mind but would find another opportunity to speak of it, and took his leave.

To bring matters to a focus, the President called a Cabinet meeting and invited the two clergymen to be present and prove their case. They came and they declared that in all they had done their object had been to save the administration of General Jackson from reproach, and the morals of the party from contamination. They offered to prove that Major Eaton and Mrs. Timberlake had visited a New York hotel together. The President announced that he would receive no testimony except such as demonstrated the criminality of the parties; everything else would be regarded as slander. As Mr. Campbell was proceeding to remark on the evidence, General Jackson interrupted him with marked asperity, saying that the minister had been summoned to give evidence, not to discuss it. After a further effort to explain, Mr. Campbell said: "I stand ready to prove, in a court of justice, all I have said, and more than I have said, or would have dared to say three days ago." He then bowed to the Cabinet and retired. The council broke up shortly and the President declared Mrs. Eaton a vindicated woman. But Mr. Campbell's church was no longer honored by the attendance of the President of the United States.

Again General Jackson summoned his Cabinet and lectured them, and he assured his advisers that Peggy Eaton was "as chaste as snow." Though obviously something he could not prove, he offered to guarantee it, and formally demanded that their wives should recognize and visit her. "You seem, Mr. President, to labor under a misapprehension as to who is general in my family," said Attorney-General Berrien.

The ladies persisted in their revolt, and made it nearly unanimous. The wives of John C. Calhoun, Vice President; John M. Berrien, Attorney-General; S. D. Ingham, Secretary of the Treasury, and John Branch, Secretary of the Navy, refused either to receive Peggy or to call upon her; and the wives of the foreign ministers declined to bow to her or to recognize her in any way. Even Jackson's favorite niece, Mrs. Donelson, the mistress of the White House, joined the revolt and said: "Anything else, Uncle, ask me to do, but I cannot call upon Mrs. Eaton."

The warrior's blood was up. "You can't call on Mrs. Eaton, can't you? You take the next stage and go home to Tennessee!" he exclaimed; and she and her husband packed their things and went.

He then started to discipline his intractable Cabinet. Van Buren, Secretary of State, was a widower, and Barry, Postmaster-General, was a bachelor, so they good-naturedly lent themselves to the President's wishes. They called on Mrs. Eaton, as also did Amos Kendall. Colonel Benton and Isaac Hill, prominent partisans, and Lord Vaughan, the British Minister, and Baron Krudener, the Russian Minister, both bachelors, joined the whitewashing brigade. Lord Vaughan gave a brilliant and expensive ball in the direct

interest of "Bellona," which was Mrs. Eaton's warlike nickname; but though the distinguished British Minister himself
led her to the head of the banquet table, other ladies were
persistently unconscious of her presence, and every cotillion
she joined was immediately broken up by their withdrawal.

Then Baron Krudener gave a splendid ball, and when the
wife of the Minister from Holland (Huyghens) refused to sit
by Peggy's side at supper, Jackson threatened orally and on
the instant to send her husband home.

The President's fiery soul was enlisted in Peggy's vindica-
tion, and often while he was in the White House he used to
stroll across lots to the little cottage where Peggy's mother
lived, and plan the campaign.

The women were inexorable.  The three married men in
the Cabinet refused to speak to Eaton, Secretary of War,
except as official business absolutely required it, and in the
presence of the President.  General Jackson wrote a very
plain-spoken note on the subject to Vice President Calhoun,
but only elicited from him the diplomatic reply that it was a
"ladies' quarrel," with which men could not successfully
interfere, adding that "their laws are like the laws of the Medes
and Persians, admitting neither of argument nor amend-
ment." Mrs. Calhoun snubbed Peggy publicly, and for
every snub, immediately reported to him by Peggy, who was
a constant visitor at the White House, "Old Hickory" laid
away a poisoned arrow for her husband, his associate in
office.  Ten years later one of those arrows made its way
through one of the joints in the political armor of the great
Nullifier and reached a vital spot.

Mr. Ingham, Secretary of the Treasury, being requested
in a tone of command to "make his family" visit Mrs. Eaton,
vigorously replied: "If the President chooses to exert his power
to force my family to visit anybody they do not choose to

visit, he is interfering with my duties and privileges, and no human power shall regulate the social intercourse of my family by means of official or any other power while I can resist."

It was at this time, and during the progress of this affair, that Van Buren became the pet of Jackson and his preordained successor. The President slapped him familiarly on the shoulder at receptions and addressed him as "Matty" in public.

The General charged that "the villains who circulate these base stories would not hesitate to slander the most virtuous female in the country, nay, even the Saviour." He alleged that much of the mischief was caused by "the minions of Henry Clay," and that "Mr. Clay and his wife are circulating these slanderous reports"; and he ended a vigorous letter on the subject with these words: "In the language of the Psalmist, 'the liar's tongue we ever hate and banish from our sight.'"

The exasperated champion of Mrs. Eaton now sent to Kentucky and summoned Colonel Richard M. Johnson to come to Washington and help to suppress the "assailants of female virtue," doubtless assuming that the warrior who had "killed Tecumseh" would be able to thwart the machinations of Peggy's defamers. But the hope was vain; the arm of the victor of Tippecanoe was palsied in the presence of women who had made up their minds. He investigated the quarrel, only to find that, though he had vanquished the great savage of the central plains, he was a failure as a mediator. He reported that the President "was so excited that he roared like a raging lion." When told that to expel two foreign ministers because their wives refused to dance with the lady in question might bring on a war, Old Hickory, in a frenzy of rage, shouted that he did not care what happened, "he would send them and their husbands home, and teach them and their masters that the wife of a member of his Cabinet was not to be thus treated; that he would be cut into inch pieces on the rack before he would suffer him or his wife to be injured by their vile calumnies."

The gallant killer of Tecumseh had failed to allay the storm, but he had sprung with alacrity to the championship of Peggy Eaton, and that was enough to make him thenceforth the favorite of the wrathful President. He was at once assured that promotion awaited him, and in 1837 he came to his inheritance — the Vice Presidency of the United States in Van Buren's administration.

Old Hickory could not control even his own best friends. Duff Green's administration "organ," the Telegraph, spoke slightingly of Peggy, and Jackson at once threw it overboard and called Francis P. Blair from Kentucky to start a personal organ for him, the Globe, which, by the aid of Peggy's partisans, sprang into instant success.

Daniel Webster, watching with delight the breach in the Democratic party, wrote home at this time: "Mr. Van Buren has at this moment quite the lead in influence and importance. He controls all the pages at the back stairs, and flatters what seems to be at present the Aaron's rod among the President's desires — a settled purpose of making out the lady of whom so much has been said a person of reputation. This dispute may very probably determine who shall be the successor to the present chief magistrate. Such great events," and so forth. James Gordon Bennett wrote from Washington to the New York Herald, "I think John C. Calhoun has doomed himself to oblivion by his refusal to rehabilitate Peggy Eaton." So, indeed, it proved; and very shortly.

With the promptness which characterized him in all warfare, General Jackson, when his first term was half ended, demanded the immediate resignation of Secretaries Ingham, Branch, and Berrien, the three married members of his Cabinet, whose punctilious wives had brought mortification to "good little Peggy," as he affectionately called the lady in question.

They resigned.  He sent them home without any hypocritical letters of regret, and appointed as their successors men whose wives were understood to be willing to declare a truce with Peggy.  The new Cabinet (for both Van Buren and Eaton had now been appointed ministers to foreign countries) were Edward Livingston, Louis MacLane, Levi Woodbury, Lewis Cass, and Roger B. Taney.  Calhoun, feeling himself *de trop,* resigned the Vice Presidency and publicly espoused Nullification, drawing from Jackson his famous indignant message.

During the quarrel Mrs. Eaton was alluded to in Duff Green's administration organ, the Telegraph, as Madame de Pompadour.  At the instigation of the President, General Eaton, believing that Attorney-General Berrien of Georgia had inspired the insult, sent him a challenge to fight a duel. This was declined with derision, whereupon Eaton stigmatized him as a coward, and expressed an ardent desire to "meet him face to face."

Thomas Corwin, just elected to Congress, wrote home to Ohio: "The fair dame, Margaret Eaton, outvies the Kitchen Cabinet in interest, and attracts more attention than any other lady in Washington.  She has created nothing less than a revolution in the Government, and has scattered a very respectable group of presidential advisers to the four winds of heaven; and apparently the end is not yet."

Jackson was not satisfied with merely rebuking Calhoun and overthrowing his ambition: he wanted to make sure of securing the promotion of Peggy's diplomatic defender.  So, during his first term he wrote a letter "to be published only in case of my death," in which he definitely nominated Van Buren as his successor; and then he called him to his side as Vice President in place of Calhoun, retired. If Jackson could not always compel obedience, he at least knew how to punish disobedience.

The plain fact is that Jackson himself was chiefly to blame for the unpleasant conspicuousness which Mrs. Eaton attained. He should have known that his fervent championship of her would injure her, for a woman's good name is about the most delicate and sensitive thing in the world. The sad case of his own Rachel ought to have been a warning to him; and it would have been, if he had not been too fierce in his hostilities and resentments to be discreet — in other words, if he had been anybody but Jackson.

"Good little Peggy" comes into history only once more — or at most twice. After her husband's suicide, Lieutenant Robert B. Randolph was appointed to succeed him as purser. The accounts were found badly tangled, and the President instantly denounced Randolph as a defaulter and dismissed him from the service as "an unfit associate of those sons of chivalry who adorn our navy." Randolph violently resented the accusation, produced a full set of vouchers to prove that his own accounts were straight, and declared that it was Timberlake who had defaulted on account of seven thousand dollars he had lent to Eaton. He called for a court of inquiry, and affirmed, "I am removed without just cause to appease Kendall and minister to the black avarice and cowardly resentment of Eaton, who might long since have closed the accounts of Timberlake by returning to the Government the money and effects which he tempted that officer to take from the public funds in his trust." The court, while failing to commit itself as to Eaton's criminality, recorded its finding that Randolph had no intention to defraud the Government or Timberlake. But the President rebuked the court, refused further hearing, and confirmed the arbitrary dismissal of the officer, "after twenty-three years of honorable service." Lieutenant Randolph angrily denounced the charge as "infamously malicious," and closed with the declaration: "In signing the fiat for my dismissal the President has accommodated himself to the malignity of John H. Eaton and Amos Kendall, worthy associates of their malicious and imbecile master."

But the officially disgraced officer was not content with mere words, however vehement. In May 1833, while the President was on his way to Fredericksburg to lay the cornerstone of the monument to Mary, the mother of Washington, Randolph crowded on board the boat without an invitation, and deliberately pulled General Jackson's nose and cursed him! He was immediately seized and flung ashore, out of reach of the irate President, who begged to be allowed to kill him.

Eaton was sent as Minister to Spain, where his Peggy had a brilliant and even pyrotechnical career in the lively court of Isabella, for fifteen of the happiest years of her life. Then she brought her husband back to Washington, and here, after quarreling with General Jackson, he died. At the age of sixty the extraordinary woman married a man less than twenty-one, an Italian music teacher, who was giving lessons to her grandchildren. It proved to be the crown of her follies. He ran away with her money and her granddaughter.

She survived even this youth, after divorcing him, and died in Washington in 1879 at the ripe age of eighty-three. I remember her very well as a famous personage of the Capital — amiable, vivacious, cheerful, triumphant, in spite of her troubles, not more garrulous than her years, and attracting pleasant attention wherever she went. Her last words were: "I am not afraid at all; but this is such a beautiful world!"

I do not remember any woman who has so impressed herself on the destinies of this country as Peggy O'Neill.   For: —

1.  She drove three members of the Cabinet into an obscurity from which they never emerged.

2.  She greatly diminished the influence of Calhoun and made his promotion to the Presidency impossible.

3.  She made Martin Van Buren Jackson's favorite and successor.

4.  She brought Lewis Cass into federal politics and made him a candidate for President, securing probably the election of General Taylor in 1848.

5.  She introduced Roger B. Taney to public life, making him Secretary of the Treasury and afterwards Chief Justice of the Supreme Court, with the Dred Scott decision at the end.

6.  She called Francis P. Blair and John C. Reeves into Washington journalism, where they established the Globe, a potent influence for a generation.

Nothing succeeds like success.  Mrs. Eaton's Timberlake daughters became highly educated and accomplished members of Washington society.  One of them, famed for her loveliness, married Dr. John B. Randolph; and the other, the beautiful Virginia, wedded the Duke de Sampayo of Paris; while a granddaughter, inheriting the family fascination, became Baroness de Rothschild of Austria.

Mrs. Eaton enjoyed to the last an interest in the large property which her husband left, and there is still retained among the household treasures of her descendants in Washington the silver service used at the banquet given to Lafayette.

# VI

## A CORRESPONDENT AT THE FRONT

CAN a page or two of this chronicle be spared for a brief record of one of my gallops in Virginia for the Tribune? My first impression of Manassas as I saw it: a junction of railroad tracks in a five-hundred-acre swamp; three very shabby buildings, and the ruins of twenty more; barracks innumerable and mud unfathomable, with strips of board laid end to end from hut to hut, to keep the unhappy inhabitants from premature burial; an acre or two of broken-down and deserted wagons — mere ancient scows with wheels put to them; twenty acres sown with wrecks of every imaginable article — broken bottles, books, provisions, shattered demijohns, rags, furniture, knives, tents, harness, arms and equipments half burnt, tracts, Bibles, musty tobacco, and more bottles; Negroes of every size groping among the rubbish.

From this point I accompanied General Stoneman's raid towards Richmond. The country was thoroughly desolated. Farms had been plundered of their stock; bridges, depots, and settlements had been burned; the carcasses of thousands of horses tainted the poisoned air while feebly enriching the exhausted fields. Deserted dogs and hungry cats whined after and followed us from barns that had escaped the torch, as if seeking their faithless masters, and here and there rose, like a grim witness, the blackened shaft that two days before had been the centre of a homestead.

It was April of 1863. We struck south of west to Cat-
lett's Station, and during the three days we rode it rained incessantly. As we advanced we found the bridges destroyed
and had to swim our horses across Broad and Kettle runs. I
remember the most vividly the experiences of our first night
out. We camped in the field under a drenching rain which
poured steadily from night till morning. We — at least the
officers' squad of Colonel Zook's 57th New York, which
kindly extended to me all the hospitality it had — lay or
crouched under a scrub oak. We brought rails from an adjoining fence and stuck one end of them up over the lower
branches while the other end rested on the water-soaked
ground. On the outside of these we laid our blankets, which
carried off a little of the rain, while we huddled on rails
beneath. It was cold, I remember, and after a few minutes
of experimentation we hustled out and got more rails and
split them up and made a faint fire at the base of the tree.
That fitful flame was an immense attraction for visitors, but
our rude wigwam would not hold all of Stoneman's army.

How we entertained ourselves in the hours of sleepless-
ness is what I most distinctly remember. I had found an
old paper-covered copy of Byron in one of the rebel shanties
at Manassas that morning, and I sat on a rail during the
night and by the wavering light of the bonfire read from
"Childe Harold" and "Don Juan." I smile now as I recall
the crowding of squad after squad around the trunk of that
tree, each wet squad bringing its quota of rails as a fire offering, and I remember what lively attention was given by the
bedraggled audience with mingled laughter and applause,
and how they insisted that the reading should go on till
long after midnight. Indeed, it was only from time to time
interrupted, not ended, till daylight superseded the light of
the embers. It certainly rendered the rain less wet, the

darkness less dark, and threw a glamour of mitigation over the dreariness of the night. At daylight we started again. The details of that cavalry ride are shadowy, although it was punctuated by a skirmish and impressed upon the memory by the loss of several men.

During the first three years of the war, Homer Byington was chief correspondent of the New York Tribune in Washington. When he was absent in the field I often left the Quartermaster's accounts to look out for themselves and ran out and lent him a hand. He beat all the other newspapers in bringing to Mr. Lincoln and the Tribune the report of the victory of Gettysburg. More than once I heard him tell the interesting story, and it ran about as follows: —

"It was the latter half of June, 1863, that I got a dispatch from Culpeper Courthouse to hurry out there, for our army was on the move. I went at once; but the army had already started north at a rapid pace, keeping between the rebel army and Washington. Hooker was in command. I went to the headquarters of Meade, at Goose Creek. He told me there was going to be a battle, and that my best way was to go back to Washington and hurry up to Harper's Ferry, where I could head off our army and find the 17th Connecticut, whose quartermaster had one of my horses. I followed his directions and he gave me a special pass, taking me anywhere. When I reached Harper's Ferry I found Hooker in a fume. I soon learned that he had demanded to have the ten thousand inactive men on Bolivar Heights attached to his own army for the battle with Lee, and that Halleck had refused. Hooker resigned that afternoon, and Lincoln commissioned Meade to command the Army of the Potomac. General Bob Tyler, of the Connecticut Brigade, was there; and he took my map and marked a red ring around on it across the Penn-

sylvania line and said: 'In a few days there will be within
that circle one of the biggest fights the world ever saw. Go
round to Baltimore and head Lee off at York.'

"Again I followed directions. I tried Baltimore, but news
came that the rebels had burnt the bridges and torn up the
tracks. I hurried to Philadelphia and got to York by way
of Lancaster, determined to be the first reporter on the
ground. The track was torn up, but I hired a minister to
carry me twelve miles in his wagon. Stuart's rebel cavalry
had visited York, raided the provision stores, and taken fifty
thousand dollars from the bank.

"Now and then I heard a gun go off in the southwest.
I ransacked the town, but Stuart had got all the horses.
Finally I found one solitary horse and buggy, and gave the
owner an order on the Tribune for the rig. I drove in the
direction of the cannonading ten or twelve miles, evaded
some rebel cavalry on the way, and got to Hanover. There
had been a severe cavalry fight there. The town had a
disorderly appearance; people stayed close in their homes,
and the débris of arms and accoutrements lay along the
road. The wounded were gathered in a church. Telegraph
wires were broken and strewn around. I stopped at the
hotel and asked the landlord if there was no telegraph operator there. 'Yes, there he is, over yonder,' said he, pointing
out a little hunchback named Tone, asleep on a bench. I
shook him and asked him where his battery was. 'Home
under the bed,' he said. 'Wires all cut everywhere; no use
trying to telegraph.' I persisted, and went over to his house
with him and pulled out the battery. After a good deal
of parleying I hired some men to go out on a hand car five
miles and fix the wires, I paying the men well and making
myself responsible for the value of the car. The battery was
brought out, the wires hitched together, and the operator

swung his hat and shouted that we had got Baltimore. It was arranged that I should have an absolute monopoly of the wire for two days.

"Then I rushed off to the battlefield some six miles south. Before reaching there I met General Howard, and he told me about the first day's fight, of Reynolds's death, and the present location of the armies. Sypher, one of the Tribune men, had followed me from Lancaster, and we sent off by our private wire an account of the fight of the first two days. It was a magnificent beat. No other account got through that night, and between nine o'clock and midnight the Tribune sold 65,000 copies on the streets of New York.

"Tone kept getting the strange signal 'KI,' 'KI.'

" 'What the dickens does KI mean?' he asked. 'I'm afraid the rebs have tapped our wire.'

"Finally we found out that we were communicating with General Eckert in the War Department at Washington. I had signed my dispatches 'Byington.' 'Who's Byington?' asked Mr. Lincoln, for he and Secretary Stanton supposed I was still in Washington. 'Ask Uncle Gideon,' I replied, referring thus familiarly to the Secretary of the Navy, Mr. Gideon Welles of our state. There was great rejoicing at Washington. 'We've got Byington's first dispatch,' said Stanton, 'and it is our first news. Send along more. We are listening.'

"For two days I sent exclusive dispatches over my wire, giving all the particulars attainable of the great battle, while the Herald, much handicapped, was running ten-mile relays of horses. I telegraphed to Secretary Stanton that the railroad was whole from York to Baltimore, and the government at once sent out trains for our wounded. The surgeon told me that our railroad saved General Sickles's life.

"After the battle I got a horse and hurried on after the

rebels, wondering why Meade did not pursue. They were all broken up and demoralized, the roadside strewn with sick and wounded men, with dead horses and abandoned muskets and spiked cannon. Next day I came up with Lee's main army. It was huddled together in a horse-shoe bend of the Potomac at Williamsport — in a valley surrounded by hills on one side and the swollen and rushing river on the other. It would have been easy to bag them all. Their flight was fatally interrupted. The pontoons they had crossed on were swept away and they had no immediate means of recrossing. By a friend who accompanied me I sent back to President Lincoln and the Tribune the somewhat premature dispatch, 'We 've got Lee's army tight. It cannot escape.'

"After waiting there awhile I turned back to meet Meade's army, which I supposed must be rapidly approaching down the road. In vain I looked and waited. It did not heave in sight. Finally an old man came up out of the valley where the rebels were encamped, driving a sorry Virginia outfit — a ramshackle of a wagon, a dying horse tied to it by tow strings, and in it, besides the native driver, a woman and children, each wearing apparently a single garment and all sitting in the straw. He said Lee had encamped right around his house, down in the swale, and he had had to quit it. He said he supposed the whole of Lee's army would be gobbled right where it lay. I asked him what he would charge to go and tell General Meade all about the situation. He said he would do it for three dollars. I gave him three dollars which evidently seemed to him a big pile, and he moved on towards Gettysburg.

"Well, you know the rest. Lee's army stayed right there three days and then captured a lumberyard and made rafts and floated across the river at their leisure.

"I was in Washington when Meade came to report after the battle of Gettysburg. I asked Secretary Welles about the interview.

"He said: 'I was there when he came in. "Do you know, General," Mr. Lincoln suddenly broke out with a laugh, "what your attitude towards Lee after the battle of Gettysburg reminded me of?" "No, Mr. President — what is it?" asked Meade. "I'll be hanged," said Lincoln, "if I could think of anything but an old woman trying to shoo her geese across the creek!"'

"After that day Meade never quite recovered his own confidence or that of the army."

Before the outbreak of the Rebellion I had met and formed a pleasant acquaintance with Mr. Cornelius S. Bushnell, an ingenious and public-spirited resident of New Haven. He was a contractor and a rather reckless speculator, for all his geese were swans and he had too active an imagination for uniform success as a practical business man. He had several bees in his bonnet and behind his back was frequently, if not generally, alluded to as "a crank." After Fort Sumter was fired on Bushnell developed a fantastic hobby — the notion that a war vessel could be so clad in railroad iron as to be practically invulnerable. His friends ridiculed the idea from the start. Secretary Welles took no stock in it. But a spy suddenly returned from a hasty visit to Norfolk and Richmond and reported that the rebels were secretly preparing to assail the Union fleet in Hampton Roads with a strange device which they believed would overwhelm and destroy it. This report, though vague, compelled attention and set Mr. Lincoln and his Cabinet to thinking vigorously.

Bushnell at once drew plans for his floating battery, and

he then went to Washington and strove to induce the government to advance money on it. Secretary Welles declined to build such a vessel unless the government was indemnified against possible loss. Bushnell camped in the Navy Department and besieged its venerable chief with tireless importunity. Persistence had its reward. Bushnell returned to New Haven and collected and borrowed money enough to enable him to give to the government the indemnifying bond. In the money required to execute this bond was the whole of his own fortune, for his confidence in the success of the experiment was unlimited.

Bushnell named the low-lying vessel the *Galena,* and, having finished a working drawing of it, he prudently called on Captain John Ericsson in New York to advise with him and assure himself of the requisite buoyancy and stability of the vessel under the stipulated weight of iron armor. The ingenious Swede inspected the drawing with profound interest. "No other man," said the Yankee, "had ever examined every detail of my projected boat with so much care." Then Bushnell was to be astonished in turn, for Ericsson led him to a shed adjoining his workshop and exhibited to him the working plans of a vessel which was intended for the same purpose and which he had named the *Monitor.* He had already applied to the French emperor, Napoleon III, and exhibited to him plans of a partially submerged vessel encased with iron, with guns in a revolving shot-proof cupola, placed centrally on deck. The ruler of the French declined to profit by the suggestion.

Mr. Bushnell was satisfied at once that Ericsson's twenty-five years of thoughtful experiment had resulted in the perfection of a plan for an impregnable warship. Lack of funds no longer prevented the immediate construction, and a contract was accordingly signed and the inventor gave him carte blanche for the construction of the vessel at Green Point. The Navy Board at Washington was so incredulous as to the value of the novel craft that it refused to accept her unless she could be built within one hundred days and the contractors had signed a guaranty that she should "prove a success."

The *Monitor* was finished and afloat in just ninety-nine days, and arrived at Fortress Monroe while the uncouth *Merrimac* was engaged in destroying the Union fleet. The result is known. From that day the Confederates abandoned their pretense of a navy. The "cheese-box on a raft" revolutionized the marine architecture of the world. The next mail carried to European nations news of a wonderful combat, involving their own destinies; and the admirals of many victories were startled to think how helpless would be their stoutest sloops of war before the iron beak.

The important part which Bushnell took in the construction of the *Monitor* is but little recognized and scarcely known. He boldly risked his fortune and those of his friends on a venture that was an experiment in which few believed. But even the Naval Board at Washington had at last waked up to the perils surrounding our fleet in Hampton Roads, and in response to hurry-up messages from the government, Bushnell drove his men night and day to get the little craft launched on time. The result justified his confidence and repaid the generous enthusiasm which superseded his own plans by those of another.

The illustrious Swede, John Ericsson, was one of the men I wished to see, and one morning I called on him. I found him in his disheveled office just above the City Hall and near the Five Points — where no other well-known man dwelt and where no other man could be found who was in independent circumstances and not a saloon keeper. Fifty years ago it was the centre of New York's gentility. The

THE MERRIMAC AND THE MONITOR

Hoffmans and Van Rensselaers lived there, and near by Washington Irving had his city home. All around the residence of Ericsson were aristocratic mansions in a state of decay — mansions of thirty or forty feet front with vast parlors turned into tenements or cheap stores, and porches, once imposing with their half-moons of radiating glass above the doors and long narrow windows of many-shaped glass flanking them, with doors now smudged and crippled and the handsome windows broken. The house of the great inventor was about the only one in good condition in the seedy neighborhood. On tables about the parlor were models of the curious machines he had made — the solar engine, the caloric engine, and a dozen other elaborate contrivances in polished brass and steel and glass. A wilderness of cylinders, pistons, wheels, and reflectors.

Ericsson was jubilant — celebrating his eighty-first birthday. A man stout and sturdy, six feet high and straight as a post, of firm hand grasp and rosy face and the sparkling eye of youth, hair black as a coal growing from his own head and enticed across his crown in a thinnish thatch, and each cheek bearing a thick clump of rather obtrusive mutton-chop whiskers — this was Captain Ericsson. He dressed in a half-clerical Prince Albert, the sleeves pulled up and turned back as if he were at work, and around his neck was a high Yankee dickey — bosom, collar, and "stock" in one. When he spoke it was in stentorian fashion, with voice of Blunderbore which rang through the house like a trumpet. I supposed he was deaf, and toned up my own vocal organ accordingly; but his secretary afterwards told me, "Why, no. He always talks that way; but he can see as far and hear as well as when he was a boy." Captain Ericsson talked freely about his inventions and devices, about his constructing the famous little *Monitor,* a picture of which hung on the wall; but when I asked about himself and his youth and growth, he shied, say-ing, "Never mind me. It is n't of consequence. Let's stick to the machines."

Among these was the first application of the screw to steam craft — an invention which was rejected by the British Admiralty fifty years before on the ground that "such a ves-sel could not be steered." Disgusted with the decision, Ericsson came to America, and here the first application of the screw was adopted. Although it came to be used by all civilized nations and acknowledged a tremendous success, the bill for $26,000 which Ericsson presented to Congress had never been paid. It is a disgraceful fact, too, that he never received a dollar for the invaluable service he rendered in producing the *Monitor,* which saved our battleships at the beginning of the Rebellion and turned defeat into victory and despair into exultation. Not a dollar! Is this any-thing less than dishonor, and does it not justify the declara-tion that "this nation is the most unscrupulous debtor and most exacting creditor in the world"?

The solar engine, one of the last of Ericsson's inventions, seemed at present scarcely more than a toy. It was in the back yard and looked like an inverted umbrella spread ten feet broad. It was intended to be run by steam from water expanding or air heated by a concentration of the sun's heat. "It is especially needed in Mexico," said Ericsson, "where the sun is hot and wood and coal are very scarce. The time is not distant when the solar engine will be in general use through the rainless regions of the earth. It would easily pull a train of cars across the desert of Sahara or over the arid sands of Egypt. Of the caloric engines run by hot air, 3500 have been sold and are now in use."

On a bench in one of the rooms was a model of a strange-looking locomotive. I asked if it was the "Novelty." Yes, it was — one of the first locomotives that ever ran in the world. In 1829 the Liverpool and Manchester Railroad offered a prize of $2500 for the best locomotive, and appointed a day for the trial. The Stevensons, father and son, were there with the "Rocket," and John Ericsson made his appearance with the "Novelty." The "Rocket" made fast time, but the "Novelty" beat it quite out of sight, making thirty miles an hour.

# VII

## POETS AND WRITERS

DURING these tumultuous years Walt Whitman occupied the second-floor hall bedroom of the house where I boarded. One morning when we met on the stairs he told me he had been dismissed from his clerkship by Secretary Harlan. He did not know the cause, but the Secretary made no secret of the fact that he had turned the "good gray poet" out of office because he considered *Leaves of Grass* an indecent book, the circulation of which ought to be diminished instead of increased. Of course the purpose miscarried, and a new edition of the improper book was immediately called for and exhausted. Whitman laughed at the alleged salacity, and he was restored, or rather reappointed to another place within a year by Attorney-General Speed, who did not classify the book with erotic verse of an extreme type. In the resulting excitement Whitman was called to the lecture field, but the call was not a very loud one. His long and flowing white hair and beard made a picturesque halo around his face which his extravagant linen collar and cuffs emphasized. But all Byronic affectations did not avail, and he was never a success upon the platform.

Whitman has always seemed to me to be greatly overestimated, especially as a poet. Hundred of his contemporaries produced much more beautiful and even more virile verse, whose names are absolutely unknown. He was an agreeable companion, but his best writings never moved me greatly. He had emotions, no doubt, but he despised art, and a true poet must be not primarily perhaps, but finally an artist.

Edmund C. Stedman was a Washington clerk at this same time, but he was an artist always, and Walt could no more have produced "The Sleigh Ride," or "Gettysburg," or *Victorian Poets,* than he could have flown.

I recall how one noon about this time I met six of the Treasury's literati at the little lunch table spread in the lower west corridor of the Department. The venerable poet John Pierpont and I, who greatly admired him, went downstairs together from our adjoining desks, — and it was something of a climb for the old man of eighty before the elevator era, — and there, seated on a bench near the door, taking rolls and coffee, were Edmund Stedman, A. B. Johnson, Sumner's private secretary, and John J. Piatt, also a fertile and delicate mind, afterwards useful in diplomacy. They were congenial companions. As we were taking off the edge of the midday appetite, Walt Whitman and W. D. O'Connor, his enthusiastic laureate, appeared and joined the group. All of them had produced something notable, and all of them except Pierpont did much better work afterwards.

One trifling detail of the luncheon I remember: Piatt ate mince pie, at which Stedman expressed his mocking horror and Pierpont said, "Piatt, is that the ambrosia you eat when you go to Parnassus? When I eat it, I go to Tartarus!" It is perhaps not odd that I never go out of the west door of the Treasury Department without thinking of Pierpont, Stedman, Piatt, Johnson, O'Connor, and Whitman, and the mince pie of that noontime long ago.

This small and studious coterie of clerks met weekly at this time to familiarize themselves with the French language. To one of them Victor Hugo kindly sent advance proofs of *Les Misérables,* and they employed their evenings in translating the novel orally into English, passing the proofs from hand to hand for that purpose. Whitman was the most expert interpreter, and when the rest were stalled with the thieves' argot, he was usually called on to clear away the obstruction and keep the story going.

One evening Whitman was an hour late, and on arriving explained that he had just come from the police station. He was walking quietly along F Street, he said, when a policeman grabbed him and charged him with being in disguise and wearing a mask. He was amazed and angry, but in the darkness he was sternly held as a dangerous law-breaker and taken to the station. On close inspection the lieutenant on duty at once released him, but the officer who had brought him in tried to explain: "You looked so queer; your long white hair and whiskers, sir, and your eyes set well back, and your pink face looking as if it was painted." "Well, well, never mind!" said the good-natured prisoner; "we all of us wear masks."

Charles Sumner, Johnson's employer, was a purist. His ears demanded nice accuracies of expression, and his delicate taste was shocked by any defacement of English, whether in pronunciation or in grammar. Henry Wilson, a graduate of the shoemaker's bench, was not so punctilious, and he sometimes spoke of his distinguished colleague, in the downeast lingo, as being "pernickety." While they were both walking to and fro in Washington and occupying a large space in the public eye, I heard a remark attributed to Mr. Wilson which was thought to indicate this difference between them. "The fact is," said Wilson, who then was Vice President, "Sumner always resents the conduct of the hoot owls in Massachusetts in not saying, 'To whom! To whom!' "

Another poet I saw while in Washington — thenceforth a pleasant remembrance. I got the first glimpse of him from the Press Gallery. He was standing in a corner of the Senate, leaning forward and patiently trying to pick a bit of the thread of current business from the bewildering tangle. Obviously he was a lion; for Sumner, Hamlin, Sprague, General Halleck, and other such advanced to greet him. It was Henry Wadsworth Longfellow — illustrious poet, linguist, and traveler. He was not tall; his dress was scrupulously neat; his hair was dark, with whiskers and moustache flowing together unmutilated. It would not have been surprising if they had been white as snow, for it was just after the awful accident in which his wife lost her life by fire. From a calm face he smiled welcome and good will on all, and maintained, through the formality of introduction and the running fire of conversation, an unflagging interest in the proceedings. Even from the gallery his identity was unmistakable.

The next day he called on Dr. Pierpont at the Treasury. As my desk was only ten or twelve feet further off, I earnestly hoped and rather expected that Pierpont would do me the honor of introducing me; but they seemed to have a thousand Boston topics and people to discuss, and my great wish to meet our greatest poet was not gratified. Finally the visitor consulted his watch; whereupon they rose together and sauntered out — the Divine Comedy wafted to the door by the Airs from Palestine.

Dr. Pierpont made an ideal president of the Washington Lecture Association. His wit was always scintillant and on hand; his good nature imperturbable. He attributed his long life to abstemious habits. His teeth were sound till old age, for he never chewed tobacco, his digestion unimpaired, for he never smoked it; he enjoyed all the odors of spring, for he never snuffed it; his eyes did not need the glasses at the optician's, for they never sought the glasses at the corner grocery.  He wrote as long as he lived, and even his last verses gave forth the scream of the wild eagle.

I am reminded here that General Grant's death was no doubt hastened by the strain occasioned by his work on his great biography and the necessity of finishing it.  He wrote it with his own hand.  It would have been better to take a good phonographer and talk to him, chronologically and as connectedly as possible, about the war, leaving the talk to be put in shape by some expert friend.  But he found it most difficult to dictate, and when he knew that his words were being taken down it clogged his tongue.  Very few men dictate well or easily, even if they are accomplished writers.  The best dictator I ever knew was "Private Miles O'Reilly" (Colonel Halpine), whom I have seen dictate a straight column in half an hour, and send the phonographer's transcript to the press without changing a word.  Secretary Chase was, in his prime, an easy writer by dictation, having the knack of saying the right thing in the right way.  He had uncommon "facility" — that gift which oftenest comes of journalistic training.  He liked to write his own letters, especially on matters that concerned him personally, but he could dictate freely and tersely, even epigramatically.  Mr. Lincoln disliked dictation as much as General Grant.  "I can never think except with my fingers," he would say.  So he did the wise thing — saying conversationally what he wanted to reply to a letter, and trusting Nicolay or Hay or Neill to put it in shape.  If he had had training when young, Horace Greeley would have dictated well, for he thought clearly and rapidly and conversed brilliantly; but he always stumbled over his phonographer.  I remember trying to help him add something to one of his lectures.  He stam-

POETS AND WRITERS 113

mered and halted, struck out paragraphs and began again, till finally he brushed me away from the desk impatiently and said, "Here! Get away! Let me come there!" and he seized the pen himself. But I had to appeal to him again when it came to disentangling his terrible manuscript.

# VIII

## ABRAHAM LINCOLN, 1861–1864

I HAVE never known so great a change to take place in any man's appearance as in Mr. Lincoln's during the three years following the day when I first saw him — March 4, 1861. He was never handsome, indeed, but he grew more and more cadaverous and ungainly month by month. The terrible labor which the great war imposed prevented him from taking systematic exercise, and he became constantly more lean and sallow. He had a very dejected appearance, and ugly black rings appeared under his eyes. I well remember how weary and sad he looked at one of the inevitable receptions as he stood near the folding doors where the central corridor empties itself into the East Room.

As there was a pause for a moment in the stream of visitors, I heard a lady standing near him ask if the incessant handshaking was not even more fatiguing than his work up in the office.

"Oh no — no," he answered. "Of course this is tiresome physically; but I am pretty strong, and it rests me, after all, for here nobody is cross or exacting, and no man asks me for what I can't give him!" And he gave his hand to the next in line.

During the last two years of his life, he was constantly threatened with assassination. Of course no public notice was taken of the menaces, and he alluded to them only to protest against the military escort which he could not always escape. When Secretary Stanton or General Hitchcock warned him of danger, he said, "Nobody can escape assassination by dodging. Moreover, if they kill me, the next man will be just as bad as I am! Under a republic no man can defend himself with a bodyguard. If I had a platoon with drawn sabres always at the door, they would cry out that I was aiming to be emperor!"

He was always exposed to personal attack. There were at least two doorkeepers to pass before getting to his room, but they did not consider it necessary to be vigilant after office hours, and I often walked into the White House unchallenged and went straight up to the private secretary's room adjoining his own, without seeing any person whatever. And it was no uncommon thing for him to go alone out of the house at almost any hour of the day or night, and walk across the lawn to the War Department for a consultation or to seek some news.

During the search that succeeded his assassination it was ascertained that very complete arrangements had been made to kidnap him, and the gloomy cellar of the old Van Ness mansion down by the river had been prepared for his prison.

Notwithstanding his constant exposure to danger, Mr. Lincoln often said, "I am physically a coward, and should very likely run if great danger threatened me. I 'm afraid of a gun." His estimate of his physical courage is hardly consistent with the fact that, when challenged to fight a duel by the intrepid General Shields in 1834, he promptly accepted, and thus defined the conditions: —

"First, weapons: cavalry broadswords — size precisely equal in all respects to such as are now used by the cavalry company at Jacksonville.

"Second, position: a plank ten feet long and from nine to twelve inches wide, to be firmly fixed on the ground as the line between us which neither is to pass his foot over on forfeit of his life. Next, a line drawn on the ground on either side of said plank and parallel with it at the distance of the whole length of the sword and three feet additional from the plank, and the passing of such line by either party shall be deemed a surrender of the contest.

"Third, time: Thursday evening at five o'clock."

The seconds prevented a collision.

If not afraid on his own account, he certainly had some fear for his family's safety, and early in the war he sent them to Philadelphia out of harm's way. He was not only prudent, but he was somewhat superstitious, for one day he telegraphed: —

MRS. LINCOLN, PHIL.: THINK YOU HAD BETTER PUT TAD'S PISTOL AWAY. I HAD AN UGLY DREAM ABOUT HIM.

A. LINCOLN.

Mr. Lincoln came to the Presidency under circumstances that would have tried the toughest fibre; and it is now well known that his was not exactly of that kind. He was not aggressive. He was essentially a man of peace. There never was a ruler who disliked contention more. He was always behind his party instead of being ahead of it — a follower and not a leader. Instead of being inspired by hate, as his enemies declared, and probably supposed, he was moved by an uncommon forbearance that seemed to many of his friends to be born of fear. Instead of being the rampant abolitionist he was frequently called, he was not an abolitionist in any sense, and was in favor of the Crittenden Compromise, which secured the permanency of slavery and its extension through half the national territories. He had shrewdness enough to call around him stronger men than himself, like William H. Seward, Salmon P. Chase, and Edwin M. Stanton; and when Sumter was fired on and captured during the second month of the dominance of his party, he began to see that the spirit of the strange revolt was one that could not be trifled with or cajoled.

Whether Mr. Lincoln was the best man to be at the head of a great people at such a time will always be matter of controversy. He was possessed of a lively sense of humor and that great tenderness which generally accompanies it, but was in no other sense a hero. While not deficient in personal courage, he was painfully deficient in self-confidence and self-assertion. His mood was passive, not active. He seldom imposed his will on others. If he had been in the position of Napoleon in Paris in 1795 he would have distributed coffee and gingerbread to the mutinous national guard, instead of blowing them to atoms with his artillery. If he had been Frederick, he probably would have left Maria Theresa in Silesia as justice required. It is now well known that his comical complaint that he had "no influence with his administration" was something much more than a joke; that all of his Cabinet were more or less insubordinate; that he was swayed by Seward's masterful spirit; that Chase managed to circumvent him and have his way; and that the imperious Stanton even went so far as boldly to countermand his orders, given to oblige some tearful suppliant, whenever he thought they interfered with the good of the service.

More than once during the war, when the Democrats of the North held peace meetings and resisted enlistments and the draft, Mr. Lincoln fell into despair, acknowledged to his confidential friends a fear that the Rebellion could never be crushed, and expressed the apprehension that posterity would hold him responsible for the heaps of slain and the misery caused by the fratricidal struggle. He was a man of ideas rather than of affairs; of conscience rather than of force;

of contemplation rather than of action.   He had the temperament of a poet and the heart of a woman.   He liked dearly to tell a humorous story; he could repeat pages of Shakespeare and half of "Childe Harold's Pilgrimage," and he was fond of crooning over Holmes's "Last Leaf."

If Mr. Lincoln had weaknesses they were of an amiable sort that "lean'd to Virtue's side" and excited a vast amount of sympathy, love, and grateful enthusiasm, which recruited the Union armies from the ranks of those who hated battle, and were moved to enlist only by the highest purpose.

He never was quite as sad as he looked, and amid his heaviest responsibilities he generally decorated the situation with a story, an allegory, or a joke — though the latter were less broad than reported.   And on occasion he was not without real vigor.

Of a committee that came to protest against making the South so angry that it would never reunite, he asked, "Would you prosecute the contest in future with alder-stick squirts, filled with rose water?"

To a visit of Louisiana planters who complained of their great losses and besought him to get them back into the Union without further injury, he remarked, "Broken eggs cannot be mended.   Louisiana has nothing to do now but to take her place in the Union as it was, barring the already broken eggs."

An acquaintance of mine asked Mr. Lincoln to appoint his son to the position of paymaster.

"How old is he?" he was asked.

"He is twenty — well, nearly twenty-one," said the applicant.

"Nearly twenty-one!" shouted Mr. Lincoln.   "I would n't appoint the Angel Gabriel paymaster if he was n't twenty-one."

Mr. Lincoln had a good deal of trouble wrestling with contumacious newspapers that criticized him sharply for going too fast, or for not going fast enough. When one of these editors called, the President got rid of him with a "little story": —

"A traveler on the frontier found himself out of his reckoning as night came on in a most inhospitable region. A terrific thunderstorm came up to add to his trouble. He floundered along in the mud till his horse gave out, and then got out to lead him. Occasional lightning afforded the only clue to the path, but the peals of thunder were frightful. One bolt, which seemed to crush the earth beneath him, made him stagger and finally brought him to his knees. Being by no means a praying man, his petition was short and to the point: 'O Lord! If it's all the same to you, give us a little more light and a little less noise!'"

One day Marshal Ward Lamon, Lincoln's close and courageous friend, called to get a pardon for some deserter. When Lincoln was about to write his name, he looked up and said, "Lamon, I'm overdoing this pardon business. Did you ever hear how Patagonians eat oysters? You didn't? They open them and throw the shells out of the window till the shells get higher than the house; then they move. I think of it often, nowadays."

Frank B. Carpenter, the artist, dropped into the Treasury Department one morning and invited John Pierpont, Ed Stedman, and myself to go over to the White House and see the portrait of Mr. Chase which he was just finishing in the great historical group on which he was engaged — "Signing the Emancipation Proclamation." The large canvas was propped up against the wall in the state banquet room. It was the opinion of a majority that Mr. Chase's unfinished portrait promised to be more lifelike than that of the

President or any other of his Cabinet.  Mr. Lincoln was the severest critic the artist had.  He was not present on this occasion, but Mrs. Lincoln paused in passing through the room and said to the old poet, "What puzzles me is, what on earth we are ever going to do with it?" — evidently having a vague idea that it must somehow be got into the little wooden cottage they had left in Springfield, Illinois.  Nobody could conjecture that Mrs. Elizabeth Thompson would come forward and pay $25,000 for it and give it to the country, so that it would find permanent place upon the walls of the Capitol.

Day by day it became clearer to Lincoln's mind that the Rebellion was a slaveholders' rebellion and that it was necessary to keep the border states on the side of the Union.  So he proposed a scheme of gradual emancipation by which these states would be paid the full value of what they called their property.  Congress objected that the remedy was too expensive.  He proposed that $400 each be paid for slaves, including all men, women, and children.  This was a tremendous price, but he knew it was much cheaper than prolonging the war.  There were $750,000 worth of slaves in Delaware.  The cost of the war was $2,000,000 a day.  So, for a third of one day's expenses, all the slaves in Delaware could be purchased.  He proposed to apply the same policy to the slaves in other border states and ultimately to all the states. He was wiser than his time, wiser than the American people. The North was so indignant and the South so mad that his advice was unheeded.  Congress was too deaf to hear and too blind to see.  Of course we know, looking backward through the vista of years, that it would have been the wisest possible settlement of the quarrel.  If we had had as much sense as Japan and Russia have manifested, or as Norway

A MASON AND SLIDELL CARTOON

BULL: "*What are you about, sir?  Picking pockets, eh?*"
JONATHAN: "*Don't get wrathy, now!  You should n't be carryin'
skunks about with you, John!*"

and Sweden have still more recently shown, it would have been far better for all concerned.

As the end of the slaveholders' rebellion approached, Lincoln became even more conciliatory. To satisfy a few fault-finders at the North he went down the river to Grant's headquarters and met some Confederate commissioners. He said to them, "You are rebels in arms; if the South wants peace, all it has to do is to stop fighting." One of the commissioners cited as a precedent that Charles I had negotiated with rebels in arms. "Yes," said Lincoln, "I remember to have read about it. If I am not mistaken, Charles I lost his head."

In critical moments Lincoln's judgment seems to have been superb — superior to that of his generals. Had McClellan followed his advice, he would have taken Richmond. Had Hooker acted in accordance with his suggestions, Chancellorsville would have been a victory for the nation. Had Meade obeyed his explicit commands, he would have destroyed Lee's army before it could have recrossed the Potomac.

No death ever caused such a convulsion of terror, of anger, and of grief in America as the death of Mr. Lincoln. It seemed for a month as if the sun had been blotted from the sky, and yet — was it not Azrael, the angel of death, who was called the good angel? Perhaps the coward stroke that bore Lincoln down was the most merciful thing that could have happened to him. Suppose he had not been slain? Suppose he had lived, and lived to bear upon his tired shoulders the vast burden of Reconstruction — the great race problem? Suppose he had gone back to Springfield, Illinois, and hung out his little sign again — "Abraham Lincoln, Attorney at Law"? Suppose he had had to mix again in the turmoil and squabble of local politics, to decide who should go to the Legislature from Sangamon County? What

would Fate have had in store for him?    Upon what pedestal
would he stand — he, who is to-day the nation's great hero
and martyr?

In Washington during the war I was acquainted with an
accomplished violinist named William Withers.    I met him
afterwards and asked him to tell me the story of Booth and
Lincoln, as I had heard that he was present on that dreadful
night.    "Well," he said, "you know I was leader of the
orchestra at Ford's Theatre.    That night when Lincoln came
in and took his seat in the proscenium box up at my right he
acknowledged with great cordiality the cheers of the audience.    He stood for a minute or two bowing.    Every bow
seemed to say, 'Lee has surrendered!' and every cheer to
answer, 'You bet he has!'

"Laura Keene was on in *Our American Cousin,* and I had
written a song for her to sing that night.    When she left
it out I was mad.    We had no cue, and the music was thrown
out of gear.    So I hurried round on the stage on my left to
see what it was done for.    I was just giving the stage manager
a piece of my mind when Spangler, the scene shifter, came
forward to the gas box and took hold of the handle with
which they turn the gas out.    Knowing he had no business
there, I pushed him away, and saying, 'Get out of here!    Go
back to where you belong!' I closed the box and sat on the
lid.    I sat there a minute talking, then started down the
stairs to my place.

"That minute I heard the pistol shot and ran back.    Wilkes
Booth was rushing madly across the stage towards me,
brandishing a knife and shouting, 'Out of the way!'    He
ran to the gas box, but was unable to turn out the gas for
some reason, and jumped aside against me.    He must have
thought I struck him, for he made two savage passes at me
with his knife, cutting me both times — once on the shoulder

and once under the arm.  I fell, and he sprang to the door and was gone.  I was the first man arrested, and I told them the assassin was Wilkes Booth.  I knew him intimately, and we had played billiards the very night before.  I also knew Mr. Lincoln pretty well, for I had taught little Taddy how to play the drum, and he used to drum for the guards."

At the beginning of the Rebellion the chief administration organ of the country was the New York Tribune.  Its editorials were read with avidity by the supporters of Mr. Lincoln, and its advice was often taken.  As the summer approached, however, a clamor arose for a more energetic prosecution of the war, and the Tribune gave vent to this feeling in the editorial exclamation, "On to Richmond!"  This was repeated and reiterated till it seemed like a battle cry.  The more conservative of the Republicans deprecated this exhibition of impatience, and it was no secret that it seriously embarrassed Mr. Lincoln in his purposes.

One day he said to Mr. Byington, then in charge of the Tribune correspondence bureau at Washington, "What in the world is the matter with Uncle Horace?  Why can't he restrain himself and wait a little?"  The correspondent reminded the President that one man did not write everything that went in the paper, although he was responsible for it.  "Well," continued Mr. Lincoln, "I don't suppose I have any right to complain; Uncle Horace agrees with me pretty often after all; I reckon he is with us at least four days out of seven."

His echo in the West in this matter was Joseph Medill of the Chicago Tribune, a man whom Mr. Lincoln esteemed and confided in second only to Mr. Greeley himself.

## IX

## THE TRIBUNE

In the autumn of 1863, discontented with the dull and monotonous routine of office work, I resigned my position in the Treasury Department and returned to the North to resume my favorite occupation. During the next seventeen years I had a varied experience in journalism, which may be outlined as follows:

1863–64    Rochester (N. Y.) Democrat
1865–67    New Haven (Conn.) Palladium
1868        New York Tribune
1869        Chicago Republican
1869–71    Chicago Evening Post
1871–75    Minneapolis Tribune
1876–80    New York Graphic, World, Tribune

In 1866 I found time to write *The History of Connecticut During the War* (800 pp.) in collaboration with John M. Morris, and in 1869 to prepare *A Helping Hand for American Homes* (800 pp.) in collaboration with the Honorable Lyman C. Draper, with an introduction by Horace Greeley.

The preparation of the introduction to *A Helping Hand* involved considerable correspondence with Mr. Greeley, and when the volume appeared I obtained the position of reporter on the New York Tribune. We were in the old building, fit only for kindling wood, on the site of which Mr. Whitelaw Reid erected the handsome tower of to-day, and the spacious editorial room on the second floor was reached by climbing dark flights of stairs in the rear.

This room was occupied — I might almost say inhabited, for they were present almost all hours of day and night — by a singularly interesting group of writers. In the front corner was an alcove occupied by Mr. Greeley himself. Near by was Mr. John Russell Young, who had earned an enviable reputation as a war correspondent. Next to him was the seat of William Winter, for nearly fifty years the Tribune's dramatic editor and critic. Touching his desk under the window was that of Clarence Cook, for a quarter of a century its art editor and editorial writer. Next to him sat George Ripley, even then getting venerable, and one of the most versatile and able writers of his time. At the end of the room was the desk of Bayard Taylor, who was seldom present, but whose name and fame were among the Tribune's most valuable properties. Taylor was a large man, with a frank and manly countenance, and so Oriental in appearance that he seemed like an enlightened and scholarly pasha. At a farewell banquet which had just been given to him on the eve of his departure for Europe, Oliver Wendell Holmes, in proposing the principal toast, exclaimed, "Reporter, correspondent, editor, traveler, translator, lecturer, poet, novelist, diplomat — it takes nine men to make a Taylor."

On the remaining side of the room above mentioned were the desks of Amos Cummings and Homer Byington, two of the most active members, presiding over the city staff. It was under their supervision that I had two most interesting experiences. When I had been in the Tribune office three or four months, doing my best to merit promotion, I became conscious that my industry had attracted the eye of Managing Editor Young; and I felt a pardonable pride when, one afternoon, I saw him talking with Mr. Greeley and looking over

at my desk.   As I was leaving he called to me and said, "I
have watched you work; you are not afraid of it; do you think
you could run the telegraph desk?"   Joyfully I told him that
I could and that I had had experience with telegraphic copy,
whereupon he invited me to dine with him the next day,
when we would "arrange it."   I dined with him as appointed,
and we arranged it, greatly to my satisfaction.   I was to
report next day for service, at an increased salary.   At the
appointed hour I appeared, and was surprised to see a
stranger at the coveted desk, vigorously sharpening a pencil.
"Oh, yes!" said Young nervously, as I asked an explanation.
"Yes; it 's all up, but don't blame me for it.   I could n't help
it.   Ben Butler came in last night dragging that fellow with
him and he went for Greeley, and Greeley, for some unac-
countable reason, gave him the place.   He 's a relative of
the General, I believe.   Very sorry indeed."

I was disgusted, and I drew my balance of pay, shook the
dust of the antique rookery from my feet, and departed with
bitterness in my heart.

I lived to see the intruder at the very bottom of the hill.
Within a week about half of the Associated Press news dispatches were missing from the Tribune one morning, and
investigation revealed them in the wastebasket weighed down
with an empty bottle which exhaled the secret of the failure.
He never came back to the office, either to apologize or to
enquire.   He spent every cent he had, and borrowed from
everybody who would trust him.   He strayed into John
Chamberlain's place at Saratoga one morning, looking very
tired indeed, and asked to borrow twenty dollars.   Being refused, he made it one dollar, then fifty cents, then "a quarter."

"No; I won't give you any more," said the proprietor.
"Every cent I give you hurts you.   Not another cent from
me."

*Leslie's Weekly*

THE EDITORIAL ROOMS

*Leslie's Weekly*

THE NEWSBOYS

"Well, never mind the cent," pleaded the visitor; "make it a dime."

"No! Not another dime, you fool, you! Get out!" was the inexorable answer.

The doomed man groaned and shaded his eyes with his hand as he turned to quit the gorgeous den, and it was thought he even shed tears; but as he reached the door he suddenly grabbed the clock of ormolu that stood ticking away the wicked hours on a convenient mantel, and ran, shouting back as he went out the door with it, "Well, ta-ta! Time is money, John!"

Chamberlain and his guests were paralyzed with astonishment and laughter, and the fugitive got away and pawned the sumptuous timepiece for four dollars on the next corner.

Horace Greeley was a queer compound of bone, brain, and self-will. The current impression that he lacked pluck and pertinacity is entirely without foundation. He had indomitable self-assertion, and was game to the last. He cared not a cent about fashion in speech, manners, or dress. While I worked under him, although I saw him every day and heard his voice through the open doors, I never once heard him say "Good morning" or "Good evening," or "How d' ye do" or "Good-bye," or inquire about anybody's health. But he scrupulously answered every letter that came to him, and generally tilted his chair forward on its legs and answered it on the spot, so that the writer could get a reply in the next mail. His conscience was abnormally developed on that one subject, and he probably wrote many thousand letters which did not need writing, and which shortened his life. On the street he seldom spoke to his nearest friends unless he had business with them. He would enter a street car down town, sit by the side of a friend, and ride a mile without speaking, then suddenly nudge him and say, "Let me take your paper."

He would read the paper for another mile, watch for the friend's house, hand the paper to him just before reaching it, and part company without speaking to him or looking at him. He did not believe in that expenditure of force which conventional civilities require.

In manners he seemed uncouth and uncivilized. In money matters he was a child. Commodore Vanderbilt had a wayward, half-imbecile son, named Cornelius Jeremiah, an epileptic, indolent, ignorant, and fond of the gaming table. His father kept him on a small allowance, hoping to compel him to work. This ne'er-do-weel applied to Mr. Greeley for money when his father would not let him have it, and Greeley gave it to him and continued the reckless habit until the loan was some forty thousand dollars. Vanderbilt wrote protesting letters to the editor, but they did no good. One evening he climbed the stairway to the sanctum, and, facing the occupant, exclaimed, "Greeley, see here! I now tell you for the last time that I never will pay back a single cent of the money you keep lending to Corneel." Greeley swung round in his chair, shook his hand at the intruder, and cried, "Who the devil asked you to pay it back, you damned old skinflint?" Greeley's prodigal habit did not prove as disastrous as it might have done, for, after the Commodore was dead, the friendly services of Whitelaw Reid induced William H. Vanderbilt to pay to Horace Greeley's two daughters the $75,000 which Corneel had borrowed.

Among Greeley's characteristics were an extreme irritability and a keen sense of justice. He was a careful political statistician, and nothing disgusted and enraged him more than an error in election returns. One morning, on looking over the Tribune, he saw that an important error had escaped correction. In great rage he climbed to the composing room and wanted to know who had set up that table. Tom Rooker examined the proofs and found that James Bayard had set the matter. The editor charged on Bayard's tripod.

"Jim, you 're a damned fool. Will you never learn anything? Look at that!"

"What 's the matter with it?"

"Matter? Why, Great Scott! It's all wrong!" (Only Greeley was never known to apostrophize as humble an individual as Scott.)

"Mr. Greeley, I did n't do that."

"You lie, Jim! Who did?" was the absurdly impatient response of Greeley. "Here you 've made a damned fool of yourself and me!"

Bayard examined the paper and said he was sure he had followed copy.

"Followed copy! Followed copy!" mimicked the employer angrily. "That 's your get-out! That 's what you always say when you make a blunder! Come into the proof room, Jim. There 's a blankety-blank jackass lying round this office somewhere that ought to be kicked from here to Sing Sing. I 'll see whether it 's you or Clark!"

Clark, the proofreader, brought out the copy, and the moment Mr. Greeley's eye fell on the reprint, he recollected that he himself had cribbed the table from the Express and sent it to the composing room. He collapsed, called Bayard into the group, turned round facing the window, and exclaimed, "Here! Kick me, all of you! Kick me! Kick me!"

Clarence Cook, one of the most conscientious and intelligent art critics in the world, quit the Tribune on account of some difference of opinion with Mr. Reid. I recall a funny incident about Cook and Greeley. When I first went to work in the Tribune office in 1868, I was considerably awed by the line of distinguished desks along the side of the big room, where sat the members of Mr. Greeley's staff —

William Winter, Clarence Cook, George W. Smalley, Bayard Taylor, Charles Congdon, and, lastly, George Ripley in the front corner where lay the big piles of books. Especially was I awed by the little room in the corner through whose half-open door I could see Mr. Greeley at work.

One day John Russell Young, then managing editor, said "Mr. Cook, I should think you'd go in and see Mr. Greeley. He speaks of liking your work, and you've been here now four or five years and have never spoken to him, I believe."

Cook laughed and said, "I'll go in if you really want me to. You've asked me to do so two or three times before, but it didn't seem worth while and I have waited till I had business with him. If he sent for me, that would be another thing. However, as you urge me, I'll go. Here, Jake!"

He called to him the office boy and sent in his card, following it presently. Cook told me about the interview afterwards.

"Greeley was scratching away for dear life, his back to the door. My card was on his desk. He had apparently not seen it. I sat down on a haircloth sofa. He kept scratching away. At last I said, 'Mr. Greeley.' He answered in that high, squeaky voice of his, 'What is it?' but kept hard at work. 'I am Mr. Cook,' I said. 'Mr. Clarence Cook of the Tribune.' 'Busy now!' he exclaimed, without looking around, and I retreated.

"I did not try again for years. But when I returned from Europe in 1871 I wanted to get a letter of introduction to A. T. Stewart, to try to interest him in that great picture, Raphael's 'Apollo and Marsyas,' then for sale, but since bought for the Louvre gallery in Paris, for $50,000, instead of being captured for this country as I wished.

"I went in to the sanctum to see Mr. Greeley. He was scratching away as before, his nose almost touching the paper. I said, 'Mr. Greeley!' He looked up at me, but evidently did not know me. 'I am Mr. Clarence Cook,' I said. He scratched away again. He did not say 'Good morning' or 'How do you do?' but only, in that strange high-pitched voice, 'What do you want?' I told him. He reached out and grabbed a piece of paper and wrote: reached for an envelope and scratched. He handed it to me and resumed his writing without a word. He had written: 'Mr. Stewart: The bearer of this, Mr. Clarence Cook, is well known to me as a journalist and a gentleman, and as one who never wastes anybody's time.'

"I found a porcupine in Mr. Stewart's marble mansion — a porcupine no doubt developed by the constant attacks of beggars and swindlers. I sent up my letter. When he appeared in the reception room, where I waited him, he made no sign of politeness. He did not ask me to sit down, but he put his hands rigidly behind him and said, 'What is your business?'

"As briefly as I could I told him that I had seen a very remarkable picture in Europe and wanted to tell him about it.

" 'I don't buy any pictures,' he said.

" 'You have not been asked to buy it,' I answered. 'I am not authorized to negotiate.'

" 'I don't buy any pictures,' he repeated.

" 'Nobody asked you to buy any!' I exclaimed, now thoroughly angry.

" 'What's your motive in coming here?' he asked suspiciously.

" 'My motive, as far as I have one, is patriotic,' I said, 'but I see that I have no business with you,' and I turned to go.

"Surprised at my abruptness into a conciliatory mood, he said, 'Hold on; wait a minute. Just glance at some of my statuary here.'

" 'Now's my time,' I thought, and followed him back.

" 'This,' he said, rather grandly, waving his hand towards a well-known and very commonplace example of the stone-cutter's art, 'this is Powers's "Greek Slave!" '

" 'Yes,' I said, 'I have seen that once before; and nobody who has seen it once will ever want to see it again.'

" 'This,' he said, after some hesitation, turning to another example, 'is the "Fisher boy." '

" 'Oh yes,' I said. 'I 've seen that before, too,' and came away without another word."

Mr. Greeley tried in vain to keep his sanctum to himself. There was no intermission in his attempt to keep the door of his little quadrilateral locked, or at least shut. But he was always in a state of siege. Charles Congdon, the Tribune's greatest satirical writer for many years, puts it cleverly as follows: —

"Almost always overworked, he was naturally irritated by intrusions upon his privacy. For a long time, his efforts to cloister himself up were humiliating failures. All sorts of people, with the greatest possible variety of bees in their bonnets, managed to evade the slight barriers, get into his presence, and interrupt his industry — people with machines of perpetual motion, with theories about spiritualism, with notions about the next election, with business plans requiring only a small loan to launch them upon the full tide of dividend-paying experiment. There were others with a passionate desire to borrow small or large sums of money; with anxiety to become writers upon his newspaper; with manuscripts which they wished to have him recommend to some book publisher; with new religions; with schemes for the abolition of every religion whatever; with mining stocks sure to pay 1000 per cent; with stories of personal destitution harrowing to listen to, and yet requiring only the loan of a few shillings to enable the petitioner to go to his friends; widows

whose sole claim on him or on anybody was that they were
widows; orphans, sometimes suspiciously well grown, who
had nothing to plead but their orphanage; Irishmen who
had lost everything in a desperate attempt to give the Green
Island a better government; Negroes who perhaps were born
free, and were merely fugitives from Maine or Massachusetts
— all these and many others besieged the sanctum and devised
tricks for swindling its occupant. If Mr. Greeley could have
locked his door and kept it locked, he would have died
a much richer man. He would try sometimes to be ex-
tremely stern and repellent, but it was always a lamentable
failure."

He could generally protect himself pretty well from full-
grown masculine mendicants, but women applicants for
money were the pest of his life, for he could not order the
janitor to throw them downstairs. A woman in black called
one afternoon and by a circuitous passage got into his room.
"No, no! Nothing! Go 'way!" and he kept on writing
while she kept on begging. "Go 'way. I'm busy. Let me
alone! Go 'way!" And he did his best to keep on writing.
She gave him no peace till finally he jumped up, went to the
speaking tube which connected with the counting room, and
shouted, "Sinclair! For God's sake send me five dollars
this minute!" This response quieted the applicant, and he
had bought rather dearly the right to use his own time.
When she occupied some more time in prolonged thanks, his
stern voice relaxed and a smile illuminated his benevolent
face.

Mr. Greeley has been so misrepresented by malignant or
ignorant writers that there seems to be a prevalent impression that he was a weak and foolish man. On the contrary,
he was perhaps the most powerful and practical editor and
controversialist that this country has seen. He was certainly
awkward, and his manners never improved. His clothes

did not resemble the fashion plates. They were not generally well brushed, or his shoes well blacked. But Thackeray would not have said of him, as he said of George IV, that "he had on his person an overcoat, a dress coat, a waistcoat, and a flannel coat, and that was all there was of him." Mr. Greeley seemed to have no idea whatever of the value of money, but he was undoubtedly the chief sufferer from that defect. No other editor this country has ever seen has put his personality so vigorously into his newspaper. The Tribune was always Greeley — echoing not only his principles, but even his personal habits and literary methods. He was fond of beginning a paragraph with a dash and a noun with a capital letter.

If he had been elected President in 1872, as he expected he would certainly be, he could have done the country no harm, and would probably have taught it some useful lessons. He would have reconstructed Reconstruction and he would have introduced a kindlier feeling between victors and vanquished, while surrounding himself with a Cabinet of statesmen at least as wise as those whom General Grant summoned to his side.

An acquaintance of mine told me this story of an incident about the time it occurred: "Packard and I were invited to breakfast with Greeley one morning at nine o'clock. We reached the dining room of the hotel first, inquired for his table, and sat down. Pretty soon he came in, handed his hat and overcoat to a waiter, and, without looking towards us, went over into a corner, sat down, and ordered a breakfast for one — a poached egg, some milk toast, and a cup of tea. I went over and spoke to him. He looked surprised and asked us if we had eaten breakfast. We told him we had not, and we ordered the same that he had done and sat down with him.

*Leslie's Weekly*

A Cartoon Entitled "A Pleasant Neighbor," Showing Greeley Dumping Reforms into Grant's Yard

" 'What paper you got?' he inquired. 'Anything in it?'

" 'Not much except an article attacking you,' said Packard.

"It was a column long, but Greeley read it through. 'Absurd!' he said, 'to take so much space for that. It is n't good journalism. It all ought to have been said in a quarter of a column. That article ought never to have been permitted to go below there,' he said, indicating a place with his finger. He did not allude to the substance of the attack at all, but bitterly denounced the slovenliness of using so much space. We hurried through our breakfasts and departed."

I knew a lady who was intimately acquainted with the Greeley household for twenty years.

"Mrs. Greeley," she said, "never had the knack of making a home. She was always clean, but never neat — never neat in appearance, I mean, — because she was always washing something and was always disheveled. I have seen her take her children without a garment on out into the street and pump water on them to wash them. When I was there one day the servant washed an apron of her own and hung it out to dry. Mrs. Greeley jumped up, seized the carving knife, rushed out and cut out of the line the piece containing the apron and flung it to the girl with, 'How dare you hang your apron on the same line with my baby's clothes?' There was neatness for you! Yet when they lived on Nineteenth Street she kept three goats in the house for the children to play with, and when I let one of my servants go there to live, she came running back to me saying, 'I won't live there, Missis, never!' I asked what was the matter. 'Sure, I have no bed at all, but must just bunk down on the pile of hay they got for the goats!'

"Mr. Greeley asked me one Sunday to come round in the morning and go to Chapin's with him. I went, and when I got to the house there was a fracas in the vestibule — he and his wife and the children and the goats all mixed up together.

" 'The question is,' said Mr. Greeley, 'whether the goats shall go up Broadway with us. Mother insists that I shan't go to church unless at the head of a procession of children and goats. It seems like a secular following.'

"I believe we got off at last without them, though Mrs. Greeley said, 'It's only your miserable pride.'

"Mrs. Greeley had an antipathy to kid gloves. She would never put them on. I remember a bout she had with Margaret Fuller on this subject. We all met on the avenue, and instead of saying 'Good morning,' or some such human salutation, Mrs. Greeley touched Margaret's hand with a little shudder and exclaimed, 'Skin of a beast! Skin of a beast!' 'Why, what do you wear?' inquired the astonished maiden from Massachusetts. 'Silk,' said Mrs. Greeley, reaching out her hand. 'Silk!' Margaret just touched it and shuddered, crying, 'Entrails of a worm! Entrails of a worm!'

"I was once in a stage with Mrs. Greeley going up Madison Avenue when she suddenly pulled the strap, whisked a tin pail out from under her shawl, and, reaching it to the Reverend Dr. Brett at the other end of the bus, to whom we had just bowed, said, 'You get out, please, and run to that bakery on the corner and get me two cents' worth of yeast!' Mr. Brett laughed aloud, but he good-naturedly got out, hurried to the shop, and brought back the coveted bread exhilarator, the driver waiting meantime, his serenity broken only by a smile. When the messenger returned, he handed the little pail to Mrs. Greeley with the remark that bread was evidently kneaded, to which she replied, 'H'm! Old joke!'

"She was very eccentric — Mrs. Greeley was. Greeley once told me that the day before, while going down to Staten Island on the ferryboat, she walked calmly up to a passenger who was smoking, snatched the cigar out of his mouth, and flung it overboard. 'I expected to be knocked down on the spot that minute,' said Greeley.

Before the birth of Raphael, their oldest boy, she told me that she lived on raw rice altogether. She would take it by the handful and chew it up soft. 'I can grind it just like a mill,' she said. When Raphael was taken with his last illness, a severe form of croup, the physician fought it for days, and finally made it yield. 'Now he will probably live,' he said to Mrs. Greeley, 'if you keep him from taking cold. If he catches cold, he dies. Keep him warm. Keep the air from him. Try no experiments. Any little exposure might be fatal.'

"In two days the mother sent for him again, and on arriving he found the child all choked up with a cold. 'What's the matter with him?' he asked. 'What? My God, what have you done? Taken off a warm woolen shirt and substituted a thin cotton one! The child will die. What did you send for me for? Why did n't you send for an undertaker?'

"Raphael died that night. She lamented him deeply. She didn't mean to hurt him, of course, but the clean devil had got hold of her, and her frenzy for cleanliness was stronger than almost any other feeling.

"She once gave me some advice as to how to bring up my children. 'Let's see,' said I. 'How many children have you?' 'I have two,' she said. 'And how many have you had?' 'Nine,' she answered. 'Then, thank you,' I said, 'but if it is all the same I think I'll bring up my children my way.' 'Oh, very well,' she exclaimed. 'I didn't raise children for this world, but for the next!'

"She always called her husband 'Greeley,' whether speaking to him or of him. He was rather afraid of her, but once in a while would say his say. I remember once we were assembled at Greeley's on Saturday evening.    Dr. Ripley, Margaret Fuller, George William Curtis, Dana, and half a dozen others, discussing the practicability of associated homes.    We talked of turning the Gramercy Park Hotel into a nest of them.  'It won't do,' said Mrs. Greeley.  'Everybody will be falling in love with Mrs.——,' naming me.  'Well, Ma,' said Mr. Greeley, 'you 'll offset that!' "

# X

## JOURNALIST AT LARGE

I LEFT the Tribune in 1868 and shortly after accepted an offer of a salary from a reputable publisher in Cincinnati, to join Dr. Draper at Madison, Wisconsin, in preparing the book already mentioned. We were just finishing it and putting it in type, after hard work for eight months, when a dispatch informed us that our publisher had suddenly gone into bankruptcy. The blow, totally unexpected, quite staggered us. No more remittances were to be expected, and the checks that had been sent went to protest when presented. I was left almost penniless, with a family on my hands, in the midst of the hard winter of 1868–69.

I at once went to Chicago, as the great newspaper centre of the West, and resolved to find work before returning. Though I did not know a soul connected with any journal there, the intention seemed promising. To the Tribune, to the Times, and to the Journal I applied successively. Of course there was "no vacancy," as, indeed, there ought not to be on any newspaper properly conducted. Then I thought it over and tried a new tack. I told the editor of the Republican, Mr. David H. Mason, that I was away from home and rather lonesome, and asked that I might be permitted to take some of the papers scattered on the floor.

"Certainly," he said. "Help yourself."

I took half a dozen home (to my hall bedroom), examined them, found several announcements of interest, and wrote out comments on current news, making them as lively as I could.

These I carried next day to Mason (eight paragraphs in all, I believe), saying as I left them, "Some subjects that I am interested in," and helped myself to more papers.

The next morning I was much gratified to find in the paper one of my small contributions to the editorial columns.

I mentioned my discovery to the editor, and he said, "Yes — very timely."

I took another armful of papers and in the evening brought in six paragraphs. Of these two were used, and he called my attention to them and said, "Thank you!"

I carried away more papers in a hopeful frame of mind. But the Republican next morning contained nothing whatever of mine, and I was correspondingly depressed.

On the following day, however, three of my squibs appeared, also my short article on the current tariff, and the quicksilver rose in the tube.

So affairs went on for another week. My funds were getting very low, but neither of us said a word about pay or place, and I do not remember hearing Mason say anything during that time but "Good morning" and "Thank you." Sometimes as many as six or eight of my trivialities found admission. I determined to stay there till I made a place for myself.

One afternoon he said to me, "You 're a newspaper man, I see."

"Yes," I said. "I 've worked on newspapers."

"Out of a job?" he asked.

I acknowledged it.

"One of our reporters is sick to-day; there 's his desk, if you want it."

I thanked him, and took assignments from the city editor

gladly. Meantime, I brought in two or three editorial paragraphs a day, humorous in character, for such had been revealed as the editor's preference.

I earned my ten dollars that week.

Three days later the scribe got well, to my great regret, and suddenly reappeared and took possession of the desk.

I thought I was out in the cold, but the genial Mason at once offered me twelve dollars a week as his assistant. I accepted, and sent some money to my family when Saturday night came. My salary was raised to fifteen dollars and then twenty dollars a week, within a month. Then I was surprised by an offer of twenty-five dollars a week from Mr. David Blakeley, owner of the Evening Post. In future promotions the reader is not interested. I had got "on my feet," and I mention the method thus in detail only in the hope that other youths out of a job may profit by my experience.

On the editorial staff of the Post I found some gifted and brilliant writers, and there I spent several profitable years. While I was thus engaged, the terrible fire came and swept three square miles of the splendid city from the face of the earth. For a time it was almost as if the place had never been. No description can add anything to the startling picture of that ruthless conflagration that still survives in the imaginations of men. All of the newspaper offices were consumed, and Chicago seemed to have turned backward and become once more an uninhabited prairie. Mr. Blakeley found a job office and some of his wandering type-setters and exhibited tremendous energy in getting out the next day's paper — one page — on time.

Simultaneously, and when the fire had not yet reached the height of its fury, I received orders from two New York newspapers to send dispatches "unlimited."  I saddled a horse and rode through the still-burning district as far as the streets were traversable, only to learn that the telegraph office had been burned after sending the orders to me.  I could not reply.  All wires were down.  I went out of the city till I found a railroad train, and at once started for Detroit.  I filled a block of letter paper on the way and from Detroit sent four columns to the Herald; then, finding the wire obstructed, I continued my way to New York.  Of course I employed every minute of the time in writing, and when I arrived in the metropolis I wrote all night and furnished seven columns more to the Tribune, Herald, Sun, Times, Mail, and Standard.  With what marvelous rapidity the vanished city was recalled to life, all the world knows.

In the spring of 1872 I attended the Liberal Republican Convention at Cincinnati that nominated Horace Greeley for President.  My seat mate on the trip down from Chicago was Joseph Pulitzer, a delegate from St. Louis, and a reporter for Carl Schurz's newspaper.  This tall, rawboned youth was twenty-four years old, had a nose like Julius Cæsar, and had already acquired a picturesque history.

Pulitzer was born in Budapest, Hungary, and there during his teens he had obtained a showy and nearly useless education.  Sadly in need of money, he fled to America in the steerage, and in New York enlisted in a German regiment for the war.  He rose to the rank of corporal, I believe, and when mustered out he knew scarcely a word of English.  Without delay he started west, resolved to go as far as his money would take him, and when it was exhausted he found himself entirely penniless on the east bank of the Mississippi.  The spires of St. Louis were visible across the river, but it was a case of "so near and yet so far," for he had

not the price of the ferriage across.  He enviously watched
the big flat-bottomed boat as it lazily came and went, and
finally he gathered English words enough to ask the captain if
he might work his way across.

"Yes, if you go three trips as a stoker," that official said.

The bargain was closed, and the lank Hungarian shoveled
coal so energetically that he skinned his hands and got a
job for a week as fireman.  At the end of the week he had
fed the fire under the boilers so much to the satisfaction of
his employer that he was engaged as a permanent stoker.
This answered as a transient potboiler, but the hot air, fierce
flame, and confinement proved intolerable, and at the end
of two months he obtained an easier berth on a river steamer
plying to and from Keokuk.  He left this job after a while
and went to work on the St. Louis levee with a gang of stevedores and roustabouts.  In this association he remained a
year, learning English with great enthusiasm and building
himself up for better things.  Along the wharves and up
and down the river dives he acquired a great reputation as
a man of learning and obtained influence as a leader of his
fellows.  The stevedores came to regard him as a prodigy
and gathered eagerly about him to listen to his conversation
and stories concerning current events, Reconstruction, and
affairs in his native Austria.  He strove hard to get remuner-
ative work, but his scant English and already impaired eye-
sight handicapped him.  For several months he served as
coachman and drove a carriage for a wealthy lady in the city.

Finally he began to write short paragraphs concerning
daily events upon the wharves, and this led to his occasional
employment as a reporter in the humblest place.  Then, in a
lucky moment, in the stress of St. Louis journalism, he felt
around and got the refusal of a news franchise, and, watching
his opportunity, he paid $2500 for it and sold it for $30,000.

Mixing his franchise and his audacity with his brains, his fortune was speedily made. He bought one of the papers he had worked for, started the Post-Despatch, and its profits in three years were $120,000.

When did the illustrated daily first appear? I do not know. I ask the question, but put forth no claim of precedence, for the pictorial efforts that were made under my initiative were so very crude, raw, and rough-hewn as to be classed not at all as art and hardly to deserve the humble name of caricature. It was in 1870, when I was managing editor of the Chicago Evening Post, that the notion of producing and illustrating a series of comic articles came into my head. They were intended as a burlesque of current topics, and were signed "Peleg Wales." Each column contained three or four illustrations. There was not an artist in the city who had ever done any work like that required, and how to produce wood engravings that would answer was the dilemma we had to face. I sought advice in the press room and stated the case to one of our bright workmen.

"Why, certainly; what's the matter with that?" he answered, and turned over in his palm an oaken advertising cut. "Can't we carve the thing on that?"

Easier said than done. But he offered to try, and, armed with jackknife and a small chisel, he brought back that same evening the rough inverted block on which I had penciled the reception of the Grand Duke Alexis.

We printed it the next day, but as I turn to it now in my scrapbook I am convinced that it is the worst picture that has ever been made since the first man stuck an edged tool into wood. What astonished us most was the enthusiasm with which that clumsy and barbarous series was daily received by our public. Little escaped us: Logan's canvass for the Senate; Sitting Bull's raid; intrigues at Washington; the great fire; the tours of the Russian prince; Greeley's quarrels with Grant — such events were duly and daily presented in cartoons which, though incredibly rough, attracted wide attention and amusement.

On exchanging the Chicago chair for one in the editorial room of the Minneapolis Tribune, I also transplanted the pictorial ambition, and local episodes, like the capture of Lord Gordon-Gordon, were there portrayed in the same audaciously unskillful fashion on reversed advertising blocks. This may not have been the first attempt at cartooning in daily newspapers, but I know of no other so early.

At any rate, it was this blundering effort that brought to me an attractive offer to join the editorial staff of David B. Croly, of the New York Graphic. Croly was a progressive and fearless thinker, just retired from the editorial chair of the Daily World. Though radical in his tendencies, and a promoter of all new discoveries and inventions, he was always conciliatory, tolerant of adverse opinions, conservative in his methods, sociable and amiable in his demeanor, and a miracle of industry. Whitelaw Reid said of him that he was "chockful of days' works." And he demanded news and wanted novelties. He had committed to memory J. B. McCulloch's definition of journalism: "The art of guessing where hell will break loose next and having a reporter on the spot."

When I reported to Croly he told me at once that his attention had been attracted by my "pictures." When he said "pictures" we both laughed, and he promptly added, "Yes — no art, and no beauty, and no skill, but other valuable stuff." I soon learned that Mr. Croly prized "suggestions" and hints far above any technique of performance, and that his assistants were useful to him in proportion to their ability in roughly outlining the first-page cartoon.

I was assigned a desk in a room ten feet by twenty or so, containing some remarkably brilliant young men — Prentice Mulford, associate of Bret Harte; James Davis, California novelist; George T. Lanigan, humorous balladist; William L. Alden, author of *Domestic Explosives;* Mortimer Thompson ("Doesticks"), and Robert H. Newell, whose whimsicalities as "Orpheus C. Kerr" so amused Mr. Lincoln and lightened his burden during the terrible stress of the Civil War.   Besides these members of the regular staff, Mrs. Croly also made her headquarters at a desk there, from which she projected her "Jenny June" letters of fashion and genial gossip to all parts of the country.   Hers was the first regular syndicate of letters ever furnished to newspapers, but they were not illustrated.

It was a high privilege to have Newell's acquaintance for six years.   He was not only a man of all-round culture and learning, but he was so delicate, sensitive, and refined as to seem out of place in the rough-and-tumble of Bohemian life. His principles were almost Quixotic, and his habits most exemplary.   With a woman's temperament he possessed that keen sense of incongruities — seeing likenesses in things that are different, and differences in things that are similar — which constitutes the humorous.   He was reticent, even shy, and not a "good mixer."   Notwithstanding the tremendous popularity of his "Orpheus C. Kerr Papers" during the war, it must be said that he was a poor judge of human nature, easily imposed on by his playful acquaintances.   Scarcely any word ever fell from his lips that could not have been uttered in any parlor; in fact, as I look back, my acquaintance with him seems like an acquaintance with an intellectual, jocular, high-minded, and self-respecting girl.   Mainly on account of his chivalry and simplicity he was the victim of a grotesque romance which cast a shadow over all his subsequent life.

Mr. Croly was a great editor. He was not a great writer, and disliked exceedingly to write if he could use anybody else's hand and constructive brain. He possessed the true executive power — the ability to avail himself to the utmost of the services of others. He was a stanch friend, a loyal ally, an able antagonist, and a man of strong convictions, which he maintained with a respectful dogmatism. He was essentially a man of ideas, unhampered by any reverence for conventionalities. It was a luxury to meet so much intellectual honesty and fine independence. He had prophetic instincts and always looked forward to the good time coming, even from the midst of a life that was not without moral and social disappointments and physical miseries.

He was essentially a domestic man, fond of home and family. For many years Mrs. Croly gave Sunday evening receptions — the pleasantest assemblies of the city. There were to be met throngs of famous men and women — brilliant Bohemians, authors, actors, lecturers, critics, poets, editors — whom it was a privilege to know. It was the shrine of positivism, where were gathered the disciples of Auguste Comte — a delightful fraternity of visionaries, always engaged in the Sisyphean effort to harmonize optimism and pessimism. Croly edited a humorous paper, but he was the reverse of jocular. He was habitually grave, and even when he was preaching altruism, his face was often shadowed by a saturnine solemnity. Mrs. Croly had a more joyous mood, and was never so happy as when surrounded by distinguished guests in her Sunday evenings "at home." It was Jenny June's popular fashion letter that fixed my determination to write a weekly illustrated personal and social letter to a

large syndicate of papers.  Pictorial journalism was not yet
born, for the masterful work of Strother — "Porte Crayon" —
was confined to magazines.  My experiment was financially
a success from the beginning.  Some attractive cartoons I
purloined and condensed from the Graphic; the rest I bought
from first-class artists — Weldon, Hopkins, Thomas Nast,
Gribayedoff, Gibson, Frost, Gray Parker.  I had their work
blocked in New York and sent direct to my twenty papers.
Valerian Gribayedoff — "Grib" for short — was a curious
specimen.  He had learned six languages and acquired art
without instruction.  And he came to New York from Russia
via Chili, where he had patriotically beaten a drum in a
prevalent revolution.  He was generally impecunious, but
had a remarkable gift of sketching likenesses and furnished
some of the best portraits and most telling groups.

Richard Henry Stoddard was at the head of the guild of
New York poets, and he wrote occasionally for the Graphic.
"Oh, yes, I knew Edgar A. Poe," he said to me one day as he
went out to lunch.  "In fact, I had a little business with him
once," and the later poet laughed.

I asked him how it was, and he went on: "I was a young
fellow and had begun to dabble in verse a little.  Among
other things I wrote an 'Ode to a Grecian Flute' and sent it
to the Broadway Journal, which Poe was then editing.  After
waiting a week or two I called around to learn its fate.  Poe
was not there; they told me that he was at home sick.  I got
the address and in a few days called and found him in his
house on Amity Street — him and his heartbroken, most
unfortunate cousin-wife.  Poe received me kindly and told
me that my poem was accepted and would appear.  I waited
a month, and finally became impatient and went around to
his office.  Poe was there, sound asleep in the editorial chair.
I did not know at that early day what Poe's somnolence meant,

so, after waiting half an hour or so, I gently woke him up.
He glared at me most rudely and impudently and shouted,
'Who are you?' I told him my name. 'What do you want
here?' he cried. 'Who the —— are you?' I told him that I
came to see about the poem that I wrote, the 'Ode to a
Grecian Flute.' 'You're a liar,' he shouted. 'You're a liar!
You never wrote it. You lie! Get out of here, or I'll kick
you downstairs!' I was too much astonished to protest. I
heard afterwards that he thought it was a European production — possibly Keats's 'Ode on a Grecian Urn' — and
I was trying to palm off a fraud on him. Poe's peculiar
temperament and habits made him sometimes very eccentric."

While I was at work upon the Graphic, Mr. Goodsell, the
proprietor, asked me if I could not get a signed article for our
Christmas number from Mrs. Langtry, the "Jersey Lily," who
had recently come to town and whose presence was making
a sensation. I went in search of her and met her in the lobby
of the hotel, and was presented to her by a friend who
happened to be in her company. I briefly hinted at my
business, and she said, "Come up to Wallack's at one o'clock.
I have now an appointment, but will be there at rehearsal."

I went and made my way through the darkness back of the
stage. She was in street costume and was at the footlights
going through the rehearsal of *Galatea*. I stood in the wings
and regarded her with sundry reflections. Just as I had
arrived at the conclusion that she would rank about the
27,000th among the handsome women I knew, she came up
the stage and greeted me.

I told her we hoped she would be able to help us out. "Oh,
I couldn't write anything that anybody would want to read,"
she said with a laugh. I murmured something about her
ability being doubtless equal to her modesty, when, without

noticing it, she went on: " But you could.  See here!  You could write something and I could sign it.  How would that do?"

"I am very much afraid that it would n't do at all," I answered.  What we wanted, I told her, was some sketch of herself and her friends and her school days and her going on the stage, and all that.

"Ah, well, yes: then Mrs. Labouchère here will write it for us — won't you, dear?"

I had met Mr. Henry Labouchère, the fearless London editor, at one of Jenny June's Sunday evenings, and was now presented to his lady.   That worthy chaperon said she would try — "And we can fuss it up together."

"A hundred pounds, you said," mused the beauty demurely.

I corrected her and said, "One hundred dollars, if you please — twenty pounds."

"Oh, that 's nothing!" she broke out — "For a whole column, too!"

I assured her that it was a good price for the service; that no paper would probably pay any more; at any rate, I was not authorized to increase the offer.

"And just think, dear," she exclaimed, turning to Mrs. Labouchère, "I got a hundred and thirty-two pounds, you remember, for just signing my name to that certificate of soap last week.  I remember the amount because it was exactly my weight, pound for pound!"

I pleaded that this would be very different; that it would be a part of the record of the honors she had won, the chronicle of her professional talent and personality.   "Signing a nice article all about your genius — your taste — your home — your ambitions; different from soap, don't you think?"

She opened her big blue eyes and glanced with pathetic inquiry at Mrs. Labouchère, then back at me.  "No, I could n't undertake it for a shilling less," she said. "What 's the difference?"

I saw that she was becoming bewildered as to the relative importance of things, and turned sadly away.

The Graphic was never very firmly established. It was unique in character and make-up. Some of its pictures were admirable, and it was the only illustrated daily in the world. But it was very expensive and had great difficulty in making both ends meet. One Monday morning a notice was laid on my desk that my services upon the paper would not be required after the succeeding Saturday. I did not know the reason, but I afterwards ascertained that I had written something which the proprietor did not like. When I went to lunch that day I dropped in at Mouquin's — the restaurant where I knew Mr. David Bonner took his midday refreshment. I had met him several times and, without hesitation or too much modesty, I told him that I could improve the Ledger if he would give me a department on it which I designated. In ten minutes he had accepted the proposition. As I already had an engagement to furnish frequent matter for the Tribune and the World I thought my nourishment would somehow be provided for. I then called upon the gentleman who had dismissed me, thanked him for his consideration in giving me a week's notice, and told him of the arrangements I had made with the other papers. It is not too much to say that he was surprised. I mention this incident somewhat exultantly perhaps, because it was one of the triumphs in a life that had met with many disappointments.

I once made myself superserviceable on the Ledger. Remembering that Mr. Bonner had been for years an ordinary typesetter on the Hartford Courant — or, rather, an extraordinary typesetter, for he took the prize as the most rapid typesetter in New England, — and remembering also that he had just paid Longfellow twenty dollars a line for a second-rate poem, it seemed to me that the Ledger ought to be, typographically, a more attractive-looking sheet. When I had been working on it for five or six months, I went to Mr. Bonner and told him what I thought. "Yes," he said, as I proceeded to explain.

"Yes, I understand. You think the Ledger ought to be handsomer."

I explained more fully.

"I catch your meaning — I think so, too!"

I thought I had made a hit and given the owner of Maud S. a new idea.

I began to amplify the fascinating suggestion.

"Yes, I understand," he said, turning towards me. "The Ledger would look better that way. I know it would. But I would n't make the change for five thousand dollars."

I was amazed, till he went on and explained: "Newspaper readers are awfully sensitive to changes. The human eye is the most conservative organ in the human body. It will not be trifled with. The Ledger would look better, if that change was made, but my bank account would n't look better, for the readers would n't stand it. I should lose a hundred subscribers a day. So we shall have to keep the old thing as it is." He thanked me for the suggestion with a laugh, and returned to his desk.

One of the most active, ambitious, and vigorous newspaper men in New York was John Swinton. Throughout the war he was an editorial writer on the Sun and shortly became its managing editor. He resigned at the close of the war on the death of Mr. Raymond, and became a leader in all the movements for labor reform. For some years he received ten thousand dollars a year as managing editor of the Sun, but his position became untenable on account of his ardent advocacy of socialism. Mr. Dana strove to repress his radical tendencies, but his efforts were vain, and the headstrong editor, now become a recognized champion of the movement, resigned his position and started an organ for the expression of his views named *John Swinton's Paper*. He thought that all socialists, single-taxers, and the army of the discontented would at once rally around him and make the new journal a success. When he tendered his resignation, Mr. Dana, though unable to restrain him, gave him some advice. "John," he said, "you are mistaken. The laboring classes will follow you and will listen to you, but they will not support you. I have seen this experiment often tried, and I myself tried it to my great detriment after Brook Farm. Your enthusiasm excites my sympathy, but it does not sway my judgment. You will find that our friends to whom you appeal merely want to get their reading matter for nothing. How much ready money have you got?"

Swinton frankly declared his resources. Mr. Dana, with equal frankness, said: "John, I'll give you six months in which to become a bankrupt. I will retain you during that period on half your present salary." The rest is known. John Swinton waited in his office next day for the inrush of subscribers. They did not come. He walked up and down the city inquiring of his agents how many copies had been sold, and he was bitterly disappointed and distressed when he got the reply, "None, or next to none. There is no demand for your paper, Mr. Swinton." But he had to believe his treasurer and his bank account. *John Swinton's Paper* was a failure from the beginning. The laboring men did not support him, and he thereafter lived a precarious life in Newspaper Row.

## XI

## NEW YORK TRAFFIC IN 1879

DURING my whole newspaper life I have given abundant hospitality to novel inventions and discoveries and all devices aiming at industrial improvement. One day while on the Tribune in 1879 I heard Horace Greeley say, with sundry expletives not necessary to repeat, "It is just about as much as my condemned life is worth to get out of this blamed island and into it again!" And then he declaimed vehemently against the vile street-car accommodations and worse omnibus lines. His angry denunciation against prevalent means of urban transit set the office to thinking, and City Editor Amos Cummings shortly gave me an assignment covering the whole subject.

I found that New York City had about the worst street-car system in the world. Feeble and disjointed efforts had been made to supersede it with other methods, underground and above the surface. Under City Hall Park the Beach tunnel had been excavated for a few rods and abandoned. On Greenwich and Vesey streets had been reared an awkward and rather offensive scaffolding foreshadowing the ultimate elevated road. There never had been a wheel or a rail on it, and this bit of enterprise had also been abandoned, and was rapidly rotting away.

On Lower Broadway, Melville C. Smith, a young Minnesotan, had established the offices of what he called the Arcade road. This device contemplated disemboweling Broadway

from the Battery to Harlem, removing the entire surface
for twenty feet in depth, restoring the wagon roadway to its
old position on an iron framework, and filling the new underground street with a four-track rapid-transit road.   Senator
William Windom was president of the company.   There
were to be sidewalks on both levels opening into two sets
of stores, and "doubling the commercial capacity of the
street."   The project was splendid, and the projectors asserted
that it certainly could be realized by a total expenditure of
$10,000,000.

The young man Smith did not hesitate a moment on
account of the magnitude of the enterprise.   It rather seemed
to stimulate him.   He studied the map and growth of the
city; walked the streets with his eyes open; estimated the
inflow from lateral streets; counted the people leaving and
entering by different avenues; inspected the capacity of ferry-
boats; studied and collated the reports of the horse-car companies; forecast the future for ten, twenty, fifty years; and
then he stood on Broadway and said, "This is the backbone
of the island — the watershed and artery of trade; this street
must be torn up from end to end and another street built
below it for a four-track railroad — express and passenger
trains each way; then this upper pavement must be relaid on
an iron arcade without impeding travel; and the road beneath
must hide within itself all the sewers, gas and water mains,
and telegraph wires, and its trains must be capable of carrying a million passengers a day."

Almost alone he went at this stupendous and complicated
project.   He was ridiculed or ignored by the newspapers
and laughed at in the Legislature.   But he stuck to it.   He
got the bill through one house, and spent all summer in
canvassing.   The next year he got it through both houses, and
asked Governor Hoffman to sign it.   Governor Hoffman

smiled and vetoed it.  Smith kept up the fight.  He organized and addressed meetings in its behalf.  He called on editors and explained it.  He issued pamphlets, wrote and circulated petitions, made speeches, answered objections, left no stone unturned.  At last he got his bill through both houses again.  Governor Cleveland vetoed it.  The young Minnesotan calmly began the campaign anew.  In two years he got his bill through both houses again.  Governor Hill vetoed it.  Nothing daunted, Smith called a dozen millionaires about him, got them to put up $25,000 apiece as a starter, engineered his measure through both houses again, — this time by an almost unanimous vote, — and twisted it a little so that the recalcitrant Hill could sign it and save his pride in "consistency, the vice of little minds."

The bill as finally passed and signed authorized young Smith to construct at once a four-track railroad beneath Broadway from the Battery to the Harlem River at 160th Street, and a branch from Madison Square up Madison Avenue to Harlem.  The trains were to be run and lighted by electricity, and the express trains were to dip under the way trains so that passengers could enter cars without crossing a track.  Then the battle against the Arcade was renewed with tenfold vehemence and violence, the largest property holders bringing suits for injunctions based on the allegation that the Arcade would ruin their property.  They were defeated in court, but they brought suit again and again, and the gallant young champion of rapid transit died overwhelmed with disappointment and chagrin, a victim of the foolish apprehensions of men who could not see where their own interests lay.  If he had lived barely six years longer he would have seen his magnificent dream crowned with victory in the tunnelings and constructions of the mighty subway.

A Projected "Atmospheric Elevated Railway for City Transit"

Besides the Arcade there was a very ambitious scheme, the object of which was to facilitate the entrance and exit of western trains by a double tunnel under the North River with terminus at Union Square. This tunnel had been already excavated and clasped in a steel tube for half its length. At this point the work had ceased, and the completion of the subaqueous highway had been indefinitely postponed.

I made ample notes of the condition of these gigantic enterprises and wrote a half-column article for the Tribune. Cummings declined the responsibility of printing it, and said "Better see the old man." Into the sanctum I carried my report. Mr. Greeley was busy; indeed, I never saw him a minute when he seemed unoccupied. He was usually sitting at his low desk scratching in a desperate hurry, with his nose within four inches of the paper, as if eating his words, but now he was at his standing desk. He did not notice my presence, but when I spoke he said, "Yes; well! What is it? What is it?"

I told him what it was and he exclaimed, not as impatiently as the words might imply, "Well, go ahead! Go ahead!" I went ahead while he continued his writing, and he interrupted every sentence or two with an exclamation. "Yes! Of course!" "Arrangements couldn't be worse! Smith's Arcade? Destroy Broadway? Four sidewalks? Hey? Double its commercial facilities? Quadruple tracks, hey? Harlem in ten minutes? I don't know!"

At this he paused in his writing, or attempt to write, turned around, and said, "Astor won't stand it. How many hundred or thousand buildings has he got right around here? 'Spose he'll let the streets be torn up clear up to the building line? Why, see here, young man, don't you know he has already begun more than a dozen suits for injunctions and damages against that elevated scarecrow across yonder for injury to property? Real-estate men will never allow the streets of this city to be torn up or built on, for any project to facilitate travel. Never! However, you 've got some interesting figures and something must be done, and we 'll print the stuff, and see what response we get."

The statistics and conjectures were printed next day and became about the first definite installment of the rapid-transit literature of New York City.

While the Arcade road was struggling for life, I tried to complete the assignment which Cummings had given me.

Twenty-four years had passed since the enormous enterprise of tunneling the great river between New York and Jersey City was practically begun, and its progress had been a tragedy from the beginning. Its yawning mouths seemed like dragons waiting for more victims. Watching it was like watching the grave of buried hope. Trenor W. Park, after sinking a million and a half of dollars in fighting the inexhaustible supply of treacherous silt, died of a broken heart. The original projector of the scheme also died, in despair of ever finishing it. A rich Frenchman came, inspected it, and committed suicide. Several wealthy Englishmen lost all they possessed in the venture, some of them bitterly denouncing it on their deathbeds as a "robbery." It certainly was not that; it was merely a vast project, of unknown extent, novel and without precedent in engineering, constantly obstructed by natural impediments that could not be foreseen or adequately understood. And now the blanket mortgage had been foreclosed; the long hole in the mud had been sold at auction and bought up by the bondholders' committee, and it was announced that "work will begin again in a few days and electric cars, crowded with passengers, will run through the tunnel in the spring." They did not say which spring. The "original proprietors" must lose everything.

The "property" consisted of a double tunnel three thousand, one hundred feet long, needing one thousand, three hundred feet more to complete it. It was announced that only a million dollars more was required. The tunnels ran side by side, and each one was eighteen feet high, sixteen feet wide, with fifteen feet of earth between the top of the tunnels and the bed of the river. Cars would run about fifty feet below the keels of ships. When finished according to estimate, it would be over a mile long; but when the excavation ran up to Union Square and to the middle of Jersey City, so that cars could make entry and exit from nearly level ground, it would be twice as long.

I went to inspect the tunnel and report on it, curious to know how a cavern under the river would look, and how the aggressive water would be kept out. I called Cummings's attention to the fact that it had collapsed and filled with water once, but he did not offer to "sub" for me.

Up to Morton Street, opposite Bleeker and next to Christopher Street ferry, I went, and applied at a midget of a shed, between the roadway and wharves, which seemed to shelter nothing but a wheezy little stationary engine. Presently Colonel DeWitt C. Haskin made his appearance, mentioned his name, and offered to show me the way. Stepping off from the barrel head under his feet, he lifted it up and disclosed a black tube leading straight down into the ground — a narrow well with a ladder on its side. Down this we clambered single file a good way — perhaps forty feet or more. At the bottom the well widened a little, so as to give us standing room, and then my escort, cheering me up with the remark, "Don't be afraid, now!" touched a spring or lever, and a circular door swung towards us, revealing another black interior, which looked like the inside of a hogshead.

"Here we go!" exclaimed the vivacious Colonel, and, stooping, he crawled into the conveyance, if such it was, and asked me to follow him. I doubled up and, executing the "Georgia squat," got in by his side, he pulling the iron door to and carefully fastening it after us.

"There! Damn it!" he said, as his candle, which had enabled us to discriminate the darkness, went out entirely, and the queer caboose shook itself, uttered a fearful yell, and started. Whither? I wondered if we were going under the river to Hackensack or to Tarrytown, or Tartarus, and whether we should ever see daylight again.

It required the utmost confidence in science to accept the situation calmly. Pitch darkness. A trembling and shaking and jumping of the vehicle, as if it were rushing somewhere in a desperate hurry. A continuous frenzied yell, like that of many locomotives, which increased to such a tremendous pitch that I put my fingers in my ears, fearing that it would make me permanently deaf. I spoke to the Colonel; screamed to him, but it was like whispering in a hurricane. I shouted. I could not hear my own voice. That experience seemed to be a quarter of an hour long, but very likely was not many minutes. Then the screech began to diminish, the rocking to subside; I heard the Colonel shout something, and presently the door opened at the other end of the hogshead. Light! A man!

We crawled out and found ourselves on a slippery shelf or wall on the side of what looked like a huge mine. We were obviously in the caisson. I could hear the noise of hammering and shoveling. Far below us men were slowly moving about with torches. I heard a donkey bray and felt reassured. We climbed down another long ladder and then another and got to the bottom of a tunnel where were railroad tracks extending towards Jersey City, sustaining undersized cars, and long beams shoring up the sides. Indeed, the shell of brick was already built into a cylinder two or three hundred feet long. At the extreme end under the river was a flat shield of heavy casting fitting the enclosure and being pushed forward a little, day by day, as the silt and mud were removed from in front of it and cautiously admitted to the interior. The pressure of air upon our ears was painful. The hogshead, as I have called it, was, of course, an air lock into which compressed air was forced till the pressure was fifty pounds to the square inch, instead of the normal pressure of fifteen, and this was continued inside the tunnel. The entry and exit of air were what caused the terrific whistling inside the lock, and the same pressure it was which now held the iron shield up against the bank of silt and kept the fluent mud from oozing through the crevices and open panels and drowning the outfit.

I asked my escort if men did not find the pressure on their ears unhealthy or dangerous.

"Oh, no," he said, "some have been here several years and their hearing and breathing apparatus are as good as ever. See here! What do you think of these?" he added, leading me along to a place where, under the shadow of a pile of brick, two mules stood calmly eating hay.

"Mules!" I exclaimed. "How did they get in here?"

"Through the other lock," he answered. I inquired how they got them out at night.

"Don't get them out," he replied. "Those mules have been here two years."

"Under this pressure?"

"Oh, yes; they like it — have grown fat on it."

"Suppose your air pumps up above break down, Colonel?"

"They don't," he answered laconically.

"Would n't this whole concern give way and the Hudson River and Atlantic Ocean rush in here and take possession?"

"We have not tried it," he said with a smile, "and we do not intend to."

I told him that I was not afraid, as I took a fleeting glance at my watch.

"But you have an engagement?" he inquired.

I admitted that I had a pressing engagement up town and would like to take my leave of the shaky-looking brick cylinder, the trundling wheelbarrows, the shield, and the mules. And I added that I was not a glutton for air anyway; that fifteen pounds to the square inch, or foot, or whatever Nature had provided, was enough for me — as good as fifty. I quietly edged off towards the exit, but he detained me by the button.

"Before you go," said the Colonel, "let me show you how we prevent congestion — of mud. All the mud that comes in front of the shield we liquefy to a certain state of fluidity, and then we stick a hose in it with the other end up in the sewer, and the pressure of air in here squirts that mud up through the hose in a perpetual fountain. How 's that? Is n't that fine?"

Yes; I agreed that it was one of the finest contrivances I had ever seen, and hinted that I should like to inspect it at leisure from the outside.

At that moment a thunderous blast went off near by. I confess that I jumped. Not a mule's ear twitched, though the echo was long and reverberant.

"There is not the slightest danger," said the Colonel, laying a hand gently on my shoulder. Perhaps I looked anxious. I answered that I was not the least afraid. As I said this I quietly slipped towards the lock, and presently followed my guide through the diabolical trap that let me in.  I got out safely and looked up at the sky and was glad.

A few months afterwards an awful calamity befell.  The fissures let in too much water; the pumps got clogged; somebody neglected something, and the terrible river rushed in and filled the tunnel at midday.  Twenty-one men were drowned in a minute.  Even the shield proved futile.

After that dreadful day the tunnel was again pumped out and some progress was made from year to year.  But the financial resources failed for the tenth time; another of the chief backers died of disappointment; the unpaid workmen crawled out through the lock; the river made a triumphant attack and took complete possession, and both tunnels were filled full to the mouth.

But nothing can withstand human energy and the resources of time.  I never harbored doubts that the pumps would again start; that the mules would again be got in; that the shields would be renewed, and that the tunnels would be finished stronger and more effective than the original projectors ever dreamed of:

The early vicissitudes of tunnel building under the North River rather increased the discontent with prevailing methods of transportation.  When I was engaged in editorial work on the Graphic I reverted to the subject frequently, and in short paragraphs presented arguments for some kind of a revolution in street transit.  One day Mr. Croly sent for me to come to his room.  There I was introduced to Colonel Horace Porter, whom a glance took in as a tall, blue-eyed, handsome man, with sandy, drooping moustache and goatee, a quick military movement, and abundant *savoir-faire*.  It occurred to me that this must be the young man who won his spurs and a wound at Fort Pulaski and who was Grant's Chief of Staff through the battles of the Wilderness, and later his

Secretary of War. Mr. Croly said to me, "You've been dabbling in railroads, I believe; Colonel Porter wants you to dabble for him."

The visitor explained that some articles recently published in the Graphic had attracted his attention and he wanted to arrange with the writer for similar service elsewhere. Croly said to me, "It's all right. Go ahead!" So it was arranged for us to meet later.

I had heard Colonel Porter's name as that of the brilliant after-dinner speaker and story-teller, but now I inquired more particularly who he was. They said he had fought through the war in important commissions; that he had chief command of the artillery that reduced Fort Pulaski; that he was successively chief of ordinance in the Army of the Potomac and the Army of the Cumberland; that his name was often allied with the magnificent phrase "gallant and meritorious services"; that he was by the side of General Grant through the Wilderness, Spottsylvania, Bethesda, Cold Harbor, and James River, and that he now looked about ten years younger than any man ought to look who had passed through such experiences.

According to appointment I met the Colonel in the afternoon at the office of the Pullman Company, of which he was Vice President. He explained to me that the obstacles to pushing forward the elevated road which had been persistently made by owners of real estate seemed at last to be nearly removed, and the Company wished a series of articles to be prepared for immediate publication in the other dailies of the city to create a favorable public opinion. He wanted me to take the job in hand and report to him with three or four articles every morning. I was willing. I heartily believed in the elevated road system, and so, as the arrangement seemed to be satisfactory all around, we went ahead. Sometimes he gave me an important hint as to what points it was desired to make the next day; usually I followed the line of my defense of the projected road in the Graphic.

It was not difficult to show that Manhattan Island was a *cul-de-sac* into which Westchester County emptied itself every morning like potatoes into an overcrowded bag; that the traffic of New York City was more congested than that of London, which I had examined; that consequently life and limb were everywhere in peril; that the movement of in-tramural freight had become so difficult that millions of dollars a day were lost by delays caused by its obstruction; that no conceivable injuries that could be inflicted by noise and darkened windows would approximate the injuries suffered by pedestrians every hour; moreover, and finally, that the courts were open for redress and that the Company introducing the great improvement was able and willing to pay liberally for all damages resulting from the partial occupa-tion of streets.   These statements in various forms were put forth aggressively and profusely.   Every day some paper published an article explaining the tremendous advantages which the elevated road would confer on the city by relieving the congested thoroughfares, and some days every one of the five largest newspapers of the city appeared in harmonious accord advocating the undertaking.   To ring the changes on this chime of propositions was not arduous or exhausting labor, and for a month or more there was music all along Newspaper Row.

One day when this desirable result had been reached, Colonel Porter appeared at the office in hilarious mood. "Very well," he exclaimed; "very good.   We seem to be mov-ing.   Public opinion has veered around.   The newspapers will hereafter run the campaign without assistance.   How much do we owe you for helping to bring things up to date?"

I preferred to leave it to him, I said, if I had been of any service. He laid before me a sum much greater than I should ever have thought of mentioning, and then he said, "I feel like giving you a piece of advice. If that sum is sufficient, you are at liberty either to accept it or take its equivalent in stock. Now this elevated road is going to be a gigantic success. We foresee a magnificent future for it. If I were you, I would take the stock instead of the money, for the stock will probably double a good many times in a few years."

Right at this point I made a mistake. I thanked the Colonel for the generous sum mentioned and for the alternative, and added that, while I should like to be rich, I did not suppose I ever should be; that I knew nothing whatever of stocks, but that I did know something of money and how much I needed it, and if it made no difference to him or the Company, I would take the money. I did. Our pleasant coöperation and association were at an end.

Before taking temporary leave of the Colonel — for when I next met him he had been promoted to be General Porter and had become the President of the West Shore Railroad — I venture to record an incident of the campaign now at an end. One morning as I went upstairs I heard him laughing before I got to his room. "Did you see the alderman?" he inquired, trying to control his risibles. I told him I was not aware of having seen any alderman.

"The distinguished gentleman from the Fourth Ward, O'Flaherty," he explained, and laughed again. "You must have met him on the stairs. He wants to help us build our road."

I waited for such explanation as he saw fit to give and he went on: "He said that our elevated structure in Battery Park was a bad defacement — 'an eyesore,' he called it. I told him that we did n't think it was as bad as that, by any means, but we would do anything we could to improve its appearance. If the Board of Aldermen wanted it painted, we would paint it; and I asked him what color might be preferred.

"He said the matter had been discussed by several of them and it was thought that painting would not conceal it sufficiently. It might be better, he said, to plant some trailing and climbing vines along the four or five hundred feet in the Park. Well, I agreed to that. I told him the Elevated Road Company would at once set our men at work planting Ampelopsis, Virginia creeper, and ivy, so as to disguise it completely; and I thanked him for calling our attention to it so promptly.

"He remarked that I did not seem to catch on — that I did not take the exact meaning of his proposition. Vines were needed, but to have them effect the desired purpose the city would have to plant the vines. He allowed that this would naturally incur some expense, and he had called to see me about it.

"I asked him about how much the foliage would cost.

"He said some figures had been made by an expert landscape gardener, and it was thought that the work could be done in a manner satisfactory to all parties for the sum of $100,000.

"I hope I did not show my surprise. I assured him that I would think about it and confer with the officers. I was thinking about it when you came in. That's why I was smiling."

I watched for those vines for years. O'Flaherty went out of office. I watched for them when the aldermen put forth their annual report. I watched for them when General Porter went as Uncle Sam's ambassador to France. I always watch for them when I get off the elevated road at Battery Place.  At last accounts they had not budded.

Since that day miracles have been performed on Manhattan Island.  Impossible things have been done between the two rivers and under them.  The mules have been imprisoned in the lock again, and the complaining valve has uttered its unearthly yell.  Trenor Park's tunnel has duplicated and multiplied itself.  The "one-legged monstrosity" on stilts has crept over the island and made its way into contiguous states, and Melville Smith's beautiful idea of underground passenger traffic has grown from the potential Arcade to the practical gigantic subway, and in its realization the great city has not been destroyed.

I wonder what Beach and Colonel Haskin and Senator Wendon and Greeley and Melville Smith would say if they could return to the glimpses of the moon and drop a ticket at the box office.

## XII

## MARK TWAIN

About the middle of the nineteenth century there came into American journalism a remarkable group of brilliant and gifted Bohemians: R. H. Newell ("Orpheus C. Kerr"); Mortimer Thomson ("Doesticks"); David R. Locke ("Petroleum V. Nasby"); and that rare coterie of fun-making Westerners and poets: Samuel Clemens ("Mark Twain"); Edgar W. Nye ("Bill Nye"); George H. Derby ("John Phœnix"), Cincinnatus ("Joaquin") Miller, and Bret Harte. Of this humorous and whimsical fraternity, Mark Twain's name alone survives, after three quarters of a century of delightful banter and badinage that have filled the world with laughter.

I heard one of his first efforts as a lecturer. That is, he called the performance a lecture, but it was not a lecture much more than it was a sermon, a story, a panorama, a magic-lantern show, a song, or a concert by a brass band. It was disjointed and incoherent, yet its very novelty made it piquant, and its supreme absurdity drew the crowd and held it, expectant of what he might say next. It was in Chicago. The hall was crowded and five hundred were standing when the lank, frowzled, lantern-jawed, and impudent Californian strode upon the stage as if it were a steamboat deck and, getting near the footlights, rubbed his bony hands together and gazed around.

A thin man, of five feet ten, eyes that penetrate like a new gimlet, nasal prow projecting and pendulous, carroty curly hair and moustache, arms continually in the way, expression melancholy, he caresses first one hand and then the other, and then stares inquisitively and anxiously here and there and cranes his long neck around the house like a bereaved citizen who has just come from the deathbed of his mother-in-law, and is looking for a sexton.  For something like a minute — and it seems five minutes — he says not a word, but rubs his hands awkwardly and continues the search.  Finally, just as the spectators are about to break into giggles, he opens his capacious mouth and begins in a slow drawl — about three words a minute by the watch: —

"La-dies — and — gentlemen:  By — the request of the — chair-man of the — com-mittee — I beg leave to — intro-duce — to you — the lecturer of the eve-ning — a gentleman whose great learning — whose historical ac-curacy — whose devotion — to science — and — whose veneration for the truth — are only equaled by his high moral character — and his fine personal — appearance.  I allude — in these vague general terms — to myself.  I — am a little opposed to the custom of ceremoniously introducing a lecturer to the audi-ence because it — seems — unnecessary where the man has been properly advertised.  But as — it is — the custom — I prefer to make it myself — in this case — so that I can get — in — all the facts.  In matters — of this kind — I don't like to take any risks.  I never had but one introduction — that seemed to me just the thing — and the gentleman was not acquainted with me, and so there was no nonsense.  He just said: 'Ladies and gentlemen, I shall waste no time in this introduction.  I know of only two things about him: first, they say — he has never been in State Prison, and second, I can't — imagine why.' "

Mr. Twain then "hedged towards his subject," as he called

it, and took his auditors on a flying trip to California and the
mining regions, giving alternate glimpses of humor, burlesque, sentiment, and satire that kept his audience in a
thoroughly sympathetic mood. He never dipped into pathos
and never rose into eloquence, but he kept sledding right
along in a fascinating nasal snarl, looking and speaking like
an embarrassed deacon telling his experience and punctuating
his tardy fun with the most complicated awkwardness of
gesture. Now he snapped his fingers anxiously as if he had
forgotten what he was about to say; now he rubbed his hands
softly together, like the catcher of the champion nine; now
he caressed his left palm with his dexter finger, like the end
minstrel man propounding a conundrum; now he put his
arms akimbo, like a disgusted auctioneer; and now he churned
the air in the vicinity of his head with his outspread hand
as if he were fighting mosquitoes at Rye Beach. Sometimes
he got his arms tangled in a bowknot, but he untied himself
during his next anecdote.

It was plain to see that Mark Twain's success as a platformer
resulted, first, from his being a genuine humorist, with
audacity and imagination, secondly, from his slow and
solemn speech and his sanctimonious bearing. He had a
lively sense of incongruities, which is the soul of humor, and
the style of his delivery gave all the effect of spontaneity.
The jokes were uttered as if he had thought of them only a
second before and did not perceive the point of them quite as
soon as the audience.

I saw the lecturer next morning, and on the subject of the
convalescence of the then Prince of Wales, he said frankly,
"I am glad the boy's going to get well — mighty glad, and
not ashamed to own it. For he will probably make the worst
king Great Britain has ever had. That's what the people
there need. They need a bad king. He'll be a blessing in

disguise.  He 'll tax 'em and disgrace 'em, and oppress 'em, and trouble 'em in a thousand ways, and they 'll gradually go into training for resistance.  The worst kind of a king is the best king they can have.  He 'll cultivate their self-respect and self-reliance and their pride and their muscle, and they 'll finally kick him out of office and set up for themselves." Forty years later the lecturer, grown to ampler proportions, was summoned to an audience by King Edward, and the court gazette was terribly shocked to record that in a moment of inadvertence he punctuated one of his far-West stories by slapping his Majesty familiarly upon the back.  The details of their conversation are not given, but perhaps the king of humorists congratulated the king of Great Britain that he was still holding down his job.

I met Mark Twain one day in the press gallery of the Senate.  "A good deal changed," he exclaimed, glancing at the photographs of some of the so-called successful editors and correspondents hanging on the walls, "and it seems a hundred years ago."  I asked when he was here.

"I had a seat in the press gallery, — " he meditated, "let 's see, — in 1867, — and now I suppose all the veterans are gone — all the fellows who were here when I was.  I was here last," he went on, "in 1868.  I had been on that lark to the Mediterranean and had written a few letters to the San Francisco Alta that had been copied past all calculation and to my utter astonishment, and a publisher wanted a book — or thought he did.  I came back here to write it.  Why, I was offered an office in that ancient time by the California senators — Minister to China.  Think of that!  It was n't a time when they hunted round for competent people.  No, only one qualification was required: you must please Andy Johnson and the Senate.  Almost anybody could please one of 'em, but to please both — well, it took an angel to do that.

However, I declined to try for the prize. I had n't anything against the Chinese, and, besides, we could n't spare any angels at that time."

"A pretty good place to write," I remarked as we took seats.

"Some things," he said, "but an awfully bad place to write a book; or, at any rate, for such a newspaper man as I was to write such a book as the publisher demanded. I tried it hard, but my chum was a story-teller and both he and the stove smoked incessantly. And as we were located handy for the boys to run in, the room was always full of the boys, who leaned back in my chairs, put their feet complacently on my manuscript, and smoked till I could n't breathe."

"So that is the way you wrote *Innocents Abroad?*" I asked.

"No, that is the way I did n't write it. My publisher prodded me for copy which I could n't produce, till at last I arose and kicked Washington behind me and ran off to San Francisco. There I got elbowroom and quiet."

"It may have been wise," I concurred, "but you could write here now, and this is exactly the place for a man like you. If you don't come back here to live it will be the only big mistake of your life, Clemens"—for only his intimate friends addressed him as "Mark" and I never heard of one who had the courage to address him by his middle name, which was Langhorne.

"You must certainly select Washington for your permanent residence," I continued. "Why, all over the United States, people of leisure and culture are —"

"Yes, I know, I know," broke in Clemens, "but don't tantalize me. Do you take a fiendish enjoyment in making me suffer? I know perfectly well what I 'm about, and I appreciate what I am losing. Washington is, no doubt, the boss town in the country for a man to live in who wants to get all the intellectual pabulum he can in a given number of months, but I was n't built that way.  I don't want the earth at one gulp.  All of us are always losing some delight that we might have if we could live everywhere at once.

"I lose what Washington has to offer for the privilege of saving my life.  My doctor told me if I wanted my three-score and ten I must go to bed early, keep out of social excitements, and behave myself.  You can't do that in Washington.  Nobody does it.  Look at John Hay.  Just fading away amid these scenes of revelry.  No, the best place for my wife and me is quiet and beautiful Hartford, though there is a great deal here that I should like."

"You seem to have been pirated a good deal," I said to Mr. Clemens.  "I do not mean by illegal publication of your works so much as by private individuals claiming to write your writings.  You have probably suffered more than any other author in this way."

"Oh, yes," he said, "considerably — a good many cases. One ambitious individual in the West still claims to have written *The Celebrated Jumping Frog of Calaveras County,* and another is dead sure that he produced that classic and immortal work of mine known to the world as *Jim Wolf and the Cats.*  I suppose either one of them would face me down with it; and their persistence has led me to conjecture that a man may possibly claim a piece of property so long and persistently that at last he comes honestly to believe it to be his own.  You know that poor fellow in New Jersey, so weak-minded as to declare that he wrote 'Beautiful Snow,' and going to his coffin with tearful protest?  And who was it that claimed to have written Ella Wheeler's beautiful poem, 'Laugh and the World Laughs with You'?

"But I have n't been bothered that way as much as I have by personators.  In a good many places men have appeared representing that they were Mark Twain and have corrobora-

ted the claim by borrowing money and immediately dis-
appearing. I am out a good deal in that way. Such frauds
don't always borrow money. They sometimes seem to be
actuated by a kind of idiotic vanity.

"Why, a fellow actually stopped at a hotel for a week in
an English city, registered as Mark Twain, struck up a
warm acquaintance with the landlord and guests, recited the
Schweitzerhof incident for them in the evening, and actually
accepted a public dinner of welcome to the city, when some
mere accident exposed him and he lit out. Yet I myself was
well known in the town. His effrontery was exceptional."

"Did he resemble you?"

"I do not know. I have tried to believe that he did not.
The same thing happened in Boston, Toledo, and several
other cities. It was not pleasant to have bills coming in for
money lent to me in Albany, Charleston, Mexico, Honolulu,
and other places, followed by my calm explanation that I was
not there at all, bringing sarcastic letters in reply. 'Oh, of
course not! I did n't see you with my own eyes, did I?' and
I resolved that I would follow up the next swindler I heard of
and put him in jail. I had not long to wait.

"A dispatch soon came from Des Moines, Iowa: 'Is Mark
Twain at home?'

" 'Yes, I am here. Have not been away,' I answered.

" 'Man personated you here — got $250 from audience.
Shall I catch him?' came back, bearing the signature of a
lawyer.

" 'Yes,' I telegraphed in reply; 'have sent you check for
expenses.'

"He went ahead. He was a good while catching him —
some weeks, — and then he made me an elaborate report
giving the route of his labyrinthine and serpentine chase of
the swindler, the money he had expended, for hotels and

railroad rides, and the information that he did not entirely and completely catch him, though he 'got near him several times.' Of course I was out hundreds of dollars — am ashamed to say how much.

"I was disgusted, and shortly I got another dispatch — from New Orleans, I think it was: —

" 'Man swindled audience with pretended lecture here last night, claiming to be you. What shall we do with him?' I telegraphed back, 'Let him go! Let him go!'

"I'd give a hundred dollars, though, to see one of these *Doppelgängers* who personate me before an audience and who speak my pieces, just to see what the liar looks like."

I dodged into the back room at Chickering Hall one evening to get a word with Mark Twain and Cable during their breathing spells. The great American story-teller was on the platform spinning his yarns at the moment, and the Creole novelist was on tiptoe at the fly, waiting his turn. Almost before a word of greeting and congratulation could be spoken there was a cordial racket of palms and boot heels and our humorist backed upon us through the half-open door. He looked grayer, but not otherwise older than when I first heard him fifteen years before. His abatis of moustache and his porcupine eyebrows were as straggling and bristling as ever, and his rebellious and tousled hair looked as if it belonged to somebody else and had been borrowed for the occasion. I reminded him that the last time I saw him he told me that he hated the whole entertainment business and had quit it forever. "Yes," he said, "but I found I couldn't get along without being amused. No lecturer can be as amusing as an average audience. I shall not keep it up, though. I like audiences, and I like spinning my yarns. It is agreeable. When the evening is over I don't like to quit it, but that accounts for only two hours out of the day. What shall I do with the other twenty-two? That's the question. This business involves too much standing around. If, when I get to a town, I could rush in and play billiards till eight o'clock, it would be fun; but, no, I have to coddle myself. That's what I hate. And I can't accept the hospitality of a friend anywhere. Traveling, too, is an awful trial. If I could be shot all over the country in an air gun, or if I could go to sleep in the morning and sleep all day, that would be tolerable, perhaps, but I haven't any place to go and so I wander around disconsolate. Just hear that last sentence of Cable's; isn't that fine? See there! He's an orator and a genius. Here he comes. Bully for you, Cable! Let's see, what's mine? — Oh, yes, 'The Interviewer'" — and he sidled out upon the stage, book in hand, smiling grimly to the audience's salute.

Mr. Cable came off. To my remark that it was pleasant to find him such a mimetic interpreter of the Creole dialect, he said, "It cannot be a greater surprise to anybody than to me. I didn't know I could read acceptably at all till I launched out. The business is very exacting. I am tired all the time. Have no time to write." These platform partners were not much alike. Twain was of robust frame, large face, slow speech, and what would seem an unexcitable temperament; while Cable was somewhat undersized, with delicate and refined face, and a temperament evidently borrowed from his mother. Yet the novelist said in reply to a remark, "Yes, Mark doesn't find it all fun; he dislikes the stern discipline which the platform imposes. To have any success you have to keep quiet, decline all invitations, and not let anything or anybody intrude. I seem to stand the unpleasant phases of the business better. What isn't a drop to me is a whole shower bath to him. Isn't he a delightful companion, though?" The running comment of laughter in the hall was broken by

Mark's coming off again, while Cable entered through the door. It was a strong team — too strong, perhaps, to hold together.

They told me down in Bermuda a good story at the expense of Mr. Clemens. The prince of humorists was not very fond of practical jokes, but a member of his party was a shameless wag. At first Mark did n't "see any fun" in such business; then he was annoyed; then he was exasperated; and finally he got real mad and invented a scheme for revenge. One morning Mark sauntered down town and bought half a dozen pairs of India-rubber shoes; then he went to a giant India-rubber tree that sprawled all over the main road and sent its horizontal branches into the opposite gardens, and he hired a boy for "thrippence" to hang the goloshes around on convenient limbs. Then he quietly returned to the hotel, one beaming smile. Presently he called out to his tormentor: —

"Say, Buckley! Let's go and see if the India-rubber shoes are ripe."

Buckley smiled, and asked the humorist what he was talking about.

"Why," said Mr. Twain, "nothing, but I hear that these curious trees do actually bear a crop of India-rubber shoes, and they are generally harvested this month."

Of course everybody laughed at the fantastic notion, and Buckley answered: —

"We have ordered a strait-jacket for you; it will be here presently."

"Now, look here, Buckley," continued Mark, earnestly, turning on him, "you don't know a thing about these islands. I know what I'm talking about. I got my information from a man who lives here. And you are so funny about it that I'll bet you a jam-up champagne supper for our whole party that if we walk down to the nearest tree we shall find a crop of India-rubber shoes fit to pick."

Buckley wondered where the catch was; but he reflected that he had had so much fun that he could afford to pay for the supper, so he boldly accepted the wager. "Now, come on!" shouted the humorist. The party rallied for the excursion. Down the hill they swarmed, passed the banana palms and the pawpaw groves, to where the colossal India-rubber tree spread its gnarled gray branches and lifted up its polished leaves to the sun. The author of the joke came lagging along behind so that the discovery might have time to mature. He was a little surprised that nobody laughed, and still more surprised when they called out, "Where are they, Mark?" Then he carelessly glanced up; he carefully inspected the vast green canopy overhead, moving this way and that, so that no strange fruit might escape his eye; then he shouted in unfeigned astonishment: —

"Great Scott! Gone! Some d— d— d— infernal thief has got away with 'em all!"

Alas! So indeed it was. They had vanished. Some local laborer had harvested. Mark Twain presided gracefully at the champagne supper and in a little speech he said: —

"My blamed, blasted, confounded luck, ladies and gentlemen! If I had bet that that tree was there, a hurricane would have twisted it up while we were looking at it, and flung it out into the Atlantic before we could have got down the hill."

# XIII

## SOME LADIES AND AN OPERA

I DID not know Anna Dickinson when she first leaped into public life. Few did, for she was only fifteen years old when she began to express herself for the instruction of the universe concerning the deepest problems of existence. Even her careful mother afterwards confessed that for a year or two she did not know the precocious child who left the grammar school at fourteen, marched to the platform in the Philadelphia convention, and vigorously repelled an insulting and offensive tirade against women.

She was not a handsome girl after the ordinary pattern, for she had the unmistakable chin of a crusader; but her aggressive lower face was finely balanced by steel-blue eyes, a comely but ample mouth, and delicately curling hair that framed a noble white forehead. She was attractive and even fascinating. She spoke with facile ease and her words were chosen with felicity. When I first met the gifted young girl she had already astonished and thrilled audiences with her oratory, which combined the demureness of the Quaker with the white-heat vehemence of the religious champion.

"I don't see," she said, answering my question, "how I ever dared, uninvited and not wanted, to face that audience. It was not courage, exactly; it was both more and less than courage — an audacity born of the taunts of that despicable man who walked up and down the aisle and shook his finger at us." The undaunted girl was filled with an instinctive passion for human rights, and, carrying it like a religion in her inmost soul, she never compromised the great questions of which she was an evangelist.

She had spoken several times and had made an immense impression before her identity was known outside of her own home. Her reticent and delightful old Quaker mother was greatly pained at her daughter's unseemly conduct, till she made a tremendous sensation at the yearly "Woods Meeting," and received an offer of five thousand dollars to go and carry New Hampshire and Connecticut for the Republicans. These were doubtful states that year, until after the unknown maiden had spoken in Hartford and Concord. William Lloyd Garrison came from Boston to hear her. After the state elections she received a thousand dollars a week for services in other states. In her political appeals she revealed a soul of passion, sometimes emitting almost volcanic upheavals of dramatic fire. On moral questions she was emotional and easily brought tears to her hearers' eyes.

Her subsequent exchange of the platform for the stage was a distinct disappointment both to her friends and to herself. Instead of moving great throngs to rapturous applause, and adding forty thousand dollars a year to her bank account, she lost money and spoke to less responsive audiences. Many friends who wished her only happiness and good fortune advised against the new departure, not because they feared she would fail, for that was hardly possible, but because no success within her reach would add to the triumphs she had already won. Her extraordinary precocity had given rise to hopes that could not be realized.

I called on Miss Dickinson a week before her first appearance in *The Crown of Thorns*, a serious play which she herself had written for her début. "I shall succeed," she exclaimed earnestly.

"Yes, she always succeeds," spoke up her loyal brother.

"I know I shall succeed," she repeated. "I feel it intuitively — feel it in my blood, just as I did that mad night when I scandalized my dear folks by suddenly getting up in meeting down in Philadelphia. Then I have certain assets."

"You certainly have," I acquiesced, "a matchless series of personal victories, and some millions of friends and acquaintances."

"Just so," she said, "and other assets. I know how to face audiences and what to do. Then the newspapers will stand by me — at their head, the Tribune. And the Graphic," she hastily added, tossing to me a smile across the parlor. "You have seen it rehearsed — how does it strike you?"

I answered with some reserve that it was a forcible composition and an interesting plot, but nobody short of omniscience could forecast the effect of any play on any audience.

*The Crown of Thorns* made the circuit of the country and was followed by *Mary Tudor,* also her own play, and then by a full line of Shakespearean tragedies. Her venture was received with considerable applause in many places, but largely on account of her personality. She never felt quite at home upon the stage, — many newspapers, the Tribune to her utter disappointment and dismay at their head, going back on her, — and after an experiment of two years, not wholly satisfactory, she returned with pleasure to the lecture platform. Here her presentation of *Joan of Arc* was received with real enthusiasm. She wrote a tragedy, *Aurelian,* for John McCullough, and a highly successful comedy, *An American Girl,* for Fanny Davenport. To these she added several novels and economic works.

I am sure that Anna Dickinson is the most eloquent woman

orator that this country has produced — approached but not equaled by Lucy Stone and Ernestine L. Rose. The trials of her life had made her tones somewhat pessimistic, but when I last saw her she was cheerful to a degree and not without hope for her country or the human race. She wanted to be a great actress, instead of a great lecturer; as Forrest wanted to be a great comedian and Burton a great tragedian; and did not Raphael aspire to be a poet instead of a painter? And did not Dante and Goethe mourn because they were not artists instead of poets? Evermore it is as Browning says: —

> What of Rafael's sonnets, Dante's picture?
> Does he paint? he fain would write a poem, —
> Does he write? he fain would paint a picture.

George Lake discovered Emma Abbott. He was a millionaire merchant down by the City Hall, and one of the pillars of Chapin's Unitarian church. She was the soprano soloist in the choir and very young. One evening the Lakes gave a little dinner to Miss Abbott, and at that dinner she was suddenly surprised by the announcement that he would send her to Europe to study music for an indefinite term. She went and applied herself so diligently that she was brought out in grand opera in Paris and achieved a splendid triumph, Through George Lake, New York was kept informed of the movements and successes of "honest little Emma," as he always called her. I am responsible for the first elaborate sketch of Emma Abbott that ever appeared in the American press, consisting of a four-column biography in the Graphic. It included an ardent forecast of the future of the girl who was still studying in France and told of her early privations, her pathetic need, her courage, her assiduity, her refusal to sing in *Traviata* for moral reasons, her high ambition, her steadfast friends, her quarrel with her Parisian impresario, and her successful début.  Miss Abbott was not handsome, but she was a dramatic singer, possessing a voice of large compass, and corresponding sweetness, and a sympathetic manner that captivated her hearers.  On her return to New York she more than repeated her foreign triumphs.

An immense reception was given in her honor by A. J. Johnson, the wealthy New York publisher.  The strongly literary character of this reception made it memorable.  Hundreds of distinguished editors, poets, and musicians vied with each other to do honor to the little *cantatrice*.

In the cloakroom I met William Cullen Bryant, who was bewailing the loss of his boutonnière, pinned on by some loving hand, and was looking for it under the chairs and tables.  Against his pleasant protest I gave the venerable poet a bunch of violets from my own lapel and attached it firmly before he descended the stairs.  Near the middle of the saloon parlor and opposite the great pier glass Miss Abbott held court, and, as Wetherel had not yet come on the scene, George Lake, the Lord Bountiful, stood near her presenting her guests and admirers as they came.

At one end of the spacious drawing-room, against another pier glass, stood the honored but diminutive Bryant, and at the other end Bayard Taylor, then at the zenith of his fame.  And there they both remained and "assisted" the prima donna all the evening.  Among the well-known guests were Generals Grant, Schurz, and Howard, Edwin Booth, Charles A. Dana, Richard H. Stoddard, Edmund Stedman, Rossiter Johnson, Edgar Fawcett, the Bunces, the Crolys, Colonel Morse and his lady, and all the generous entertainers who often brought the *littérateurs* of the metropolis together.  It was a great evening.

Shortly I had occasion to call on Mr. Bryant at the office of the Evening Post concerning a business matter, and I took the opportunity to mention "Thanatopsis" and ask him whether at the age of seventeen he had intended to introduce any definite religious reflections into that poem.  He said, "No, certainly not," and added, "I probably know what you allude to, for a lady wrote to me several years ago and asked me if I could not substitute the word 'faith' for 'trust' in the closing lines, adding that they were obviously meant to be synonymous.  But they are not synonymous at all.  The poem is wholly terrestrial.  I have of course, written poems with a theological cast, like 'Lines to a Waterfowl,' but the 'trust' mentioned in 'Thanatopsis' is a confidence in the processes of Nature and the peaceful and silent rising and passing away of generation after generation."

When next I met the prima donna I asked her about her relations to Patti, suggested by something I had seen in the papers.

"Oh, we are the best of friends," she said.  "We always exchange calls when we can.  Dear Adelina is a first-rate fellow!  Why, she first introduced me to the public, and my earliest engagement resulted from a letter in which she said, 'Her voice is lovely.  The *mezza voce* and sustained notes are simply perfect.'  That was nice of her, was n't it?  But I have n't always agreed with her.  She said, 'You must have an Italian name.  You can never succeed as Emma Abbott.  No American name will answer.  Try Alberti.  That is respectable and it is foreign — which is indispensable.'  I told her No, I would go ahead as Emma Abbott, and if I ever won any laurels it should be under my own simple family name.  So here I am — still Emma Abbott."

I asked Miss Abbott to tell me the range of her voice.  "I can sing three notes higher than any other living prima donna excepting Sembrich," she replied.

"How high is that?" I asked.

"To F *altissimo*.  Listen," she added, and, raising her head slightly, she sounded the note A above the staff lines, ran easily up the scale to C and then, with no apparent exertion, struck C sharp, D, D sharp, E, and finally F, holding the last note long enough to turn to a piano and, striking the same note, verify the correctness of her voice.  I congratulated her, when she laughed and said, "You may be surprised to know that I have transposed the score of *Il Trovatore* up in order that I may sing it with greater ease."

What Emma Abbott made of herself resulted from conscientious application — unremitting hard work.  She was probably the most versatile artist on the stage, having appeared in thirty-eight different operas, ranging from the merry and coquettish Zerlina and the tender Juliet to the passionate and blood-curdling Borgia and the sorrowing Bride of Lammermoor.  One chief secret of her success was her phenomenal animal vigor and strength.  She said to me, "My health is perfect.  I hardly ever had a headache in my life, and never disappointed an audience.  My throat and vocal organs are tough, too.  I am the only prima donna in the world who sings publicly seven times a week.  I suppose no money or eulogy could induce Patti to sing two nights in succession."  Miss Abbott became rich — worth two or three millions, probably, with no expensive habits, except an ultimate marriage.  Through shrewd and lucky investments she had attained an income of a thousand dollars a week.

Speaking of operas stirs me all up and fills me full of melancholy reminiscence.  For I once wrote the book of an opera myself — a "comic opera" it was called.  What? You have never heard of *Deseret, or A Saint's Afflictions?* Oh, you must have heard of it, but it passed into your forgettery. Yes; it was presented.  It was put on the stage at the Fourteenth Street Theatre, New York, with much expensive scenery and great expectations.  To bring it out the first night cost four thousand dollars.  It had a run of a fortnight in New York, and was sung a week in Brooklyn and also in Philadelphia, Baltimore, Washington, Cincinnati, Chicago, and Detroit.

Then and there its performance was suddenly "suspended." That is what Hart Jackson, the manager, called it, and I feebly acquiesced.  The unfeeling boys of the dramatic press amused themselves by remarking that it was "busted," "petered out," "gone up" — it makes my blood curdle to recall their brutal language.  It seemed to be going along very successfully when it suddenly stopped.

Why it suspended — that is what racked my sconce.  Why was there not a public clamor for *Deseret,* as the friends of the author and the composer had predicted?  Why?  It was quiet and refined, moral and chaste, and could have been given in any boarding school for girls.  It was strictly and even painfully American — and an American opera was what there had been such a clamor for.  Mormonism was the droll theme it played with — for the first time, I believe.  It was well put on the stage and admirably sung.  Elder Scram had some thirty or forty wives, — thirty-five, I think, to be exact — and they made it lively for their husband.  Why did the opera fail?  It was composed by the most gifted and eminent American musician, Dudley Buck, and the libretto was written by another ditto ditto, whose name modesty forbids me to mention.  Yet it had a brief existence — a few weeks only — and then the demand for it ceased.

I never understood its premature doom.  I saw the howling idiocies of Rice's "Surprise Party," "The Rag Baby," "The Painted Dog," and "The Tin Soldier" received with universal acclaim.  Women shouted for them.  Children cried for them.  Bald men hired opera glasses and sat in front, yet *Deseret,* which was coherent, intelligible, and respectable, came to grief in one short lustrum — no, I don't mean lustrum; I mean lunation — month, you know, or a little over. My brain still reels when I think of the wreck.  The score was by a composer of the highest reputation, and was spirited, tender, humorous, virtuous.  The libretto was as good as the music, if not better.  It displayed high dramatic skill and literary talent.  I know what I am talking about, for I wrote it myself.  It was everything it should have been, and perhaps more.  I cannot permit the question to be discussed.

And the manager was an able manager.  I know he was, for he told me so himself.  How came *Deseret* to fail to captivate the American public, then?  I lay it to the profound stupidity of the human race.  It was too intellectual for theatregoers of that time.  Like Wordsworth's poetry and Bacon's philosophy, it was written for the future, and the question how soon it will rise from its premature slumber and go forth to conquer depends on how soon the world becomes enlightened and acquires the love for the beautiful.

I am thinking of writing another libretto.  If I do, it will be different.  There will be so much kicking and jumping in it that a castiron theatre will have to be built expressly for it, and so much howling and yelling that the fire department will turn out every five minutes and adjoining blocks will be uninhabitable.  Dudley Buck declines to compose the music and profanely declares that "if that is what the present generation wants, the p.g. can go to Halifax" — though he does n't say Halifax.  Whenever we get together we sing the solemn song: —

> The world of fools has such a store
> That he who would not see an ass
> Must stay at home, and bolt his door
> And break his looking-glass.

I never wrote often or much for magazines.  Perhaps it was because I lacked patience.  Having worked during my whole newspaper life where what I wrote was always printed, I could not get accustomed to rejections.  When an article was returned to me with kindly words ending with "not exactly adapted," I generally flung it aside and did not repeat the application.  Only once did I ever send the same article to more than two magazines.  That exception was in 1870, and it is perhaps worth speaking of.

Among my casual acquaintance in the West I came upon a gentleman who possessed a highly interesting album.  In fact, it was unique, for it contained nearly forty autograph letters written by presidents of the United States and as many more by the most distinguished statesmen, and all upon one subject — the painting of their portraits!  They were letters generally written to the artists themselves, and included all the presidents, with two exceptions, from Washington to Lincoln.

These most interesting letters I framed into an article for a magazine and named it "Before the Camera."  I offered it with confidence.  It was declined — more than once.  At last I disposed of it for $125.  Still it did not appear.  I was working on the Graphic.  One evening I went to the Lotus Club, whose president, the genial poet and novelist Dr. J. G. Holland, the editor of *Scribner's Monthly* was in the chair.  During the evening I was surprised by being called upon for "A speech!  A speech!" after the uproarious habit of that intellectual circus.  I hesitated, not being primed with a speech, and the president suggested a story instead.  To this I had to respond, and while I was getting on my feet it occurred to me that I should give them the history of "Before the Camera," especially as the presiding officer knew something about it.  So I ran on somewhat as follows: —

"I wrote an article once which I thought would make eight

pages in a magazine — if it got a chance. I concluded to give the *Atlantic Monthly* the benefit of it — because that was a superb creation of the human intellect and ought to be encouraged. [Merriment around the table.] I hastily sent it to that periodical, calling attention to its merits which would be sure to make a sensation, and asking the editor to send me the hundred dollars by draft or money order. In three weeks it came back, to my utter amazement, with the printed notice that it was excellent, but not exactly adapted, and so forth.

"My opinion of the *Atlantic* and its editor underwent a radical change [cheers round the table and cries of satirical approval.] I immediately sent it to another well-known magazine, offering it for fifty dollars. It came back in two months, just when I was looking for it to appear. I am happy to say that this magazine shortly went into bankruptcy. I then sent it (price fifteen dollars) to a first-class weekly which was just then running presidential literature not half as well written as mine. [Applause and encouraging remarks round the table.] Again I received it back. [Laughter.] At first I could not believe it. It did not seem possible that our periodical literature was decaying so fast.

"I thought of offering it for nothing, but my pride saved me. [Applause.] I was angry, gentlemen. Something heroic must be done. Two years had passed. It was now 1872. There was a handsome illustrated magazine in this city which I had not tried — a beautiful work of art. I resolved to storm the citadel. The doorkeeper stood briskly aside and I was speedily ushered into the presence of a young man who inquired my business. 'To see the editor.' He himself would examine my manuscript, he said, for the editor was just going home. 'Very well,' I rejoined, 'I must have an answer in fifteen minutes, as I leave on the evening train for Boston.' He parleyed, but I was severe and taciturn, and reached for the manuscript which he had taken. 'I will see the editor, then,' he remarked.

"The chief at once appeared — the dean of the magazine corps. He was a tall, rather corpulent, slightly bald, handsome, middle-aged man. 'We will send this to you by mail,' said he, 'if it is not used.' 'I can leave it with you only fifteen minutes,' I replied. He looked surprised and glanced at the title. A boy brought his overshoes, and stood holding them. 'You can surely leave it one night,' the editor expostulated. 'No,' I answered resolutely, 'I have other use for it.' In that he evidently scented the opposition house, for he took off his overcoat (he was just going home) and said, 'I will look it over now.' [Cheers and rapping on plates round the tables.]

"This particular editor was a fine-looking man as he sat there in the dying twilight [cries of 'Oh!' 'Ah!'] — a rather corpulent, slightly bald, middle-aged, handsome gentleman. [At this the company around the table spontaneously turned towards the presiding officer, Doctor Holland, who was red as a boiled lobster, and then they roared with glee and shouted 'Oh! Ah! Yes, of course!'] He read my contribution very deliberately and then said, 'We will take this. Mr. Oliver, please make out a check for fifty dollars.'

"'What?' I asked. 'Fifty dollars? My price is $125.' [Applause.]

"'Ah,' said he, returning the manuscript to me, 'that is more than we ever pay anybody except famous writers.'

"With a feeling of resentment I took the roll of paper, delivered my bow, and turned to the door.

"'Well,' said he, calling to me, 'we'll take it at $125,' and Mr. Oliver made out my check. [Hearty cheers and roars of laughter around the table.] Perhaps I did not mention, as

I certainly ought to have done, that the editor was a tall, rather corpulent, slightly bald, handsome, middle-aged gentleman. [Roars of laughter and cheers.] He was obviously qualified for his high responsibility. The worst of it is — or perhaps the best of it, depending on the point of view — that I have not seen or heard of that article about the camera and the ancient portrait painters during all these seven years! The editor, I ought to say, was a tall, rather corpulent, slightly bald, handsome — "

The uproar at the table became so great that the sentence was never finished. When the racket measurably subsided, all parties turned straight towards the presiding officer, now recognized as the hero of the narrative, and shouted, "Holland! Holland! Timothy T.!"

He rose slowly to his feet. The crimson went out of his face and turned to the rosy flush habitual to it, and he laughed cheerfully by the time the applause and guffaws which greeted him had died away.

"The fact is," he began, deprecatingly, and there was another great roar of laughter — "yes, I well remember the incident, and the circumstances mentioned. I recall the dilemma vividly. I accepted the sketch offhand in order to keep its writer from inflicting it on some weaker magazine. [Loud and prolonged laughter.] Our house is rich. We can afford to stand in the breach. If it were not for the great and benevolent work we constantly do in buying up articles capable of injury, the mortality among magazines would be incalculable. [Loud laughter and cheers.] Yes, my friends and gentlemen, when a person with a flighty temperament comes in [laughter] we exert every nerve to get possession of the manuscript to prevent the desolation that might otherwise ensue. [Vociferous cheers and jingling of glasses.] Such an article might fall into the hands of some editor who would inadvertently print it. [Cheers and cries of 'Hear!' 'Hear!'] We protect him. We lock it up in a strong safe."

The company spontaneously rose and drank to the sagacious magazine, while Dr. Holland went on seriously declaring that he had eight immense fireproof safes full of stories and other manuscripts that had been bought and paid for, some of the matter extending back for years. "If nobody should write a word for the body of our magazine for the next ten years," he concluded, "it would appear regularly every month, and I doubt if its quality would be at all impaired."

The sequel of this narrative is that thirty years have passed since that Lotus Club dinner, and my cherished contribution, "Before the Camera," has never yet appeared.

Ever since I could vote I have been deeply interested in the movement to extend the franchise to women. At first, for many years, I warmly advocated it as a right. At last, I drifted from approval to doubt, from doubt to opposition, as I more clearly saw that all government was founded on force; that voting was not a "right," but a concession from those in power; that the bayonet and ballot must go together, for it was scarcely expedient to arm with the suffrage those who might, in some cases, be in the majority, but would be wholly unable to enforce their laws. In such a case as that, the legal possession of the ballot would be merely a mockery. Even the raid on Parliament by the vociferous and obstreperous "suffragettes" of London has not modified this conclusion.

The first speech in favor of woman suffrage that I ever heard was by Henry Ward Beecher in Cooper Union, and I vividly recall the opening sentence, for it brought down the house: "Ladies and gentlemen: Man is vastly superior to woman — as man; and woman is vastly superior to man — as woman; and both of them together are more than a match for either of them separately!"

I have generally attended woman's rights conventions, whenever I could conveniently do so, and reported their doings to the newspapers I served. If I am not mistaken it was in 1888 that the annual convention met in Washington. I strolled down to the hotel in the evening to make certain that nothing important should get away from me at headquarters.

Mrs. Cady Stanton stood at the head of the drawing-room receiving guests, and directing the social functions.

"Yes, yes, we are all, all here!" she laughingly exclaimed in response to my salutation. "And we are going to have the greatest convention we have ever held."

"No flies in the amber this year?" I asked.

"Nothing but the same old fly!" she answered, looking down the rooms to where Dr. Mary Walker perched on a sofa. "You know she's always in our way."

Mrs. Stanton was far the handsomest woman in the assembly and the convention's most remarkable attendant. Her skin was white as wax, her eyes a turquoise blue, and her large head was crowned with a peck of short white silky curls. These and a rich black velvet dress heavily draped with white duchesse, and the ample corsage filled in with point lace and a universal flutter of white all about her, made this striking personage look like a dwarf plum tree in extravagant bloom.

Dr. Mary Walker was even more conspicuous. She looked exactly like a little man, for she was in her usual masculine attire — tweed coat, white marseilles vest, and broadcloth pantaloons, and she held her cane and silk hat in her hand.

"I observe that Dr. Mary Walker stands gallantly by the cause," I said, casually indicating with my thumb the slight effigy that was talking with another fellow at the end of the sofa.

Mrs. Stanton uttered a sniff of contempt and added, "She's an awful nuisance. Nobody can keep her still. She bobs up serenely every time after being sat on by the whole convention. She hasn't any sense. She's headstrong, conceited, and ignorant. You knew how she bit me at the last convention?"

"Bit you, madam?" I asked anxiously and incredulously. "Bit you? Is this a favorite metaphor of yours to emphasize a difference of opinion?"

"Metaphor?" she said. "It is not. It is not, indeed. She bit me — bit my hand till it bled all over my velvet dress. It was sore for weeks."

"Good heavens!" I exclaimed. "Bit you! How could such a thing happen?"

"Well, we just wouldn't let her interrupt and break up the convention — and you know how obstinate she is! We had six police to keep her out of the building, but she crept in somewhere, and the first I knew there she was, right on the platform, speaking. I was presiding, and I got up and told her that she couldn't speak then and must keep still. She said she knew her rights and would speak, and she proceeded to read those same everlasting old resolutions about women's dress. That wasn't what we were there for, I told her, but she wouldn't sit down. She talked louder than ever, and though her voice is dreadfully weak, it was enough to make a great disturbance. I advanced towards her, at the same time calling the executive committee to the platform. Three or four of them came up and took hold of her and gently pulled her towards the stairs. I also pushed her and tried to persuade her. Suddenly, before I knew it, she got my hand in her mouth and bit me terribly — it was a long time before I got over it."

Other arrivals claimed the lady's attention at this point, and I turned to look for the biter.

Dr. Mary was the centre of a compact crowd who evidently regarded her merely as a curiosity. She had a soft and pleasant voice and, though she spoke fluently, she was by no means monopolizing the conversation. "Oh yes, I have about got over being a scarecrow in Washington. The police used to arrest me every little while because I wore these innocent-looking pantaloons, but I fairly laughed them out of it. When they saw that I didn't care and the judge before whom I was summoned said he couldn't see but that I was a very harmless person, they gave it up as a bad job — or a good job, and let me alone. I feel quite lonesome now, without any policeman to escort me."

I waited and waited for her audience to disperse so that I could speak to her alone — and waited and waited. Finally, an hour later, I found her with only two or three listeners. I didn't want to be abrupt, so I just said, "Doctor Walker, did you bite Mrs. Stanton?"

"Yes, I did bite Mrs. Stanton, and I don't care who knows it."

"Why did you bite her?" I continued. "Mrs. Stanton is generally considered a remarkable woman — what may be called a great woman."

She thumped on the carpet with her little cane and cried, "She is! Cade Stanton is an extraordinary great tyrant! That's what she is! She is a mean, selfish, jealous, conceited, overbearing scoundrel! That's what she is! She can't make a speech, either! She can only read it from manuscript. And Sue Anthony is no better! Not a whit! And that Lil Blake creature!  They are all a heap of rascals and they are leagued together to crush me."

"There never was a plainer case of jealousy," Dr. Mary went on.  "I was young, and I excited éclat.  Often, in conventions, audiences would call for me when Cade Stanton was wading through manuscripts by the hour.  It made them mad.  After I had prepared my crowning constitutional argument I took and read it to Senator Sumner, addressing him as the greatest statesman in the land.  He said he was astonished at the profundity of my argument. . . . Well, it was at the last convention that the thing happened.  Cade Stanton and Sue Anthony had hid policemen in the anterooms and cellars to keep me out.  I got in another way and walked on to the platform, and when I rose to offer a resolution they went for me!  The audience clamored for me to go on, and there was a great deal of éclat, but Cade Stanton and Sue Anthony and others got round in front of me and actually pushed me off the stage.  Cade was a great big thing and I never weighed a hundred in my life, and when she grabbed me by the wrist I just raised her hand to my mouth and bit it.  I bit it hard.  I bit it as hard as I could.  I meant to bite it harder, and have always been sorry I did n't."

At this point Dr. Mary recovered her vertical attitude, threw back her cutaway coat, and looked at her watch.  I took the hint and my leave, going to my couch to meditate on the vicissitudes of the great cause and the discordant notes in the diapason of perfect harmony.

## XIV

## SCHUYLER COLFAX

For many years I had the privilege and pleasure of an intimate acquaintance with Schuyler Colfax, — such friendship as a youthful admirer could have with a distinguished statesman, — from his early days in Congress when he helped to break into the Smithsonian, to the sad winter when he lost his life in a Minnesota blizzard. He had been Grant's Vice President, and later named as his Secretary of State, when he was suddenly summoned to defend himself from a vile conspiracy of which Oakes Ames was the leader.

When the Crédit Mobilier scandal, involving more than a dozen members of Congress, was under investigation, there was a check for some thousands of dollars introduced drawn in favor of "S. C.," endorsed with the same initials and marked "paid." Oakes Ames, centre of the ring, testified that he wrote it and delivered it to Mr. Colfax. This was taken by many as conclusive. Colfax indignantly denied ever having endorsed it or seen it, and the money was never traced to him, through the bank or otherwise. He alleged that it was a forgery and introduced evidence to prove it; but a persistent slander can never be wholly obliterated, and the sensitive man was seriously wounded by the falsehoods, although their inventor survived their utterance only a few miserable months. Mr. Colfax expressed to me the belief that either Oliver or Frederick Ames would, after the death of their

father, make public a statement relieving him of the stain.
Colfax was generally believed to be entirely innocent.

It is not generally known how near Schuyler Colfax came
to being the editor of the New York Tribune. Mr. Greeley's
death was a shock to the country, and his myriad friends immediately cast about for a successor. Whitelaw Reid, an
enterprising, tactful, and talented young journalist from
Cincinnati, the "Agate" of war correspondence, was the managing editor, and still had those "nine points of the law"
which possession is supposed to confer. To carry on the
paper and relieve the tense situation, Jay Gould advanced
some hundreds of thousands of dollars. Of course such a
relation was incongruous and incompatible with the history
of the paper and could not last.

While several acquisitive millionaires were considering the
situation, William Orton, president of the Western Union
Telegraph Company, took a hasty survey of the property,
made a guess at its future, bought a controlling interest in
the Tribune, and slipped off to Washington to engage Mr.
Colfax to edit it. The candidate was pleased. He had been
a successful editor all his life, keeping closely in touch with
his South Bend Register, both from the Speaker's chair and
from the Vice President's room. Moreover, he had always
been a warm friend and admirer of Mr. Greeley and generally
advocated the same public policies. Just as he was about to
close the bargain, Orton scented the extinguished calumny
and postponed action to ascertain if his new editor's reputation was injured. The delay was fatal to the arrangement.
While the chief of telegraphs was waiting and watching,
Whitelaw Reid adroitly stepped in, presented a check from
D. O. Mills, his millionaire father-in-law, and obtained the
great newspaper.

One Sunday morning about this time I walked to Plymouth Church to hear Mr. Beecher. A stranger was in the pulpit and I turned away to the Unitarian Church of Dr. Chadwick. He was a popular writer, a gifted sermonizer, a widely known poet, and an eloquent pulpiteer. His great Gothic church was crowded that summer morning with an audience of a thousand or two. I do not recall the text which the pastor selected, but the lesson of the sermon was the unprofitableness of sin, and the certainty of malefactors being overtaken by punishment even during their earthly career. To strengthen a proposition which on its face is very doubtful indeed, he went on to enumerate the famous criminals of history and show how they had met their dreadful doom, proceeding from one to another up the centuries until he had marshaled a terrible platoon of wicked men — Nero, Caligula, Judas Iscariot, Benedict Arnold, Boss Tweed, and Schuyler Colfax! I was shocked, and for the moment paralyzed at the audacity of the man. I felt that somebody ought to correct him at once, and I turned around and asked the man immediately behind me if he thought Dr. Chadwick would object to an interruption for the sake of truth and justice.

He inquired, "What's the matter? Anything wrong?"

"Yes, indeed; very wrong," I answered, "and it ought not to pass without correction."

"Well, I don't believe the Doctor will object," he said. "He's a pretty liberal man, you know. I am a deacon in the church and I don't believe he'd object if there's anything wrong."

I thanked him and waited. When the sermon was concluded and the recipients of the collection had started round the great auditorium, I walked up the aisle and ascended the pulpit stairs. The minister leaned forward inquiringly.

I said quietly, "I have come to the pulpit because this is

SCHUYLER COLFAX

a liberal church and you are reputed to be a fair-minded man. You have been misled to-day into doing gross injustice to one of the most gallant, honest, and high-minded gentlemen that ever went into American politics — Schuyler Colfax. I know his personal and political history, and the attempt that has been made to impeach his character. I have come to the pulpit to ask if you will give me four minutes in which to show your audience that you are in error and that he deserves a different classification."

The minister rose and said, "Oh, I don't believe that's worth while."

"That is not what I came to ask," I said. "Before doing such an unusual thing as to interrupt your exercises I had thought it over and concluded that it was worth while. I now only inquire if you will permit the correction."

"It would cause a disturbance and controversy," he replied, "and that would not help matters any. Already the congregation is uneasy and disturbed, you see."

I answered that I did not wish a disturbance or controversy, and I would agree that in case an answer was made to what I had to say I would make no rejoinder.

There was considerable excitement in the audience by this time, and several men moved forward towards the pulpit. Dr. Chadwick raised his hand, as deprecating disorder, and then leaned his head upon the cushion in front of him in the attitude of prayer. After a couple of minutes of silence he rose and said, "No, such a thing cannot be permitted."

I expressed regret in a word and resumed my seat in the audience. At the close of the services I was intercepted on my way to the door by a large number of the auditors who asked what it was all about. At their request I stood on a chair in the vestibule and freed my mind. Some questions were asked and answered, but there was no disturbance of any kind. The New York papers noticed the incident next day, the Sun contenting itself with saying, "Some man created a disturbance in the church by insisting on defending Schuyler Colfax from the preacher's allegations."

I have never quite satisfied myself whether my action that day was justified or not. It was certainly not conventional, and if ministers have a right to name distinguished citizens as wicked malefactors in their sermons, the interruption was indefensible. In a few days I received a letter from Colfax saying, "Thank you from my heart. I know it must have been you."

"I do not expect," said Mr. Colfax to me once, "that justice will be done to me till I am dead — perhaps not even then. You know, and a good many others know, not only that I never had a cent of the Crédit Mobilier money, but that I did not lie about it; that I was in exactly the same boat as Judge Kelly, who continued a member of Congress, and Garfield, against whom the charge of venality was never remembered; that Oakes Ames's famous 'memorandum book' was manufactured for the occasion, the item about me appearing not in the order of date, but on a flyleaf at the end; that the sergeant at arms testified that, according to his best knowledge and belief, he paid the money on the check 'of S.C. or bearer' to Oakes Ames himself, and not to me; that the stock which Oakes Ames swore belonged to me was actually bequeathed in his will to his son; and that, when he died, he acknowledged that he had 'dealt unjustly by Schuyler Colfax.' But why reiterate these facts? After suspicion has once been raised against a public man it is almost impossible for him to get the truth told."

I am not quite certain whether the Tribune gained or lost by losing Colfax and gaining Reid. On the whole, perhaps, it gained, for Colfax, though a very experienced journalist, with a comprehensive knowledge of public affairs, had turned his fiftieth year, and Reid was ten or twelve years younger. Both were characterized by unusually amiable and genial manners. Indeed, the former had such a superabundance of good nature and such an outflow of cordiality that a reporter who did not get the office he thought he deserved gave him the nickname of "Smiler Colfax."

It is certain that Reid proved equal to the large responsibility he had assumed. Two or three members of the staff who were arbitrarily superseded felt and said that he was unjust, but it was obvious that he must trust his own judgment and exercise authority equal to his responsibility. One of these called him overbearing and tyrannical, but he always seemed to me gentle and kindly, not easily irritated, and only insisting on the enforcement of measures that he thought would reinstate the Tribune in the public confidence which Mr. Greeley's curious political diversion had forfeited.

Especially he had a "nose for news." He multiplied his reporters and increased his special dispatches. He looked after local happenings. He attended to Wall Street. He compared the Tribune with other papers every morning, and woe to the managing editor who let it get behind in the race. Moreover, he had not only a nose for news, but an extraordinary liking for novelties. I was at this time writing for the Graphic some daily verses which envious curs called "doggerel," and one morning Mr. Reid asked me if I could n't do some of the same sort of thing for the Tribune, giving them a partisan turn. I could and did. I took up the daily grind of producing for the Tribune a contribution four or five verses long on the political situation of the hour. They were rather personal. Some of these so-called poems were set to music. Mr. Reid called them "Songs for the Stump."

They took.  I was greatly surprised to see them copied very widely by one party and derided and denounced bitterly by the other as "some more of the Tribune's lunacy."  I had never written anything before that kicked up such a dust. Mr. Reid seemed to enjoy the situation.  Pleasant letters were received from many sources, including President Hayes and his Secretary of the Interior, Carl Schurz.  Mr. Blaine called, with the result that the National Committee of the party ordered an edition of 100,000 as a campaign document. I had to buy a new hat several sizes larger when, in September 1879, this edition of the Bourbon Ballads made its appearance with this complimentary introduction: —

The Tribune Extra, No. 52, contains nearly all of those humorous political songs which have been written for the Tribune by Mr. William A. Croffut under the general title of "Bourbon Ballads."  These poems have been extensively copied by the Republican press of the country, and their flavor is pretty well known. Nearly all of them are written from what is assumed to be the Democratic point of view, but members of that party will perhaps hesitate to adopt the utterances as their own.  Partisan verse, used with such terrible effect in the seventeenth and eighteenth centuries in England, and effectively employed there still later by Moore and his contemporaries, as well as by caustic versifiers of the present day, has never been successfully transplanted to the American soil; for the lyrics of Freneau and Hopkinson were desultory and without persistent purpose, and the *Biglow Papers* of James Russell Lowell were devoted to the advocacy of principles rather than to the satirizing of parties.  The Ballads herewith presented have had wide approval and they are doubly interesting as showing what can be done in this almost unoccupied field even in a season of comparative quiet.

## XV

### FRIENDSHIP WITH THURLOW WEED

THURLOW WEED was often called Warwick because, like that potent statesman, he preferred to confer dignity rather than to wear it. I said to him one day that it was difficult to understand why he had never accepted office. He turned his blind orbs towards me and said, "Because my ambition never took that direction. I could have been Governor, repeatedly; Senator, probably; and a foreign mission was offered me several times. One office I held of which I am proud — because it was the most important office the country had to confer. I was Dr. Franklin's successor as commissioner to placate the wrath of Europe in time of war."

"Your service was as great as his," I ventured to say.

"The good we were providentially enabled to do," continued Mr. Weed, "was great. I attribute all to Providence — even the way in which I happened to go, — while there was, and still is, a strange mystery about the manner in which I secured royal audience in both England and France. Yes, I 'll tell you about it. It was some time after the Bull Run defeat, and when W. H. Russell's letters had greatly inflamed England against us, that the government thought it necessary to send a commission of three to Europe. A cabinet meeting was held, and three distinguished gentlemen were named for the great service. Mr. Chase named Bishop McIlvaine for England; Mr. Seward named Bishop Hughes for France and Rome, where the Bishop of Charleston had just been confusing the mind of the Pope; and Caleb Smith named Edward Everett for commissioner at large. These were admirable appointments. The three gentlemen were summoned to Washington. Hughes and McIlvaine went at once; Mr. Everett telegraphed a declination to go.

"I got a dispatch from Seward, and on arriving in Washington went straight to Seward's house to breakfast. I found him in great distress of mind. He unfolded the trouble to me. It was agreed to urge Everett to accept, but he positively refused for reasons which seemed to me punctilious. (Everett afterwards told me that that refusal to go to England was the great mistake of his life.) Seward said to me: 'There is to be a council here to-night about it. Hughes and McIlvaine will be present — also Lincoln, Chase, and Stanton. You must join us at supper.' I told him I did n't like to be present at a meeting for such a purpose, and excused myself, agreeing to come in at nine o'clock. It was Sunday, and the commissioners were to sail on Wednesday. I then found that Bishop Hughes had declined to go. He pleaded that he could not leave his people. Moreover, the third place had been offered during the afternoon to Robert C. Winthrop, and he, too, had declined, on account of dangerous illness in his family.

"I sat down on the lounge by the side of Hughes, whom I knew intimately, and when Mr. Lincoln and Mr. Chase went into another room I made a strong personal appeal to the bishop to go. 'You must go,' I said. 'You cannot afford to refuse. It is a solemn duty, to which men are never called twice in a life. Your country is in danger. All other calls upon your time are of less importance.'

"I used every argument I could think of. Suddenly he turned around and laid his hand on my shoulder, and said, 'I will go if you will go with me.' 'Very well, I will go,' I said as promptly. 'I will go as your private secretary or your valet, Bishop. I will give my services in any private way if you will go.' 'You will go as a colleague on the commission,' he said, 'and in no other way.'

"I said, 'Hush! That is impossible. Do not mention that again. Under some circumstances I would go joyfully, but there are reasons now why it cannot be. I will go as your secretary.'

"Just then Seward came into the room, looking jaded and worried. I told him that I had made the Bishop agree to go. Seward's face lighted up and he clapped his hands.

" 'On one condition,' said Hughes gravely; 'that Weed goes with us.' I repeated to the Bishop that I would go in any private capacity, but he said to Mr. Seward, 'He goes as a colleague.' Seward's glee deserted him and his bad spirits returned. He said nothing till the Bishop took his leave. When I followed the departing guest down to his carriage, he turned upon me as he drove away and said with uplifted finger, 'Remember, this programme is not to be changed.'

"I knew it must be changed, for Seward had as much as he could carry already, and with me on his back he would have been swamped. Greeley, Sumner, Lovejoy, and others were making a dead set to get Seward out of the Cabinet, and I knew it would not answer for him to appoint me to anything. When I went back upstairs I found him much agitated. 'What's this talk,' he said, 'about your going on the commission?'

" 'Don't let it disturb you,' I said, 'If Hughes insists, I will go with him, but in some private capacity.'

" 'Very well,' said Mr. Seward; 'you will go unofficially?'

" 'Yes,' I said.

" 'Without an appointment?'

" 'Of course.'

" 'And pay your own expenses?'

" 'Yes,' I said.

" 'Very well,' said Seward.   He knew as well as I did that nothing else could be thought of.

"Two days afterwards Mr. Seward met us at the Astor House to confer.   McIlvaine and Hughes were commissioned and had received their instructions.   They thought I was also.   I knew it would not do to undeceive Hughes, so they left us to go to Europe on the steamer next day, I to follow two days later.   Robert J. Minturn and Blatchford were there.   'Where are Weed's instructions?' said Minturn. 'He is not instructed,' said Seward, 'nor appointed.   He goes unofficially and pays his own expenses.'   Shortly after, Minturn and I left and Blatchford stayed.   I knew he stayed to blow up Seward.

"At the foot of the stairs Minturn made out a check for a thousand dollars and handed it to me, saying, 'Your expenses will be paid by the merchants of New York.'

"Blatchford that night wrote to Seward a letter, — a terrible letter, which was shown me afterwards, and the language of which I should n't like to repeat, — and the result was a commission and instructions by the next mail from Washington.   There were half a dozen letters of introduction to the real rulers behind the thrones of both France and England, but, oddly enough, I never had occasion to present them.   For, just as I was about leaving, a gentleman, a perfect stranger to me, stepped up and handed me a letter of introduction and said: 'You had better present this as soon as you get to Paris.'   Well, was n't that providential?   I can explain it in no other way.

"When I got to London there was intense excitement everywhere.   New recruits were drilling in front of the hotel for war with the United States on account of the Mason and

Slidell affair. The shipyards were working nights and Sundays. Clamorous crowds were yelling in the streets. The newspapers demanded a declaration of war. Our minister, Mr. Adams, was feeling very blue, but thought he could get an audience for us with Lord John Russell in a few days. I went down to Peabody's bank and arranged for drafts on New York, and as I turned away from the desk and walked through a crowd of strangers to the door, one of them suddenly stopped me, seized my hand, and said, 'I am glad you 've come. I never met you before, but I 'm glad you 've come. The peril is imminent. Is this your cab? Then I 'll ride with you.' He went along out with me and said, 'My name is —— .' He got into the cab at my side and added, 'You must see Lord John.'

" 'Oh, it's all very well to say I must,' said I, 'but I find that even our minister has difficulty in getting an audience.'

" 'You must see Lord John to-morrow,' said my companion, whose name I now remembered having heard. 'He is n't in town; he is out at Pembroke Hall. You must go out there.'

"We presently stopped and I was introduced to a member of Parliament, Kennard, who said, 'Your visit is timely. Hurry out to Pembroke Hall to-morrow, and you 'll find Lord John waiting for you.'

"I had not implicit confidence, but I went out. The Premier received me pleasantly, but he was very indignant at the arrest of Mason and Slidell. It was an inexcusable outrage, he said, and their instant release was the least reparation that would be accepted.

"The very first word I spoke after that was a confession that we were wrong in their arrest, and a promise that they would be surrendered. But I pleaded for time. I said the Americans were in hot blood now, and Mason and Slidell were acknowledged traitors to their country; and I added,

'My lord, hundreds of men not guilty of a tithe of their crime have been taken by your country from the Tower yonder to the block.'

"He was immovable. He said it was a flagrant violation of the law of nations, an insult to the British flag, and the people demanded war.

"I replied, 'My lord, that it was a violation of law, I admit; but there was very great provocation, and when you say that the insult was flagrant and inexcusable I call your lordship's attention to the fact that your country once violated our flag in precisely the same way six thousand times before we resented it by declaring war.'

"This view of the subject was evidently new to him. I then went into some particulars concerning the War of 1812. He appeared slightly mollified, and insisted on my staying and dining with him.

"When I left, an hour later, Lady Russell went with us out upon the lawn and pointed out the great historical places. Observing a little mound of earth, I asked, 'My lady, what does this round pile of earth signify?'

" 'This?' she said in a scornful tone, as she stepped upon its top and stood there, pointing with one finger down through two long rows of elms that extended in a distant vista. 'This is where that beast, Henry VIII, stood that morning, and waited till he saw on that distant tower yonder the signal that Anne Boleyn was beheaded!' She spoke with real indignation.

"Sir Henry Holland, the Queen's physician, did much to influence her mind to modify the dispatch which Lord Russell and Lord Palmerston prepared, demanding the immediate surrender of Mason and Slidell. I found out about it in an odd way. Two ladies who were at the house of one of these statesmen saw him lay down his portfolio when he returned from the audience with the Queen. They waited till he went into the dining room, then opened the portfolio and found the demand on America. The copy was much altered and toned down, here and there interlined and the most offensive words struck out. One of them, a friend of this country, ran straight down and told me, which was the first intimation we had that the threatened violence of language was certainly relaxed.

"Providence favored us the same way in France. Our minister, Mr. Dayton, was in great alarm. Napoleon was angry and threatening. He was almost inaccessible, and even Mr. Dayton had difficulty in seeing him. The little colony of Americans were in fear of what would happen next. Mr. Dayton said he would try to get an audience for us in a few days. On my way to the consulate I stopped and delivered the letter handed me by the stranger in New York. The gentleman received me very cordially, told me the situation was full of perils, and said he would call with me next day on the Duke de Morny, brother of the Emperor. We made an appointment and I returned to our minister's, where they were very incredulous as to my new friend's influence at court.

"But the next morning I met him, and, when his card was sent up, down came the instant summons and we went up, leaving a crowd of notables cooling their heels in the anteroom. The Duke was rather frigid towards me and very angry when he spoke. Evidently war was imminent. France was a paternal government, he said, and must take care of her people. Their cotton factories were stopped because they could not get cotton, the supply of which was cut off by the American blockade. 'This cannot be tolerated!' he exclaimed.

"I asked him to have a little patience; told him that wars

always injured the commercial world; but assured him that the Federal Union was going to subdue this most causeless rebellion, and then they could have cotton.

" 'Your government has permitted one crime,' he broke out, 'unparalleled in the annals of nations. It has destroyed the beautiful harbor of Charleston, and this is an outrage to commerce and an offense to the whole world. It must be restored.'

" 'I beg to say,' I answered, 'that you have been misinformed. Charleston harbor is not destroyed. It is not even injured. It is merely obstructed, and all obstruction can be removed in a week.'

" 'It was a crime against nations!' he cried out vehemently.

"I protested that it had by no means been an uncommon thing.

" 'For instance,' he said, 'you mean the blocking of the little Scheldt, which was not by any means a parallel case.'

" 'Not at all,' I replied. 'I allude to the treaty of Utrecht, which France herself signed, providing for the complete destruction of the harbor of Dunkirk, the second harbor in the kingdom; it was filled up and the forts were dismantled.'

"He rang the bell for a servant, as if to dismiss me. I took from my vest pocket a slip of paper and handed it to him, saying, 'That is the paragraph from the treaty.'

"The interview did not conclude at once. After he read it he became somewhat mollified, and was evidently more thoughtful. This was the beginning of the work which Bishop Hughes, Bishop McIlvaine, and I did to induce France and England to be patient. But the chances that enabled me to get so promptly to the ear of Lord John Russell and the Duke de Morny seem to me to have been providential."

Leslie's Weekly

NAPOLEON III

THURLOW WEED

"Who was the Duke's father?" I asked Mr. Weed.

"Hortense, you know, was his mother," he said, "Hortense, the Queen of Napoleon's brother, King Louis."

"Yes, I remember who his mother was," I said. "But his father, Mr. Weed — to whom does history impute the honor of his paternity?"

"Hortense is reported to have been a very beautiful woman," said Mr. Weed. "The Duke de Morny was an orphan — he was born several years after his father died. But I am much obliged to him for his kindness to us in 1862." He twisted his gray beard and laughed as if he had made a joke worthy of being repeated at the Lotus Club.

One morning when I called on Thurlow Weed he broke out with: —

"See here! Have you seen this message of President Hayes's? The man must be crazy. He makes another plea for the so-called 'civil service reform,' and hopes the time will come when the tenure of office in this country will be permanent."

The old man raised himself to a sitting posture on the lounge and said vehemently, "That time will never come. Never! Never! And it never ought to come. When the tenure of office in this country is made permanent, the republic will be already death-struck. He says he does not want any official assessed to procure victories for a party, but such assessments are just what elected him. When Mr. Hayes was running for the Presidency, he wrote to Governor Morgan for five thousand dollars, well knowing that the people in the Customhouse would provide it. Governor Morgan obtained it from them, and that money judiciously and properly spent, carried Louisiana and Florida and elected

Hayes to the Presidency.   Why does he kick down the ladder he climbed by?"

Knowing that Mr. Weed had obtained office for thousands of men, but had never held one himself except a commission, I asked him if the public service would not be better performed if clerks could feel that they would not be disturbed.

"No!" answered Mr. Weed.   "That very certainty would make them inefficient.   Suppose a farmer should say to his field hands, 'Now, men, I want you to do your best.   To make sure that you will do your best, I have deprived myself of the privilege of appointing anybody in your places. So your positions are permanent.'   What kind of service would the farmer get?   And would it help the matter any if he should pay them twice the wages that anybody else was paying for the same work?

"I warned President Hayes that this project could not work," continued the American Warwick, who had appointed seven thousand men to office.   "Mr. Hayes came over here when he was first elected and sat in that chair and invited me to be frank with him concerning the measures he proposed.   One of these was civil service reform — keeping appointees in office for life on good behavior.   'It is wrong,' I said to him; 'it is undemocratic — unrepublican. The men who win victories have a right to the prizes. Americans will never tolerate a monopoly of office holders. Besides,' I said to him, 'you would be the first one to violate the rule.'   He was surprised, and asked me to tell him how. 'You will violate it the first week,' I said; 'the first act of your administration will be to recall Washburne, Minister to France, and send Noyes there.   Washburne is a man of eminent ability and long experience in the very post he occupies.   Governor Noyes is not his equal by any means, and has no diplomatic experience whatever.   You are going to re-

move Washburne and appoint Noyes. The civil service reform requires that you keep Washburne there. Yet you are
going to do the very thing you ought to do. Washburne is
an exceptionally good man, but he has been Minister to
France eight years, and he ought to come home and give
some other man a chance. Noyes is your personal friend.
You are under obligations to him. So is the Republican
Party. Therefore, having requisite ability and fair fame,
he ought to go to Paris — in spite of civil service reform.'
The President smiled and said it could not be applied to the
most important offices. I replied that I thought it could, if
to any, as they were the very places where experience was
most valuable, partisan activity most likely, and corruption
most dangerous. I told him that, if consistent, he ought to
make all his Cabinet and diplomatic appointments without
any regard to the politics of the applicant."

Pretty soon the old dictator of offices spoke again: —

"The republic is founded on the interest of the people in
self-government — that is, on their activity at the polls. This
activity is caused by their expectation that they or their friends
will get office or somehow profit if the party wins. To the
majority in power belong the offices. The idea of keeping
clerks in office for life was invented in England for the purpose of keeping the penniless sons of noblemen in place as
long as they live."

I asked him if a good many people did not go to the polls
merely because they believed the success of their party would
promote the prosperity of the country.  ·

"Yes, a good many do," he said. "But there are enough
who go for other reasons to affect results. They have a right
to expect to profit by victory. And if any party dares to
ask for the suffrages of the people on the platform that if it
wins it will give the offices to friends and enemies indis-

criminately, that party is already beaten.  A policy of giving the offices to anybody that has a good memory and can answer a string of senseless and irrelevant conundrums will be sure to create widespread dissatisfaction, in all parties."

I asked Mr. Weed if he always had partisans appointed.

"Yes, for new appointments.  But there are some men in every large office whose services cannot be safely dispensed with.  So I have kept a good many Democrats in office where they had difficult positions or such exceptional ability as made them indispensable.  I have kept Democrats in office twenty, thirty, forty years, for this reason.  In fact, I am the original reformer.  I believe in promoting for efficiency in office rather than in appointing for talent displayed out of office.  I am the genuine civil service reformer, you see; these other men across the way are chromo reformers," and he indulged in a hearty laugh.

The old gentleman rose, made a disdainful allusion to educational competition, went across the room, sat down in his rocking-chair, and sniffed audibly.  He presently added earnestly: —

"Enough offices must always be given to the men who do the work in the party canvass and at the polls to get that indispensable work done.  I shall not live long, — not long enough to see this system tried, —but I wish you to put my judgment on record that the method of giving offices to partisans as the prize of victory — vulgarly called the spoils system — is the vital centre and cohesive power of the republic.

"The civil service reform, so-called, is a humbug.  Remember what I say.  I am old and shall not live long, and when I die I want you to bear witness to me, so far as to repeat my testimony.  Three fourths of all the offices ought to be taken possession of by the party that wins in the election. The rest will be offices requiring special training and extra expertness, like some places in the customhouses and the signal service, where the most competent men ought to be kept as long as possible, without regard to politics. If the theory ever wins requiring places to be filled by competitive examination and clerks are kept in place for life, the country will be the weaker and poorer for it. Offices generally ought to be held as prizes and premiums to the winning party. In no other way can men be induced to do the required work on election day."

I asked him if he was not a standing refutation of his theory, having been a tremendous partisan worker all his life without the inducement of office.

"No," he said, "I had other inducements. Success at the polls gave me other prizes. People will show little enough interest in elections if they are to get nothing for it. Patriotism is very well: it is all the stimulus some need all their lives. Love of contest is sufficient to influence some; but the rank and file of both parties will give you to understand that hurrahs butter no parsnips. They will not run their legs off and perspire to elect a President unless they have a chance to get something for it. They will not argue and contend and urge their neighbors to rally and spend thousands of dollars in torchlight processions, teams, and meetings, unless there is to be a new shake-up. If this newfangled notion is correct, why should local offices be elective any longer? Why should not the sheriff and coroner and county clerk and collector and assessor hold their offices for life on good behavior? And when a sheriff or alderman dies, why should not the vacancy be filled by competitive examination, to find out who knows most about botany and geology and chemistry, and the perturbations of the planets, and give him the place?"

When Death on the pale horse heaves in sight, nothing disconcerts the rider so much as to have the person who is to receive the visit nimbly step out ready to hold the steed, hang up the scythe, and offer any needful hospitality.

Thurlow Weed understood and practised this gruesome politeness to the last. When the venerable editor, printer, publicist, politician, philanthropist, lay on his dying bed in the second floor back, in his pleasant house on Twelfth Street, New York City, his daughter, ever by his side, was asked into the hall to see a caller.

"Who was it, Harriet?" asked the vigilant octogenarian when she returned.

"Only a young man," said his daughter. "It is time for you to take your medicine again."

"What young man?" whispered the invalid.

"A young man from down-town. Have you any appetite, Father?"

"What did he want?"

"Oh, he bothered me with all sorts of questions. Come, now, you must keep still, Father."

"What did the young man want, Harriet? Was he a newspaper man?"

"Perhaps so," and the lady rose and made an excuse to go and fetch the medicine. "Don't worry about it."

"See here! You are keeping something from me," exclaimed the distinguished invalid. "He wanted help to write my obituary, didn't he?"

"I believe so. Yes, that's what he wanted, Father!"

And, like a dutiful daughter, she gave way to a flood of tears.

"Bring him back! Send for him!" gasped the sufferer.

James, the colored boy, was dispatched without his hat, and the World reporter was overtaken and brought back. He looked embarrassed when he was led to the sick man's chamber and marched up to the side of the bed.

"Well," said the aged man, his face expressing an appreciation of the situation, "what is it?"

The youth stammered deprecatingly, and finally asked if Mr. Weed had anything to add to what was known of Morgan, the notorious great Antimason.

"Look here, young man," said the editor, "be frank and speak up. You were sent here to write my obituary, were you not?" The reporter confessed, with great relief, that it was his assignment.

"Well, I don't want you to go back empty-handed. I was once a reporter myself, and I know how it is, exactly. I can't talk much above a whisper, but if you'll make your questions direct, and write fast, and listen close down here, you may ask anything you please, except how long I am going to last."

To say that the young reporter was grateful at having struck a man who "had been there himself" is speaking but half of the truth. He succeeded in obtaining the fullest and most accurate obituary of "Warwick" of all the hundreds of columns that were printed when the death was announced.

The Herald had two obituaries of Thurlow Weed standing in type for six or eight years — one of two columns, and one of less than half a column. The shorter one was merely a condensation of the other, and was provided ready for use in case the great politician should die on a "heavy day," when the columns were crowded with news. He finally took his departure on an "off day," with his proverbial shrewdness, and the two-column notice was used.

As Captain Rynders was fond of saying, "It is the toughest patriarchs who have the last word." When Greeley's brain sickness and nervous prostration quenched his fine intelli-

gence, General James Watson Webb called on him at Alvin
Johnson's, where, shortly, he died. "Now, rally! Rally,
Greeley!" urged the General. "Hurry up and get well.
You've got to get well, you know, for Weed is still alive,
and it would n't do for you to leave him behind. If you
should die first, Greeley, Weed would remember on you
awfully." The cheerful advice was not effective.

A singular career had Mr. Weed. In his infancy he lost
both of his parents. He entered active life as a cabin boy
in a sloop. At ten he got the position of devil in a printing
office and learned to set type. At thirteen he enlisted as
drummer in the United States Army and became quartermaster's sergeant at fifteen. At the close of the War of
1812 he entered earnestly into the newspaper business, and
this became the chosen occupation of his long and eventful
life.

"It is not generally known, I think," said Thurlow Weed
to me one evening after a rubber at cribbage, — for though
he could no longer make out the faces of friends, he could
still see cards and pegs when placed in a good light, — "it
is not generally known how near Mr. Webster came to being
President."

"It is generally known," I said, "that he was a candidate
for the Whig nomination five times and missed it every
time."

"Yes," he acquiesced, "but he came a good deal nearer than
that — a good deal nearer. I had always been among his most
profound admirers, and wanted to see him made President in
1840. But it became obvious to me during the winter that
he could not get the nomination — that Harrison was in the
lead. I went down to Washington early in the spring and
met Mr. Webster in the marble room.

"'I think I shall be the Whig candidate,' he said.

"I expressed my doubt of it.

"He asked me who I thought stood a better chance.

" 'It looks to me very much like Harrison,' I answered. 'He is very popular.'

"Webster almost sneered at the idea.  He put it aside with some disrespectful remark as not worthy of consideration. He naturally had little respect for mere military men, and he exclaimed, 'It is impossible, sir, that a man so ignorant as he and so lacking in every quality of a chief magistrate can be nominated by any great party for such a place.'

"I told him that the man nominated might possibly not be the ablest in the field: it was simply a question of who could poll the most votes.  Then I got him to sit down and look over my figures.  They did n't convince him, of course.

" 'Why, you don't act as if you believe it yourself,' he said, 'for you have chosen a Scott delegation from your own state.'

" 'Yes, we have; that was to divide the opposition and prevent the appointment of a Clay delegation,' I said, 'for Clay cannot be elected if nominated.   But, Mr. Webster, I have n't come to Washington to get you to withdraw your name, but to ask you to accept the nomination for Vice President in case Harrison shall be selected for the first place.'

"The proposition stirred all his pride and irritated him greatly.  He would n't listen to such a proposal, and said that he did n't want to be buried till he was dead.  I argued, but it was useless; he reiterated his refusal to consider it with a little more spirit than I thought the occasion called for.

"So I went home again.  Harrison was nominated and John Tyler was made his Vice, and then, by the death of Harrison, Tyler became President a month after the inauguration.  Webster saw the fatal mistake he had made, and he confessed as much to me the next time I saw him. He was then Tyler's Secretary of State.

"Well, curiously enough, that was n't the last of the great man's fatal mistakes. In 1848 the very same thing happened right over again. In 1844 Clay had been defeated and taken out of the way, and now Webster thought he could walk over the course.

"It did n't look so to me. There was a great furor over General Taylor, for it was widely and deeply felt that he had been deprived of his command and his opportunity in Mexico out of mere jealousy and pique, and that the administration had done all it could to deprive him of the honors he had fairly earned by the victories of Buena Vista and Monterey. In fact, he was looked upon as a martyr to Polk's intrigues.

"So, after consultation with some friends in New York, I went over to Marshfield during the April before the nomination.

"'Well, what do you think of it this time?' asked Mr. Webster, with a smile of security.

"'I think this time,' I said, 'that General Taylor will be the man.'

"He was astounded. It did n't look so at all to him. He thought it a very wild guess and wondered what I based it on. 'Do you seriously think,' he asked, 'that such a man as General Taylor can be nominated?'

"I assured him that I thought it very probable. Taylor was then designated by those who did not admire him as 'an illiterate frontier Colonel who has n't voted for forty years,' and Webster seemed to sympathize with this view. He seemed not to understand that the people wanted a hero, especially if a little martyrdom could be mixed with the heroism.

"I then appealed to him to accept the nomination for Vice President under Taylor.  He remembered his former mistake and smiled, and said at last that he would consult his two best friends, George Ashmun of Massachusetts and Senator Williams of New Hampshire, and would do as they advised.

"They were summoned and came.  I met them at Mr. Webster's house and presented my figures.  They were nonplused at first, but finally, after long discussion, came to the conclusion that Taylor's nomination was probable, and they joined me in advising Mr. Webster to be content with second place if the first should prove beyond his reach.  He reluctantly agreed to it, and I was authorized to see the agreement carried out.  We believed we could elect that ticket.

"Just at that point his son Fletcher came home from Boston, and he ridiculed the scheme so energetically and bitterly that his father returned to the original position and refused to have anything to do with my proposal.

"Well, you know what followed.  Taylor was nominated. The Vice Presidency went begging.  The name of Fillmore was suddenly sprung on the convention and he was put on the ticket as a makeshift.  Taylor and he were elected; Taylor died in four months, and Fillmore became President, and then Webster went down to Washington and served him as Secretary of State as he had similarly served the accidental Tyler.  I think the pair of curious mishaps did a good deal to sour him and perhaps helped to make him reckless in his personal habits."

Thurlow Weed's remarkable memory seemed unimpaired to the last, and he recalled with great accuracy long lists of names of men who were politicians in the various counties when Monroe ran for President — sixty years before.

"You seem to remember as well as ever," I said to him one day.

"Better than ever," he answered. "If I had not cultivated my memory, I should have been a dismal failure."

"Did you make a systematic effort to improve it? Or did it improve by use?"

"I had to adopt a regular method, and I hit on one that was very effective. I will tell you about it for the benefit of other young men. I got married in 1818, when I was working in Albany as a journeyman printer. In a few months I established a newspaper for myself, and some of my friends thought I was 'cut out for a politician' — that is, I probably impressed my views strongly on those about me. But I saw at once a fatal weakness. My memory was a sieve. I could remember nothing. Dates, names, appointments, faces — everything escaped me. I said to my wife, 'Catherine, I shall never make a successful politician, for I cannot remember, and that is a prime necessity of politicians. A politician who meets a man once should remember him forever.'

"I recalled what had been said of Henry Clay: that he could go around a room and be introduced to fifty persons and on mingling with the company call every man by his right name. I thought also of the colored fellow who officiates at the grand hatrack in the vestibule of the Saratoga Hotel, and who, as the hundreds of guests flock out of the dining room, hands to each one instantly the hat, shawl, parcel, book, or whatever has been deposited there an hour before.

"My wife told me," continued Mr. Weed, "that I must train my memory. So, when I came home that night, I sat down alone and spent fifteen minutes trying silently to recall the events of the day. I could remember little at first; now I remember that I could not then remember what I had for

breakfast.  Finally I could recall more.  Events came back
to me more minutely and more accurately.  After a fortnight
or so of this, Catharine said, 'Why don't you tell it to me?
It would be interesting, and my interest in it would stimulate you.'  Then I began a habit of oral confession, as it
were, which I followed almost fifty years.  Every night, just
before retiring, I told my wife everything that I could recall that had happened to me or about me during the day.
I generally recalled the very dishes I had had for breakfast,
dinner, and tea; the people I had seen and what they said;
the editorials I had written, and an abstract of them; the
letters I had sent and received, and the very language used
as near as possible; when and where I had walked or ridden
— everything, in short, that had come within my knowledge.
I found I could say my lesson better and better every month
and every year, and, instead of growing irksome, it got to
be a pleasure to run over the events of the day in review.  I
am indebted to this discipline for a memory of somewhat
unusual tenacity, and I recommend the practice to all who
expect to have much to do with influencing men."

## XVI

### THURLOW WEED IN WASHINGTON

In the spring of 1881 I called again upon Thurlow Weed, to inquire after the health of that aged man, then eighty-three, and to enjoy hearing of the bygone times in which he bore a distinguished part. His tall form reclined upon a lounge, wheeled in front of a hearth blazing with cannel coal. "I was just thinking about General McClellan," he said. "I see they have started a movement to put up a statue of him in the Park, though I suppose they'll wait till he dies before unveiling it." The speaker laughed and said, "He might have deserved it better, for he could have been President as well as not, as a reward for doing a great deed." Noting my surprise and interest, he went on: —

"Yes, I'll tell you what led up to it, for it is really an important bit of history. About the middle of December, 1862, Seward telegraphed me to come to Washington. I was not surprised, for I had been summoned in the same way before. I took it as a matter of course and caught the first evening train south. I got to Washington by daybreak and went straight up to Seward's to breakfast. He was waiting for me, and after breakfast took me right over to the White House, saying 'Lincoln wants to see you.'

"We found the President deeply depressed and distressed. I had never seen him in such a hopeless mood. 'Everything goes wrong,' he broke out. 'The rebel armies hold their own; Grant is wandering round in Mississippi; Burnside manages to keep ahead of Lee; Seymour has carried New York, and if his party carries many of the Northern states we shall have to give up the fight, for we can never conquer three quarters of our countrymen scattered in front, flank, and rear.   What on earth shall we do?'

"I suggested that we could hold our own and continue to wait, and that the man capable of leading our splendid armies to victory would come in time.

" 'That 's what I 've been saying,' said Seward, who did n't believe, even then, that the war was going to be a long one.

"Mr. Lincoln did not seem to heed the remark at all, but he went on: 'Governor Seymour could do more for our cause than any other man living.   He has been elected governor of our largest state.   If he would come to the front he could control his partisans and give a new impetus to the war.   I have sent for you, Mr. Weed, to ask you to go to Governor Seymour and tell him what I say.   Tell him now is his time. Tell him I do not wish to be President again, and that the leader of the other party, provided it is in favor of a vigorous war against the rebellion, should have my place.   Entreat him to give the true ring to his annual message, and if he will, as he easily can, place himself at the head of a great Union party, I will gladly stand aside and help to put him in the executive chair.   All we want is to have the rebellion put down and the Union preserved.'   He walked vigorously up and down the room and seemed greatly excited as he spoke.

"I was not greatly surprised at his proposition, for I already knew that such was the President's view.   I had previously heard him say, 'If there is a man who can push our armies forward one mile further or one hour faster than I can, he is the man that ought to be in my place.'

"Of course I agreed to his request. I stayed a little longer, but Mr. Lincoln had nothing more to say except to amplify and emphasize his wish.

"Two days later I visited Governor Seymour at Albany and delivered my commission from Lincoln. It was received most favorably. Seymour's feeling was always right, but his head was generally wrong. When I left him it was understood that his message to the Legislature would breathe an earnest Union spirit, praising our soldiers as patriots and calling for more, and omitting his usual criticisms of the administration. I forwarded to Lincoln an outline of my interview.

"Judge of my disappointment and chagrin when Seymour's message came out — like his former messages, a document calculated to aid the enemy. It demanded that the war should be prosecuted 'constitutionally' — as if any war ever was or ever could be — and denounced the arbitrary arrest of Vallandigham and the enforcement of the draft in New York City. It insisted, in fact, that the war power should be held in abeyance till an appeal could be made to the Supreme Court as to its legality!

"Shortly afterwards Mr. Seward again telegraphed me to come to Washington. Arrived there, Mr. Lincoln authorized me to make the same overture to McClellan.

"'Tell the General,' he said, 'that we have no wish to injure or humiliate him; that we wish only for the success of our armies; that if he will come forward and put himself at the head of the Union Democratic party, and through that means push forward vigorously the Union cause, I will gladly step aside and do all I can to secure his election in 1864.'

"I immediately opened negotiations through S. L. M.

Leslie's Weekly

HORATIO SEYMOUR

Barlow, McClellan's most intimate political friend and adviser. Mr. Barlow called. I outlined to him a scheme to bring McClellan forward. He approved of it and agreed to see the General at once. He shortly called and told me he had seen him and secured his acquiescence; 'for,' he added, 'Mac is eager to do everything he can to put down the Rebellion.' The plan I suggested was to have a great Union Democratic meeting in Union Square at which McClellan should preside and set forth his policy, and this was agreed to by both Mr. Barlow and General McClellan. At the suggestion of the former I drew up some memoranda of principles which it seemed to me desirable to have set forth on the occasion of the mass meeting, and these Mr. Barlow agreed to deliver to McClellan. The time set for the meeting was Monday, June 16. Once more there seemed a promise of breaking the Northern hostility and ending the war by organizing a great independent patriotic party, under 'little Mac.' But this hope failed us, too. For, on the very eve of the meeting, I received a formal letter from McClellan declining to preside, without giving reasons. If he had presided at that war meeting, and had persistently followed it up, nothing but death could have kept him from being elected President of the United States."

This statement seemed to me so extraordinary that I called on General McClellan at his residence on Gramercy Park the very next day, and told him the story, with the purpose of ascertaining why he did not preside at the Union meeting after agreeing to do so.

He was evidently startled at the purport of the narrative. "You amaze me!" he said. "No such event ever occurred. Mr. Weed is a good old man, but his memory is failing. He has forgotten. Mr. Lincoln never offered me the Presidency in any contingencies. I never declined to preside at a war meeting. How could I when I was a Union soldier, and the only criticism I ever made of the administration was that it did not push the armies fast enough? There never was a time when I would have refused to preside at any meeting that could help the Union cause. I remember nothing about any such memoranda, and am sure I never wrote to Thurlow Weed in my life."

At General McClellan's suggestion I called on Mr. Barlow. He also had forgotten all about it and merely said, "It never could have happened."

Returning to Twelfth Street, I said to Mr. Weed, "I have seen General McClellan. Your memory seems to be at fault and it was probably somebody else who declined to preside at the war meeting in June 1863. The General says you never made such a proposition to him, and he never wrote to you in his life."

The octogenarian softly thumped upon his forehead and certainly looked worried. He repeated, however, most earnestly that the proposition had been made and the letter had been received. He doubted, however, if he had kept it and feared it was lost. He called to Miss Harriet, his faithful daughter and invaluable secretary, and told her of his trouble. She said she would hunt, and departed in search of it. The sun slipped quite a way down the sky before she was heard from, and I thought that probably the old gentleman's memory had failed him or that the letter was irretrievably lost. I tried to draw Mr. Weed out on the "good enough Morgan" controversy, but he was not inclined to take up any new subject. At last footsteps were heard upon the stairs, and Miss Harriet swept into the room triumphant, holding a letter in her hand. It ran as follows: —

(PRIVATE)

OAKLANDS, N. J.
*June* 13, 1863

HON. THURLOW WEED,
    NEW YORK.
MY DEAR SIR:

Your kind note is received.  For what I cannot doubt that you would consider good reasons I have determined to decline the compliment of presiding over the proposed meeting of Monday next.

I fully concur with you in the conviction that an honorable peace is not now possible, and that the War must be prosecuted to save the Union and the government, at whatever the cost of time, and treasure and blood.

I am clear, also, in the conclusion that the policy governing the conduct of the War should be one looking not only to military success, but also to ultimate reunion, and that it should consequently be such as to preserve the rights of all Union-loving citizens, wherever they may be, as far as compatible with military security. My views as to the prosecution of the War remain, substantially, as they have been from the beginning of the contest; these views I have made known officially.

I will endeavor to write you more fully before Monday.

In the meantime, believe me to be, in great haste,

Truly your friend,
GEORGE B. McCLELLAN

"The General has forgotten that formal letter, has he?" said Mr. Weed, laughing.  "If he had presided at that meeting, and rallied his party to the support of the war, he would have been President.  I never heard what his reasons were, either 'before Monday' or any other day.  Just see what an embarrassing time it was to refuse to preside at a war meeting.

Grant seemed to be stalled in front of Vicksburg, and that very morning came a report that he was going to raise the siege. Banks was defeated the day before at Port Hudson, and two days earlier a rebel privateer had captured six of our vessels off Chesapeake Bay. The very day that McClellan wrote the letter, Lee was rapidly marching through Maryland into Pennsylvania, and the North was in a panic. There could n't have been a worse time to decline to preside at a Union meeting. And I am sorry that the General did decline."

I took the letter and immediately returned to General McClellan with it. "Well!" he exclaimed, as he took it and carefully inspected it, "that is my writing. Yes; I wrote that and had forgotten all about it. I don't know why I declined to preside; but it was probably because I am shy in the presence of multitudes, am not in the habit of speech making, and should be certain to preside awkwardly. But why should anybody suppose me indifferent to the prosecution of the war?"

"Possibly," I replied, "because a year later they found you standing as a candidate for President on a platform which declared the war up to that time a failure, and seemed to disparage the services of our soldiers in the field."

"I never stood on that platform a day!" he exclaimed. "Everybody knows I did n't. I repudiated it in my letter, and made my repudiation of it the only condition of accepting the nomination. I told all my friends so!"

"Mr. Weed thinks," I added, "that if you had presided that day, instead of refusing to preside, and had followed it up with corresponding vigor, it would have united the North, finished the war a year sooner, saved thousands of lives, and incidentally made you President."

"Oh, well," he said laughing, "that's an interesting situ-

ation.  Nobody can tell.  At any rate I did n't, and it 's all
over now."

Shortly afterwards I mentioned these facts to Frederick
W. Seward.  "Yes," he said, "I have often heard Mr. Weed
tell about it.  Neither Mr. Lincoln nor Father expected that
the administration would be reëlected.  The President used
to say, 'I am sure there are men who could do more for the
success of our armies than I am doing; I would gladly stand
aside and let such a man take my place, any day.'  Looking
back at the Mexican and other wars, we thought some
general would succeed Lincoln in 1864, and McClellan
evidently thought so too.  We did not foresee the tremendous
victories and the splendid wave of patriotic feeling that
carried Lincoln in again."

Colonel John Hay told me that he was acquainted with
Lincoln's effort to enlist McClellan and Seymour, heard when
he was in the White House.  And Roscoe Conkling told me
it was not news to him.

One morning shortly before he died Mr. Weed said to me:
"Governor Seymour was here yesterday.  He stayed to dinner,
and we had a good talk about old times.  I spoke of the scheme
to make him President, and he remembered the details as I
did.  But he said that his reason for his action was that he
'wanted to carry on the war legally.'  He said he could n't
have carried his party with him to approve of the arbitrary
arrest by Stanton of the Northern opponents of the war.
When Seymour was sitting here I told him that he would
have been President certainly, if he had come out heartily
and unreservedly for the war in 1863; and he said, 'Well, it
is n't much matter.  I was not in good health and it might
have killed me.  It is a hard, laborious, thankless office — it 's
just as well as it is.' "

General McClellan's funeral in New York was made very

impressive by its civic simplicity. It was not a noisy public demonstration, but the dead soldier was affectionately laid away by those who knew him best and loved him most.

McClellan was not born to greatness, and he did not achieve greatness, but he came pretty near having greatness thrust upon him. Responsibility was piled upon him prematurely. Think of a quiet, and rather demure, railroad superintendent being seized by a frenzied governor and made a Major General of volunteers in four days, and in three weeks more, without having been to the front at all, elevated to be a Major General of the regular army. When he was astonished by being flung into this high place of power, he knew nothing about war, for in Mexico he did not have the command even of a company, but was on staff service.

Senator Pomeroy of Kansas told me this story: When McClellan was put in command of the Army of the Potomac, an aged aunt of his said: "George? Is it George? Are you sure it is George? Why, I thought it was Sam! If it had been Sam, now, it would have been a good appointment. He'd make things fly!" This "Sam" was George's brother, an active and energetic doctor.

Another apposite story was told me by Pomeroy: In the spring of 1862 McClellan failed to move on the enemy, as he had promised to do and as President Lincoln had commanded. The whole country was clamoring for the splendid army to advance, but McClellan, with 200,000 men, insisted that he was not ready. A distinguished committee called on the President one evening in the first week of March, composed of Senators Wade, Chandler, Pomeroy, and Wilson, and Governor Buckingham. Ben Wade was spokesman.

"Mr. President," he said boldly, "you are too slow. This stand-still policy won't answer. The people won't stand it any longer. You ordered McClellan to move on February

"Masterly Inactivity," or Six Months on the Potomac

22, and he did not obey you.  Turn him out!  A President must not submit to be overruled.  The people who are being taxed $1,000,000 a day will not be — they will be obeyed; and if you refuse to enforce their orders they will come here to Washington and enforce them themselves!"

Mr. Lincoln was greatly startled by this attitude, and he said, "Well, what can I do?  I have ordered McClellan to move with the whole army.  That's ten days ago.  And there he is yet.  Not a man has stirred.  What shall I do?"

"Tell him that if he does n't move in a week you will dismiss him from the army!" said Wade.

"Will you carry that message to him?" asked the President.

"Yes, of course I will!"  The Committee withdrew after a long conference of four hours, and from the White House they went directly to McClellan's headquarters.  It was one o'clock, and he was abed and asleep.  They rang the bell, thumped on the door, and finally got in.  The orderly said the General was asleep, and would they call in the morning?  "No, no, give the General our cards and say that we must trouble him to get up."  They waited.  He came down at last, yawning, in dressing-gown and slippers.  They made known their mission, telling him bluntly that the President had authorized them to say to him informally that his resignation would be requested unless he moved his army out of its intrenchments by March 10.  If the General insisted, the President would put the command in writing.  No, Mc-Clellan said, he did not stand on ceremony.

He dressed.  He went to bed no more.  He sent for his staff and dispatched orders to his corps commanders.  The whole army moved on March 10.

# XVII

## A BOGUS PEER: LORD GORDON-GORDON [1]

WHILE I was struggling to make the Minneapolis Tribune a newspaper worthy of that splendid city (in 1871, in fact), the State of Minnesota was visited by one of the most audacious and plausible swindlers and robbers that have taken the highway since Dick Turpin.   Indeed, for unparalleled effrontery this king of charlatans has perhaps never had an equal.   In two days his suavity of manner had won the entire confidence of Colonel John S. Loomis, Land Commissioner of the Northern Pacific Railroad, who announced that the distinguished stranger was no less than Lord Gordon-Gordon, and that he had arrived from Scotland prepared to invest a million dollars "and perhaps more" in the wild railroad lands of the state.   The nobleman was introduced as heir of the great Earls of Gordon, cousin of the Campbells, collateral relative of Lord Byron, and descendant of the bold Lochinvar and the ancient kings of the Highlanders.   It was casually mentioned that his income was over a million dollars a year.

As a matter of fact, he was a lowbred knave for whom several penitentiaries waited.   In Scotland he had been "wanted" by the sheriff, but he finally stole $125,000 worth of diamonds in Edinburgh as "Lord Glencairn," and made his appearance suddenly in Minneapolis as Lord Gordon-Gordon.   To sustain his pretensions he actually deposited

[1] From *Putnam's Magazine,* January 1910.

$40,000 of the stolen money in a Minneapolis bank. He presented forged letters of introduction from famous English noblemen to a few prominent officials and became the lion of the city. He was received on all sides with the greatest delight and deference. He was a much-desired guest, and was invited everywhere. He accepted few invitations, and was reticent. Great banquets were given in his honor. He told his entertainers that he needed immense areas of rich land on which to colonize his overcrowded Scotch tenantry, and might take as much as 500,000 acres if they could spare so much. Colonel Loomis lay awake nights thinking about it. The Northern Pacific Railroad was being pushed slowly westward under the greatest difficulty, and sadly needed help. It was understood that his lordship had come to its relief. Excursions were made to prospective town sites, and a great buffalo hunt was arranged. Lord Gordon-Gordon then announced that he was ready to go and pick out the lands required. But there were no railroads to convey him.

Then Colonel Loomis expanded to meet the occasion. He organized a gorgeous expedition for my lord, something like the excursion that Apollodorus planned for Cleopatra. It was equipped regardless of expense. During three delightful summer months the impostor traveled, feasted, and hunted through Minnesota and Dakota in the style of a king at the expense of the Northern Pacific Railroad. Twenty strong and alert men served in his retinue, and they took along thirty or forty horses. He had a secretary and valet who shaved him and who wrote his letters and flourished a seal with armorial bearings. Nothing was too good for the nobleman. Two palatial wall tents were provided for his exclusive use, and in one of them, with silver and the loveliest china, were served to him viands that would have enraptured Sam Ward or Epicurus. Fruit was brought from Mexico for him, curaçao from the Spice Islands, dry Monopole from its fragrant home. His table was like Montezuma's. One large covered wagon was an armory equipped for deer hunting, with guns and ammunition galore. Another was equipped with complicated fishing tackle to have fun with when the caravan with the magnificent Gordon should pause by the inland lakes.

A government surveyor attached to the train galloped on horseback to pick out such choice square miles as were required. He was playfully called "the land taster." Sites for cities were selected and stamped "Sold," and the historic banner of the Gordons of Scotland and the Stars and Stripes fluttered side by side before the marquee of a man who was befooling a continent. The opulent chief of the expedition at his own request was always carefully addressed as "My lord." Why should he not be, when he was declared by the equerry to have fourteen changes of costume? Loomis spent $45,000 on him that summer, and beamingly said to the directors: "He is the richest landlord in Europe. He will invest $5,000,000 with us."

His lordship saw the state thoroughly, and inspected and selected vast areas of arable land that would rejoice the soul of a Highlander. He also incidentally located and named several cities, explaining that it would be necessary to have churches and schools well organized before his colonists would flock thither in large numbers. Then he said he was satisfied and the excursion could now halt while he went to New York for money to pay for his purchase. While up at Lak Lake he had borrowed "a little change" from Colonel Loomis for daily expenses — it is not known exactly how much. Then the excursion retired to Minneapolis, freighted with great expectations. Lord Gordon deftly lifted his $40,000 out of Westfall's bank, partook of a banquet *au revoir,* and vanished from the sight of his dear Minnesota friends —

carrying with him incidentally a letter of warm introduction from Colonel Loomis to Horace Greeley.

While in Minneapolis the well-groomed visitor never made haste, but moved everywhere deliberately. He visited the office of the chief newspaper, bowed low in the sanctum door and thanked the editor for the privilege of inspecting the latest copy of the Thunderer — bowed as graciously as if he were conferring a favor. This extraordinary tourist was a man of impressive personal appearance. He was slender of build, about five feet ten inches in height, and dressed with the greatest care, usually wearing gloves, patent leathers, and a silk hat. His hands were frequently manicured, and his hair was brushed as smooth as curly hair could be. He was clean shaven, except for two tufts of side whiskers, *à l'anglaise*. He was exceedingly self-poised, calm and deliberate of speech, articulated with much precision, and posed with an amount of ceremony seldom seen on the American continent.

It was early in the year 1872 — the psychological moment to visit New York. The Erie war was raging and a battle of magnificent proportions was on. The Erie road was the centre of the conflict. Jay Gould had just fallen outside the breastworks, to his great astonishment and the bewilderment of his friends, and Generals Dix and Sickles were securely intrenched within; while Daniel Drew and Colonel Thomas A. Scott were gently bandaging their wounds. The sum at stake was more than $30,000,000.

Month, February. Scene, a magnificent suite of apartments on the drawing-room floor of the Metropolitan Hotel, New York. A gentleman calling himself Lord Gordon-Gordon is the only occupant. Charts and maps lie open upon the table. The door opens and in steps Mr. Horace Greeley of the New York Tribune, philanthropist and statesman, who is to become in three months the candidate of a great party

for President, and is to die of disappointment six months
later.   The cordiality of the meeting shows that these men
are not only intimate but on the closest confidential terms.
The visitor removes his white overcoat and goloshes, throws
his slouch hat and woollen gloves on the sofa, adjusts his
spectacles, makes a remark about the weather, and settles
down before the fire in a cosy chair, his boots on the fender,
for it is winter.   Mr. Greeley has dropped in to breakfast, to
discuss an omelette and immigration with his lordship.
The centre table is spread with the whitest damask and the
breakfast service is of solid silver, bearing the monogram
of the noble host.

Conversation ranges.   Gordon-Gordon quietly informs Mr.
Greeley that he is at that moment the owner of 60,000 shares
of Erie, and with this and the holdings of his English friends
he intends to control the next election for directors.   It is
great news, for the Tribune is for "the Gordon reform movement."

Greeley never enjoyed a breakfast better.

Before retiring he obtained my lord's permission to tell
Colonel A. K. McClure, editor of the Philadelphia Times,
and Colonel Thomas A. Scott, Vice President of the Pennsylvania Railroad system.   To half a dozen magnates the news
spread that the Right Honorable Lord Gordon-Gordon was
then in New York and had been in this country eighteen
months, during which time he had succeeded to his title and
estates; that he was an immense stockholder in the Erie
Company and controlled the stock of most of the English
holders; that, "if an amicable arrangement could be made,"
he would like to have Colonel Scott go into the direction, and
Mr. Gould remain president of the company.   Colonel Scott
intimated that he would like to see Lord Gordon-Gordon, but
was told that the noble lord was very punctilious, as all men of

his high rank were, and that he could not call first upon Colonel Scott. Colonel McClure requested Colonel Scott to send his card at once to the Right Honorable Lord Gordon-Gordon at his hotel, which would enable Lord Gordon-Gordon to call upon Colonel Scott when he should go to New York, and charged him to be particular to address the noble visitor as "The Right Honorable Lord Gordon-Gordon." It was done accordingly.

Horace Greeley and Thomas A. Scott called upon Lord Gordon-Gordon at the Metropolitan. He sent down word that it would "afford him pleasure to give them an audience shortly, as soon as he had completed his toilet." They waited and waited. The leading editor of America and the leading railroad manager of the world, whose time was worth five dollars a minute, cooled their heels in the vestibule, varying their occupation by reading the "Black Crook" posters of Niblo's Theatre, which decorated the walls, or declining to have their boots "shined," or refusing to buy morning newspapers. They waited there for nearly an hour, while this arrant Jeremy Diddler upstairs was having his hair oiled and parted and his cravat tied by his valet. Finally they were admitted. The conversation at once turned on the embarrassments of the Erie Railway and the methods by which it was proposed to relieve the management. To facilitate the discussion, the autocrat of the breakfast table set forth another breakfast. He alluded to his estates and income in Europe as being very large, and of his desire to put some of his means in this country. He spoke particularly about the immense purchases of land on the Northern Pacific which he had just closed and of buying a large tract of property near New York where he would put up a handsome country house to entertain his friends when they came to visit him. He referred to these friends of his as earls, dukes, and other titled personages, and said they were interested in his large holdings in Minnesota.

Immediately after this Jay Gould comes into the comedy. It was on March 2, 1872, one hour after midnight, that Mr. Gould was roused from sleep and called out of bed by the receipt of an important telegram from Colonel Scott. It peremptorily summoned him to a conference that morning, "sure," and Mr. Gould promptly responded in person. He was told that the Honorable Lord Gordon-Gordon was willing to see him and he must call at the Metropolitan ceremoniously and without delay. He obeyed. He called on that noble-man, took breakfast, and later, when the affair got into court, Mr. Gould gave this frank account of his visit: —

"I asked him what his interest in Erie was. He said that individually he owned thirty millions of the stock; his friends, twenty millions more; that he controlled the whole; that he was satisfied that it was best to keep the road under my management, but wanted to put in a new Board to be selected by himself and Mr. Horace Greeley — all the gentlemen to be approved by me. He told me much about his antecedents, his career and his family; stated that he entered Parliament at the age of twenty-two, and took his seat as the youngest member of the House of Lords; spoke of the great confidence the Queen had in his ability and discretion, and mentioned delicate missions that had been intrusted to him — an important negotiation with the Prussian Government, which he was sent out to attend to as the only man who could cope with Bismarck. Just then there was a knock on the door and in came Mr. Greeley."

Gordon was very suspicious. He seriously distrusted Jay Gould, and gave him distinctly to understand that something besides his mere word would be necessary to bind any bargain they might make or to carry out any project entered into. At this Gould does not seem to have been at all surprised, and he gracefully yielded to all demands.

During the next week an agreement with Lord Gordon was consummated, providing for the entire reorganization of the Erie Railway Company. Of this Gordon testified in court, where he ultimately had to make answer: "I informed Gould of my position: that, being an extensive stockholder, I could influence a great number of other stockholders, and that a change in the management of the company could be no longer delayed; that the change demanded was that the line should be restored to the stockholders. I told him that if his statements were correct he had nothing to fear, and that I, for one, if satisfied of the truth of what he informed me, would vote for him myself and induce my friends to do so also. Gould was very anxious to secure my coöperation. I declined to commit myself; I told him it required more than mere words — that he must show me by satisfactory proofs that what he stated was true. He then said that he would do so, and that if I would aid him he would willingly place his resignation in my hands. He pledged himself repeatedly to follow the honest policy I laid down, and I told him that if he did not I could not, under any circumstances, give him my support. Gould urged upon me that we should purchase more stock together. I declined and told him I was not disposed to have my crédulity and my pocket tested at the same time. To this he replied: 'I don't mean it that way; I will carry the stock for both you and myself.'

"I made inquiry next day on the subject of 'carrying stock.' A friend advised that I should have the transaction in 'puts and calls,' and he gave me a form. I then told Gould that the better way would be to put it in the form of puts and calls, and I would accept them and coöperate with him. Gould said, 'With pleasure,' and he took the form I handed to him and wrote out and delivered to me calls upon him for 20,000 shares of Erie at thirty-five dollars per share, good for six months."

Gordon represented to Gould that in making his investigations, getting bills passed, and bringing litigations to an end, he had been at a very large expense; that his bills had been paid by him personally; more legislation at Albany had also been provided for, and he considered that these expenses would be a legitimate charge against the new organization. To this Gould agreed and asked how much had been expended. Gordon said he could n't give the exact sum, because there were a large number of claims not yet settled, but it was over a million dollars.

"In view of the fact," explained Mr. Gould later, "that he had made these advances personally, and that the success of the new plan would depend very much on my good faith and his coöperation, I agreed to deposit with him securities and money to the extent of about one half of his expenses, or about $500,000. This pledge was not to be used by him, but was to be returned to me on my carrying out my part of the agreement. In accordance therewith I deposited with Gordon money and securities as follows: —

500 shares of the National Stock Yard Company
500 shares of the Erie and Atlantic Sleeping Coach Company
200 shares of the Elmira Rolling Mill
200 shares of the Brooks Locomotive Works
20 bonds of $1000 each of Nyack and Northern R.R. Company
500 shares of the Jefferson Car Company
4722 shares of Oil Creek and Alleghany Valley R.R. Company
600 shares of the Erie R.R. Company
Cash, $160,000

"When I gave him these securities I put a memorandum against each of them of their value. Gordon afterwards wrote me that there was an error in the footing, he thought; and, though there was no error, yet, not wishing to raise any question, and supposing that the money was safe in his hands, I took $40,000 more and deposited with him, making, in all, the securities mentioned and $200,000 cash."

In another deposition in court Mr. Gould added to his testimony that he asked Lord Gordon for a memorandum receipt for these securities and money, which his lordship declined to give, taking the high ground that his word was quite sufficient, and, suiting the action to the word, handing the parcel back to Mr. Gould; whereupon Mr. Gould broke off the negotiation and was about to leave the room — in fact, had reached the door — when, upon second thought, he laid the package upon the table again and accepted his lordship's word of honor as his only voucher!

The Right Honorable Gordon-Gordon in his sworn answer in court, to which he was presently summoned, said: —

"The following day Gould called upon me at ten o'clock and handed me a note and a package containing certain shares of the inside companies referred to at our interview the previous day. The note is as follows: —

NEW YORK, *March* 7, 1872

My DEAR SIR:

In our conversation yesterday you made reference to several stocks and bonds of companies connected with our line and seemed to infer that you had some doubt as to their genuineness. I beg to enclose you some shares of the stock of each of these and trust that you will accept them in good faith, and in testimony of my desire to have you personally interested in all that concerns our lines, and thus ensure your confidence and coöperation without testing your credulity and your pocket at the same time.

Yours respectfully,
JAY GOULD

"The accompanying package contained the stock given as evidence of his good faith.

"He then made reference to the great rise there would be forthwith in the Erie stock. My calls, he said, would be worth over a million dollars in six months; at which I laughed, and told him I would willingly part with them for half that sum. 'Will you?' said he, 'then I will buy them from you. I will give you other stocks and shares to the value of half a million.' I said: 'Very well; what is the value of the shares you sent in the package? I will take them as part of your own price; they must be included.' This he assented to, and, taking up a pen, he wrote a memorandum showing the price or value of some of the shares I had received to be as follows: —

| | |
|---|---:|
| Jefferson Car Company shares | $ 25,000 |
| Erie and Atlantic Sleeping Coach Company shares | 50,000 |
| Stock Yard Company shares | 25,000 |
| Elmira Rolling Mill Company shares | 40,000 |
| Total | $140,000 |

"In exchange for the money, stocks, and bonds received by me I delivered to Gould the puts and calls for forty thousand shares of Erie stock which I held. Gould was with me at my rooms on the eighth and ninth of March, arranging matters. On the latter day he delivered to me his resignation, as follows": —

I hereby resign my position as President and Director of the Erie Railroad Company, to take effect upon the appointment of a successor.

Yours, etc.,
JAY GOULD

NEW YORK, *March* 9th

Marvelous as it may appear, it is absolutely true that at this date this consummate knave was not only possessed of the entire confidence of Jay Gould, the admiration and respect of Thomas A. Scott and Alexander McClure, and the trust and affection of Horace Greeley, but he had more than half a million of Gould's securities and greenbacks in his handbag and Gould's voluntary resignation as Director and President of the Erie Railway Company in his vest pocket! Gould admitted to his associates that he had given his resignation to Gordon simply to induce his co-directors to do the same thing, and in the interest of harmony!

More than this: he had not only obtained without the pretense of an equivalent this vast sum, but he had exhibited such airs of superiority as to bring the marvelous millionaire to his knees and cause him to assume an apologetic tone and attitude when asked to give some slight guaranty of his honesty and good faith! This most extraordinary thief had so impressed his new friend with his own fidelity that when he superciliously refused to furnish any voucher for his truthfulness, Gould instantly yielded and handed over half a million dollars on "his lordship's word of honor"! And only a week had passed since he first set eyes on his lordship!

But matters were now approaching a crisis. The "Honorable Lord Gordon-Gordon" had $200,000 of Gould's cash in his pocket and 10,000 shares of stock transferable into half a million dollars in a day. Something must shortly happen. Something did happen. My lord slyly sold 600 shares of Erie in Wall Street and pocketed the proceeds. This attracted little attention, but to make a market in Philadelphia for nearly 5000 shares of Oil Creek and Alleghany produced a depression which caused a stir. Gould began to suspect that there was something crooked about Lord Gordon-Gordon. Investigation confirmed this opinion. He enjoined the further sale of stock instantly. He then hired a suite of apartments in the Metropolitan Hotel immediately

adjoining my lord's and summoned his friends. After conference he sent for the superintendent of police with a squad.
Before the superintendent he made affidavit to the facts.
Whether Gordon was a real lord or a mere fakir was not
known, but it was resolved so to act as to cover both alternatives
and, in the last resort, to storm the citadel by forcing an entrance.

This was not finally necessary, for peaceful measures
prevailed. Gould did not wish to arrest the alleged lord as
an impostor and swindler, for he did not absolutely know
but that he was in fact the man he claimed to be. Horace
Greeley as a friend of both parties was selected as ambassador,
and had no difficulty in obtaining entrance. He appealed to
the Scotchman, as a gentleman of high rank who could not
afford to get into a vulgar controversy over filthy dollars, to
return the money at once, and abandon all intention of helping Gould or rescuing the Erie Railroad. He pleaded that a
surrender of the money would not prejudice his rights to
recover in court thereafter. Gordon was stubborn and insisted on seeing Gould. Gould as resolutely declined the
honor, but gave his ambassador in writing plenary power to
settle. At last, after some hours, Greeley received and handed
to Gould $200,000 in bank notes and most of the securities,
excepting the 4722 shares of Oil Creek stock, the shares of
Erie which had been sold, and a few others.

The next day, finding that his lordship had failed to account
for a thousand shares of Erie and other stocks, proceedings
were instituted against him in New York and he was arrested
for obtaining money under false pretenses. Mr. Gould's
counsels were Elihu Root and David Dudley Field, while
Lord Gordon was represented by Generals Dix and Sickles.
Mr. Greeley seemed still to entertain no doubt about the
representations Gordon had made concerning his own per-

sonality, but expressed to him some doubts whether he could get anybody to go on his bond for the $40,000 required to ensure his appearance in court when wanted. At that vital moment the door opened to admit A. F. Roberts, a well-known magnate, and Horace F. Clark, a son-in-law of Commodore Vanderbilt, and a millionaire, a Congressman, and President of the Union Pacific Railroad, who at once volunteered to be his bondsmen, to the profound astonishment and dismay of Jay Gould and his friends. With this new alliance the pseudo-lord at once assumed the petulant air of an innocent and much-abused man.

The case was tried before Judge John R. Brady in May. The prisoner's manner was haughty; his replies instantaneous. When asked to explain how it happened that his name did not appear upon the list of stockholders of the Erie Company, he parried the thrust in an instant with the sneering response that under the American system any man might own the absolute control of a corporation without having a single share of its stock registered in his name. Of course this was correct. He told the story of his coming to America, of his large purchase of lands in Minnesota, his immense owner-ship of Erie Railway stock, his relationship to the great Scotch Gordons, his association with many English noblemen, with such consummate nonchalance as to impress every auditor with his good faith save Jay Gould and his intimates. He asked why he was being persecuted. He was closely questioned about his Scotch relatives and gave their names and residences. During three hours of vigorous examination he sat with his legs crossed and his thumbs thrust carelessly into his waistcoat pockets, as unconcerned and unruffled as if con-versing in a drawing-room. One outburst of injured inno-cence completely captured Judge Brady himself, who instantly commanded Mr. Field to desist from further persecution and rather angrily informed him that "this kind of thing has gone quite far enough!" The Judge then appointed a commissioner to continue the taking of testimony and adjourned the hearing until eleven o'clock the next morning. After adjournment Mr. Gould cabled to the parties in England, Scotland, and France whom Gordon had mentioned, and received replies from every one in which they repudiated Lord Gordon, declared they had never heard of him, and that he was not allied with either of the great Gordon families of Scotland. With these in his pocket he appeared promptly at the eleven-o'clock hearing the next day. His friends were on hand early, as were Mr. Greeley and the confident attorneys for the defendant. Lord Gordon himself was late in making his appearance. Eleven o'clock went by and twelve o'clock came, and the injured nobleman was still detained.

In fact, he did not appear at all.

He had skipped, and inquiry revealed the fact that he was then in Canada, having left on the last night train for Montreal. Gould handed the batch of cablegrams to Judge Brady, and the case was considered ended. Gordon had returned to Gould over $300,000 in cash and securities; nearly $200,000 was under lock and key of the court in Philadelphia, and Horace F. Clark was security for $40,000 more.

Gordon had sold about $150,000 worth of securities of various kinds and got away with the money — exactly how much is not known and probably never will be.

Gould offered $25,000 for the arrest of the distinguished charlatan and his delivery to justice in New York. Anticipating a trial, he sent agents to Europe to examine the personal history of the fugitive and verify the reports that had been made to him by cable. While in this service they became acquainted with the facts hitherto mentioned concerning his robbery of jewelry stores in Edinburgh and Glasgow. The proprietors earnestly coöperated in showing up the character of "Lord Glencairn," whose identity with Gordon-Gordon was revealed by photograph.

At the time of the robberies "Lord Glencairn," then calling himself Hubert Hamilton, had a shooting box in Forfarshire in Scotland. He lived in fine style, and was clad in costly raiment. His hat was so conspicuous that it became one of the items by which the robber was identified. He was accompanied by a youth who was dressed in buckskin breeches, long boots, blue coat with gilt buttons, and an immense cockade upon his hat, which in Great Britain denotes that his master holds a commission under the sovereign. This youth was sometimes a valet, and sometimes officiated as secretary, being what is called "a gentleman's tiger."

When these facts became known in Minneapolis, half a dozen sturdy citizens resolved to get even with the pseudo-lord who had so grossly imposed on their hospitality, and was now reported to be in Fort Garry, Manitoba, fifty miles north of the line. It was immediately resolved to organize a party and "fetch him down." George Brackett, mayor of the city, and William Lochren, Eugene Wilson, and J. B. Gilfillan, prominent lawyers, conferred secretly and planned the capture of his lordship on British territory. Without a day's delay Mayor Brackett detailed his chief of police, Captain Mike Hoy, and Sergeant Owen Keegan, arming them with letters to Loren Fletcher, J. C. Burbank, and other Minnesotans who happened to be at Fort Garry. No time was lost. Fletcher and Burbank hired a team of fast horses with a light wagon. Hoy and Keegan jumped in, hastened to the cottage where Gordon was staying, seized him upon the front porch, kept him from making an uproar, dragged him to the wagon, and drove for the boundary as fast as the horses could go. They reached American soil with their prisoner and were a quarter of a mile south of the line when they were arrested by a pursuing party from Fort Garry. Gordon was released and the Minnesotans were heavily ironed and taken back. They were thrust into a dungeon and treated with great indignity. Fletcher telegraphed to Brackett, "We're in a hell of a fix; come at once!" The greatest excitement prevailed in Minnesota and it was seriously proposed to raise a regiment at once and throw it across the border. But peaceful counsels prevailed.

The New York bondsmen, with $40,000 at stake, eagerly coöperated. First they procured an opinion from their learned attorney that according to an old English statute the Minnesotans were within their legal rights in proceeding to Manitoba and taking the fugitive by force. Lord Gordon made the most of his "martyrdom." Mayor Brackett hurried to Fort Garry and sought to extricate his friends from their dilemma. There were threats and counter threats. The Government at Washington was appealed to. The Manitoba authorities resorted to blackmail, offering to release the prisoners if Brackett would pay $14,500 for a piece of land belonging to the attorney-general! He angrily exposed the offer and telegraphed it to the newspapers. The prisoners suffered greatly from the heat of midsummer. Mayor Brackett and Governor Austin hurried to Washington and laid the matter before President Grant and his Secretary of State, Hamilton Fish, with whom I had made an appointment. They were deeply interested and at once promised to effect the release of the Minnesotans when Brackett alleged that, through a mistake of the Canadians, the capture by them was actually made on the south side of the boundary. Bancroft Davis, Assistant Secretary, boldly advised that the Minnesotans go up to the boundary and sieze the customhouse officer and boundary police and hold them until redress was ob-

tained. He offered to back up the movement. To avoid
international trouble, however, Brackett and Governor Austin
went to Canada and presented the case to Sir John Macdonald,
the Prime Minister. He received the visitors very sympathetically, alleged that, while the attempt to capture and
kidnap Lord Gordon-Gordon was irregular and wrong,
there was no reason why his captors should not be admitted
to bail. His decision was at once telegraphed to Manitoba
and bail was obtained and accepted. The prisoners were
released and went home, September 15, 1873. Three of the
kidnappers were afterwards elected to Congress and two
made governors of the state.

The "international conflict" was at an end, but Jay Gould's
offer of $25,000 for Lord Gordon-Gordon still held good, and
New York City was not without adventurous speculators
who were willing to pocket it. It shortly became known
that the Honorable Lord Gordon-Gordon, cousin of the
Campbells, and descendant of the bold Lochinvar and the
Highland kings, had concealed himself in a cottage near
Toronto. His pursuers again gave chase, but were fated to
obtain meagre satisfaction. Extradition papers were quietly
obtained from Washington, two vigorous officials were employed, and the much-wanted nobleman was found, not
boldly exposed to capture on the front porch, but ignominiously asleep in the recesses of his chamber.

"Ah, yes; do you want me?" he asked, on being touched
lightly upon the shoulder. He found that he was at the mercy
of two officers stationed on each side of the bed, and for a
moment he imagined that one of them was Hoy, Brackett's
vigilant chief of police. He playfully requested permission
to sleep a little longer, as it was not yet noon, but was informed
that the exigency would not permit it. The "gentleman's
tiger" who had accompanied his lordship's splendid retinue

over the prairies of Minnesota was not at hand, and the sleepy nobleman was compelled to get out of bed without assistance and to complete his toilet by his own unaided exertions. Lord Gordon-Gordon took his arrest with the cool nonchalance which had always been his distinguishing characteristic. He surrendered at discretion. He was permitted to consult a lawyer, and was given five minutes for the conference.

"Tell me," he said, "if these papers are sufficient to compel me to go with these men and appear in a Toronto court."

"They are," answered the lawyer.

"Very well, I will go," and the prisoner smiled a peculiar smile. "Cold, is n't it? Then I must wrap up." At this moment his valet returned, not the gorgeous "gentleman's tiger" of the northwestern prairies, but another, who, though much humbler, showed himself capable of great astonishment and alarm. He followed his master into the bedroom, where they busied themselves with getting the clothing requisite for the journey to Toronto, perhaps New York.

"What have I done that I should be seized like a felon?" he asked as he vanished into the bedroom.

"Are you ready?" asked one of the detectives.

"In one moment, policeman," said the soft, indifferent voice from the inner room. "Here, Grant, help me with these boots."

There was a long silence. Then came the crash of a revolver in the little apartment and the Right Honorable Lord Gordon-Gordon fell dead across the threshold, carrying all the mysteries of his strange life with him.

Thus ended the career of a man who, while posing as a nobleman on two continents, had successfully imposed on the shrewdest merchants and ablest men of affairs of the day. He proved to be the illegitimate child of a clergyman's son, and his mother was the parlor maid in the family. From which of his ancestors he inherited his brilliancy and his vices can only be conjectured.

He certainly was a close second to the illustrious Cagliostro. He had made his own the motto of the great Napoleon: *"L'audace! L'audace! Toujours l'audace!"* And if Jay Gould was "the Little Wizard of Wall Street," to what person or thing under Heaven can we liken this consummate magician and prince of liars, whose genius was equally at home unlocking the diamond vaults of the canny Scotch, annexing the broad prairies of our Western states, or boldly invading the mortal arena of the metropolis where gladiators contend for mastery?

# XVIII

## MASCULINE SOCIETY AND THE CLUBS

A NOTABLE event was the reception given to the venerable David Dudley Field in honor of his eightieth birthday by his brothers, Stephen, Henry, and Cyrus, at the latter's residence in Gramercy Park. Around the same green breathing space were the residences of Peter Cooper, Samuel J. Tilden, General McClellan, Horace Porter, F. B. Thurber, Clarkson Potter, and Joseph Pulitzer. The assembly was the most distinguished I had ever seen. Everybody seemed to feel that the opportunity of meeting four such remarkable brothers, each distinguished in a separate way, was like being invited by Cornelia Sempronius to a dinner of the Gracchi. The mansions of Mr. Cyrus Field and his brother David Dudley, at the foot of Lexington Avenue, stood like two overgrown elephants awaiting the promised festivity, and each of them, heeding the menace of rain, stuck a long proboscis of sailcloth out upon the sidewalk. Into these the guests surged from nine o'clock to twelve, and out of them, to avoid congestion, they were from time to time ejected — a thousand or two in all.

When I got there it was early. The proboscis was empty and expectant. In the cloakroom a dozen hats and overcoats were already piled under chairs, where they could (perhaps) be found again. While I was stowing away my galoshes in my overcoat pocket, Roger A. Pryor came in and went through similar motions. His hair still swept his shoulders and was as black as when he was regarded as the typical fire eater of Congress.  Just inside the door of the great parlors stood the hero of the Atlantic cable, receiving guests as they came and passing them to his brother, David Dudley.  The guests now rapidly arrived, and it was notice-able that almost everybody was somebody.  Of leading lawyers, there were Chauncey Depew and Clark Bell. Then August Belmont, — lame from a duel he fought fifty years before, — short in stature, with a typical Jewish face, *nez gigantesque,* and a scowl ready to discharge itself.  He was one of the most bitter and cynical of men — some say quarrelsome.

DeWitt Talmage is talking with Bishop Potter when Henry Ward Beecher appears in the doorway; then the Tabernacle man pulls down his laughing face into sobriety. If he meets Beecher during the evening they will bow and say "H' are ye?" but they are not close friends and their con-gregations are in a state of armed neutrality.  Dr. Henry comes down the room glowing with the enjoyment of the occasion.

Roscoe Conkling comes along and salutes the Judge.  He looks even taller and straighter and more muscular than ever, and as he bows he seems a veritable Heenan.  His hair has turned quite gray and the famous hyacinthine curl above his forehead has entirely vanished.  His voice is smooth and rich; his words are measured and deliberate, carrying the weight of a special personal authority.  But he evidently does not feel happy and does not glow with love for the human race; for when a Boston journalist is presented and says, rather effusively, "Senator!  I have known and admired you so as a public man that I have very much wished to meet you," the great Roscoe answers superciliously, "Ah! There was a time, sir, when that confession would have deeply moved me;

but now I am impassive and have scarcely any longer, as the Declaration of Independence says, 'a decent regard for the opinions of mankind.'" It is spoken as if it were part of an oration — slowly, impressively, with oratund intoning, and the enthusiastic Boston man giggles as if he were quite self-composed and sneaks away crushed.

The drawing-rooms are soon crowded. Well-known heads loom everywhere, many of them familiar from their carica-tures. There is a terrible jam in the vicinity of the scalloped oysters and salads, the pâtés and the creams, and the cham-pagne tanks are the centres of solidity. Monsignor Capel is introduced to Russell Sage, who probably says, "Let me see what this man is like who so fascinates the women"; and Capel seizes him by the hand as if he were a long-lost brother, probably saying to himself, "This is the clear-headed boy who has scraped together a hundred millions and has twenty millions in the bank this minute." Capel slaps his friends on the back familiarly, and some he embraces, after the manner of Europe, in spite of the scarlet collar that stiffly spans his shoulders. Among familiar faces here are Heber Newton, Robert Collyer, Governor Hill, Governor Abbott, and Gov-ernor Hoyt, Secretary Windom, James Parton, Edward Everett Hale, George William Curtis, and Judge Brewer, who has come a good way to honor the compiler of the com-mon law to-night; Henry Bergh, equine laureate, who leans against a pillar near a bank of roses, his long serious face re-laxing into a smile as he looks on the multitude and listens to the racket. General N. P. Banks is here looking older than during war times — white bristly moustache, and white bristly eyebrows. He stands straight; his hand is still steady and his eye clear. Russell Sage squeezes gently through the crowd, bland and unwearied, and looking like a well-to-do farmer rather than like the Ajax of Wall Street. They shout a salute and seize each other's hands. "This is the man," said General Banks to William M. Evarts, "who made me Speaker during those hot weeks in 1855. Every evening during the five weeks of that contest we were together. I gave him carte blanche, and the result justified it. Oh, he's got a head on him. If he hadn't caught this put-and-call craze, he would have made a great politician."

They both laughed, and Mr. Sage stammered his thanks. "I was a young fellow then," he explained, "and that's what made me act so insanely, I suppose. I was thirty-two — the youngest man in that Congress."

Thomas A. Edison is present, and he excites very lively interest for the phenomenon he is. He has gained thirty or forty pounds in the last three or four years, and is no longer the cadaverous slave of the lamp that haunted the bucolic groves of Menlo Park.

Jay Gould is a centre of the greatest attraction wherever he moves, and is surrounded by a crowd of sycophants who want to take him by the hand and talk to him. He never talks to anybody — he only listens. I yield to the prevailing fascination and stand still and look at the remarkable genius who seems always to be holding an impromptu levee, judging by the crowd around him. His is a most interesting face to study. He speaks only in monosyllables. He casts furtive looks about him, then retires behind his black beard with a suspicious shudder, like a hermit crab trying to back into a shell that doesn't fit him. You look into his small gray eyes and he isn't there at all; he is in ambush, fifty miles beyond.

At twelve-thirty David Dudley Field stood, as he had stood for four hours, as straight and tall as a wild Indian.

The great club of New York for more.than a generation was the Union Club preëminently. It was said that there was not a man in the Union Club whose great-grandfather was known to have kept a pie stand or whose great-grandfather was known to have driven a dray. I do not say that the legacy of leisure went back of the great-grandparents, for one must draw a line somewhere. Everybody's family is obliged to bear the odium of an ancestor who worked at some time or other; but it seems to me that a man ought not to be thought any less of, provided that he rests systematically now and tries to make the world forget this blot of elbow grease on his escutcheon. The Union Club had a thousand members, and there were hundreds of them who never earned a meal of victuals in their lives or otherwise demeaned themselves. If they should have happened to lose their money, they would have gone to the poorhouse with as much fortitude as the savage goes to the test of his valor by laceration. Such men are the real aristocrats; and the stuff that runs in their veins is the genuine blue blood. To be blackballed by the Union Club always annihilated the victim; it was exactly as if a comet had struck him.

The Lotos (so spelled by the Club) was one of the most famous and fashionable of our social organizations, almost entirely superseding the Travelers Club in the agreeable function of welcoming distinguished strangers. As a presiding officer Whitelaw Reid combined grace, dignity, good nature, and tact, and his incumbency lent much éclat to the Club, which was formed by six young journalists in 1870.

I wonder what has become of the Greek Club. For years it flourished much under the paternity of Reverend Dr. Crosby. Mr. Dana of the Sun was one of the foremost members, and one of the inflexible rules was that nobody should speak anything but Greek at the weekly reunions. One of

the conditions of membership, besides fluent Hellenic con-
versational ability, was the production of an original poem in
Greek every year. William Cullen Bryant and Bayard
Taylor were both members of this curious and difficult club,
and distinguished tourists from Athens used to come and
laugh to hear their native tongue. This aggregation of en-
thusiasts bore the same relation to ordinary culture that the
Union Club bore to average respectability. I never went to
one of the dinners; it always wrenches my jaw to ask for
pancakes in Greek.

The Press Club was started in 1866, and Horace Greeley
was its first president and Charles Dickens repeatedly its
guest. It throve hopefully at first, but after a little while it
excited the mortal hostility of the Herald and gradually paled
its intellectual fires.

At the sixteenth anniversary of the New York Club the
dinner was given at the St. Nicholas Hotel, and it was a
notable affair because the great people who were expected
came. To see Grant, Sherman, Frémont, Commodore
Nicholson, Henry Ward Beecher, Benson J. Lossing, Stewart
L. Woodford, Admiral Porter, and other such, all in one
anteroom fifteen feet square at one moment, is a spectacle that
cannot be witnessed more than once in a lifetime.

I was writing voluminously for newspapers at this time and
thought to take advantage of this rare opportunity to interview some celebrities.

"I thought you did not like these newspaper men," I remarked to General Sherman, recalling the trouble that
three or four of them gave him in Tennessee.

"I don't and I do," he said, turning his head with a far-off
gaze as if he had his eye on the brace of garrulous correspondents whom he drove out of his army in 1863.

"There is a difference between them — you must have

noticed that yourself," he said, fixing me with his eye. "Now, for instance," remarked the General, lifting his finger to emphasize what was in his mind, "take one case that you will remember — though probably not as vividly as I do —" At that moment General Hawley twisted him around the other way and introduced some Brooklyn men to him and I was unable to get him again. I shall never know, and the world will never know, what that case was.

I was not much more successful with General Grant, though I tried hard to interest him for the sake of my business. He was left standing alone near me in a rather disconsolate way, I thought; so I said, to break the silence as it were, "I don't remember your attending any of our press meetings before, General." He merely said, "Never did."

It was probably about a minute that I waited and then remarked in my usual beaming way, "I never saw you looking in better health, General!"

He waited about half a minute, and then responded, "Never was."

I was already perspiring violently, but I hitched a little closer and said, "There will evidently be a full attendance to-night, though it is so slushy underfoot." He looked up at me in a surprised way, as if I had asked him a categorical question which needed some thought, and then he said, "Yes."

I tried to preserve a calm exterior, but mentally I was wringing my hands and shouting for help. I could feel my collar getting limp. I tried to think of something that would interest him. I had a great mind to leave him to his confounded meditations, but I pitied him, standing there alone in a kind of helpless attitude, so I took hold of the lapels of my swallowtail with both hands to brace myself, and said in an earnest voice, "General, did you ever hear about the queer way in which this club started?" He changed his weight to his other foot, reflected a while, and said, "No."

"Well," said I, leaning against the mantelpiece and at last obtaining his attention sufficiently to begin my narrative, "about sixteen years ago —" Just at this very moment Pulitzer and Amos Cummings came and carried him off peremptorily to his seat at the head of the table. Ten dollars to a cent that General Grant never found out how the New York Press Club originated. But I had done my duty.

The speeches were in the papers next morning — some of them. Two features of the banquet may be recalled. Mr. Beecher, Dr. Storrs, Dr. Field, and other clergymen were present, but nobody asked any blessing over the food or suggested it. This could scarcely have happened fifty years before.

Another memorable thing was Joe Howard's speech. Howard was known as "a good fellow," and among journalists he was a good fellow — kind, obliging, recklessly generous. He was fluent in speech — very fluent — and he never spoke more than a minute before some stranger inquired, "Is he drunk?" He was not drunk. He was never drunk. But he decorated his speech with all manner of improper frills. The presence of Grant, Sherman, Beecher, Robert Collyer, and others did not dull his tongue, but rather sharpened it.

Joe's speech was not in the papers next morning — only a euphuistic version of it. I cannot write it here. It was too rich for type. I may perhaps recall one sentence, slightly toned down: "It is disgusting to have you illustrious old cocks sit up there on your high stools and tell us that we are great men — that we are the true rulers of the country. It's damned nonsense, every word of it. We are a lot of poor devils trying to dodge the sheriff, scratching night and day to keep soul and body together — most of us glad to get thirty dollars a week.  Talk about our being the arbiters of nations!  It's damned nonsense, Sherman, and you know it."

"Joe," as all his acquaintances called him, and he knew everybody, was a man of forty, nearly bald, with rosy face, glib tongue, and capable of writing a column of nonpareil an hour.  He was a very facile and valuable man on a newspaper; well informed, quickwitted, steady, and above all ready.  He made remarks that would bring a blush to the cheek of a grindstone.  I cannot imagine what Anna Ballard of the Sun would have done if she had been admitted to the banquet, as she tried to be.

"Joe had on his high-heeled shoes to-night," I said to Henry Ward Beecher, as he was going to his carriage at one o'clock in the morning.  "Yes," he said, "he astonished even me to-night.  It was stunning, was n't it?"  Knowing that Howard's father was a deacon in Plymouth Church, I said, "I did n't suppose that Joseph could surprise you."  "Well, no," he said, "but it was paralyzing.  It would n't be tolerated a minute in anybody but Joe, but they don't seem to mind it in him.  There is no Joe but one Joe, and eccentricity is his profit.

"There is one thing, though," he added a moment later, "there is no sham about Joe.  He's a kind-hearted fellow, and always with the under dog in the fight."  Perhaps the great orator of Plymouth Church spoke from a sense of gratitude and a memory of his own trying experiences.

Joe Howard was one of the most facile, reckless, rollicking, cynical, and witty journalists in New York.  It was he who telegraphed to the Tribune the genealogy of Jesus of Nazareth during the war to keep a Times correspondent from getting the wire, and immense was the astonishment of the night editors at the New York end of the line when they read the news from the Rappahannock that Zorobabel begat Abiud, and Abiud begat Eliakim, and Eliakim begat Azor. Joe got top prices for his work — ten or twelve thousand dollars a year. A characteristic incident occurred while Mr. Dana was managing editor of the Tribune. Howard was officiating as a war correspondent at the front. A great battle had been fought, and Joe was telegraphing the description of it. He began with the exordium, "To God Almighty be all the glory! Mine eyes have seen the work of the Lord and the cause of the righteous hath triumphed," with more of the same sort, followed by the words, "The Army of the Potomac has won a great victory." A day or two afterwards he received a letter as follows: "Hereafter, in sending your reports, please specify the number of the hymn and save telegraph expenses. — Charles A. Dana."

One afternoon I was looking out of one of the windows of the New York Club when Commodore Thompson, who sat near, said, "I was just thinking, as I was looking out at that wave-washed monument to Admiral Farragut, what obstacles he met trying to get into trouble."

I made some commonplace remark about the apocryphal account of his being lashed in the rigging, when he interrupted: —

"Oh, no; I was n't thinking of that, but about the beginning of the war."

Being asked to explain, he went on, "Farragut was by birth a Southerner. When the war broke out, the Confederate authorities offered him a commission in their navy. He declined and told them plainly that he felt that his services were due to the nation that had educated him. Then the South became too hot to hold him and he went to New York. Being a poor lieutenant on half pay, he could not afford to live in the city, so he went and rented a little place at Yonkers.   Fort Sumter was fired on; the North was roused. Farragut was greatly troubled, and his anxiety caused much loss of sleep.   During these attacks of insomnia Farragut used to go out and walk to and fro on the level top of the old aqueduct for hours.   He was seen perambulating here in the moonlight by his patriotic and suspicious neighbors, and they inquired about him and soon started the story that he was 'a United States naval officer from Georgia.'   The suspicious felt justified.   Local spies followed him about and a message was sent to President Lincoln at Washington of this thrilling import: 'A rebel officer named Farragut has been seen walking up and down on the aqueduct here in the night, pacing it off and measuring distances, and it is believed to be a part of a plan to cut the aqueduct, deprive New York of its water supply, and burn the city.'   Farragut suddenly found himself watched by persons who seemed to be acting in concert, and in disgust he rushed to Washington and prayed to be put instantly into service.   When he came back to Yonkers after the war, a committee of citizens waited on him, told him how much they desired to present him a home and have him spend his life among them.   He laughingly alluded to the aqueduct-walking days, thanked the committee for its kindness, but said he had decided to live henceforth in New York.   So the fine house in the city was offered him, and he accepted."

# XIX

## IN THE PUBLIC EYE

WHEN the great scandal broke out, Samuel Wilkeson, the New York Tribune's Washington correspondent, was one of Henry Ward Beecher's most intimate and earnest friends. He was one of the chief witnesses at the celebrated trial. He became considerably involved with the famous defendant and paid him an immense sum of money in advance to write a life of Christ. Beecher made a contract to write it and furnish it to Wilkeson "as soon as possible," and Wilkeson wanted it badly and troubled the great preacher with his importunity. Five years later, when the manuscript was not forthcoming, Wilkeson brought suit for the money. The only defense Mr. Beecher set up for not writing the book was that he "had not felt like it"; he refused to pay back the money and the court held that Wilkeson had no redress, because there was no time of delivery mentioned in the contract.

I called on Wilkeson one day and asked him about this matter. He shrugged his shoulders and said, "It's a sore topic. Beecher is sick, they say. I wonder if he will die this time. I have had some remarkable experiences with that man. You know that when the scandal exploded and I, yielding to his importunity as a friend, had paid him ten thousand dollars in advance for his life of Christ I casually remarked that the trial had knocked that estimable work higher than a kite. So it seemed to prove, especially as Beecher refused to go on with the book after writing a short first chapter. I tried in vain to get my money back. I stuck to him through thick and thin, till I was tired to death and disgusted. I then sued him, with what result you know. I was deliberately robbed, and so I have never hesitated to tell him or his friends. Certainly you may print it, if you want to. He remained placid and unruffled from year to year, never doing me the slightest justice.

"At last, about a year ago, he came up here and embraced me, calling me his oldest and dearest friend, and hugging me all over the room. He said his conscience troubled him about that book, and he was now going to make amends and hand it over to me according to contract. He declared that I had been treated shabbily; that I was entitled to first consideration; that other publishers could wait; and that he would go to work immediately, that very afternoon, to make restitution. He even wept on my shoulder, reminded me that he loved me more than ever, and when he went reluctantly away he hugged me effusively and said for the tenth time, 'I will send you a chapter next week. Don't lose faith in me, Sam. You must n't lose faith! You must love me, Sam! Love me! I will send you a chapter next week!'

"Well, what do you think?" said Wilkeson. "That was a year ago, and I have n't heard one word from him since! He is the enigma of our generation!"

One of the most interesting figures in New York life at this time was General John C. Frémont, whose name and romantic career cemented two million men into the compact Republican Party. He was one of the most attractive and best-defined of our historic personages. I frequently met him on Broadway, swinging along up town like a man of twenty. The illusion of youth was further encouraged by the close-cropped hair, the form still trim, the elastic step, the rosy face, and the cheery, buoyant manner when he spoke. He generally wore a business suit of light-colored plaid. Time and trial had not soured him. It seemed impossible that this clear-eyed and agile man was that same stalwart pathfinder whose footsteps so many men followed with enthusiasm.

I called one evening on the General and his Jessie Benton, at their Staten Island villa, where they were prolonging the romance of half a century before. Mrs. Frémont was a staid-looking, matronly woman, with a remarkably strong face, resembling the portraits of her distinguished father. They already had two stout boys grown up and married, with children of their own to bother about, "and one is in the army and one in the navy," said Mrs. Frémont, "so my feelings are completely triangulated" — and she deftly drew on the table before her a triangle with its apex in New York and one leg in Montana and the other in the Southern seas.

I mentioned the General's unparalleled travels. He said, "It sometimes seems like a dream. When I take a map and pass my finger over the states and great cities of the West, it seems impossible that I traveled through them before they had any population whatever — and such a little while ago! Every large city in the West was originally my camp."

"We cannot forget," I said, "that you are responsible for the Mormons going and settling Utah."

"Yes," he said, "I suppose I must confess that. In the report of my second expedition over the central plains I called the attention of the government to the beautiful valley of Salt Lake which I was the first to explore, its fertility and general attractiveness, and I recommended that a fort be built there to encourage and protect immigration. A few years afterwards, while passing again through that luxuriant region, Brigham Young called on me and told me that my report had led him to select that place as the seat of his hierarchy."

In reply to my remark that the people of California seemed in danger of forgetting his services in conquering and holding it for Uncle Sam in 1846, he said: —

"Oh, no. There is no danger of my not getting all the credit that belongs to me. People love justice, and in the end they generally decide right, especially about their own affairs. Of course, as nineteen twentieths of the present population of California were born after I was elected Senator from that state, they cannot be expected to have the vivid recollection of pioneer days, but my taking possession of that coast in '46 is a matter of history. The English admiral was standing on and off for weeks, awaiting orders from home, and he afterwards declared to me that he would have landed and seized Monterey for the English that very day if I had not hurried in and raised the Stars and Stripes. That settled the status of the coast."

I congratulated Mrs. Frémont on being the possessor of such abounding health, as it had enabled her to be of so much assistance first to her father, then to her husband.

"No, you mistake me," she replied. "Unfortunately I have no secure health. I belong to a consumptive family, and inherit strong pulmonary tendencies. In fact, I have had hemorrhage of the lungs myself, and saved my life only by a fight of years. My father was a man of tremendous energy and resolution, and people generally suppose him to have been robust. He never was. He belonged to a family of eight children of whom five died of consumption before they were twenty."

I asked her how Colonel Benton escaped the family doom.

"When he was eight years old his father died of consump-

*Leslie's Weekly*

LINCOLN: *"Well, Master Frémont, that's rather a long reach, ain't it? You might fetch it with your sword, in the proper time, but it is n't ripe yet."*

tion, and when his brothers followed, one after another, it set my father to thinking. He had begun to practise law in Tennessee. The doctor told him he had consumption of a fatal variety and must die. He rebelled against this mandate and said that, rather than perish in such an ignoble manner, he would die on the battlefield; so he raised a company (it was in the War of 1812) and started with a detachment of young men for New Orleans to relieve Jackson. In the march from Memphis to the Gulf he walked most of the way, lending his horse to others. He marched in the rain. He waded streams. He lay down in his wet clothes and slept, and then marched on. He ate like a bear. He gained in strength. His hemorrhages diminished in frequency and severity and finally ceased altogether. He always attributed his escape to outdoor air and exposure.

"Well, after I was married, my life was despaired of, too, and the doctor intimated that my time had come. I quit civilized life at once and fled to the plains and joined the General in camp. It undoubtedly kept me alive. So it was with our youngest boy, Frank. He went into the law and had much ambition in its study, but suddenly the old familiar symptoms came upon him and the doctor told him he must quit the law office if he would live. Reluctantly he took the hint and went into the army, where he can live out of doors as much as he likes."

I said that Colonel Benton was such an incessant and profound scholar along certain lines that I had supposed his life must have been mostly sedentary — especially during the years when he edited the Missouri Inquirer.

"He always kept up the habit of much exercise in the open air," said Mrs. Frémont, "and it made him comparatively strong so that he could pursue long studies. I remember reading through to him, in French, the sixteen volumes of the

*Causes Célèbres* of France, while he made an abstract of the cases."

I asked General Frémont if John Bigelow's allusions to his duels in the Campaign Life of '56 repelled the Quakers from him, and he answered, "Not greatly, I am sure. Quakers are sensible people, and when I gathered that fine army of sixty thousand around me in Missouri several of the foremost young Quakers of Pennsylvania joined me and put on the uniform and took up the sword at the risk of expulsion from their church. I believe a few actually were expelled. I'll tell you what repelled the Quakers, and everybody else, more or less," resumed the General. "The horrible woodcuts that they made to represent me and the pictures on banners and transparencies. I am not handsome, by a good deal, but I don't feel that I have ever done anything to deserve those caricatures. To my certain knowledge the villainous woodcut of me printed by the Tribune the day after my nomination lost me twenty-five votes in one township."

"Your happening in this evening is timely," said Mrs. Frémont. "The General is just putting the finishing touches to his memoirs in two bulky volumes. I need not say it is the splendid record of a very busy life. Well, do you know, it is so comprehensive and, indeed, ponderous that he finds it difficult to get a satisfactory publisher. One excellent firm will present it to the public under its imprint if the General will erase all of the 'unessential details' — that is, all of the picturesque pages that give it animation and life. But he thinks that an autobiography without vitality would not be very valuable, even as a history, and I think so, too. How about this firm that has just put forth your history of the Vanderbilts?" she asked.

I told her something about Belford, Clarke & Co., and, briefly, the conversation ended by the General and Mrs. Fré-

mont going with me next day to the New York branch of
my publishers, where a contract was entered into under which
the first great quarto volume of the Pathfinder's memoirs was
brought out in the fall.

When these interviews took place Mrs. Frémont's hair was
white as snow, but she showed few other indications of aging,
and talked as brilliantly as ever.  She greatly resembled her
father, even in gestures and manner when animated by conversation, and, with lineaments somewhat softened, inherited
his studious and logical mind and his commanding spirit.
Her sons were both tall, black-haired, black-eyed, and
"bearded like a pard"; and both, like their sister, showed
strains of Gallic blood — the influence of their grandfather,
the poor, scholarly French gentleman who came to Virginia
at the beginning of the century and found their grandmother
in her teens.

## XX

## WHEN MILLIONAIRES CONFIDE

Is the owner of fifty millions really worth any more than the owner of one million? I have interviewed several well-known millionaires and have obtained answers to this question.

About the first man I interrogated was Chauncey M. Depew. To the question, "Does it pay to be very rich?" he answered: —

"I don't know. I have never been, but I should imagine it did, or folks would n't want to be it, would they?"

Mr. Depew was worth only a paltry two or three millions, and therefore was not "very rich," according to metropolitan standards. "However," he continued, after a minute, "they may think it is going to pay and afterwards find themselves mistaken. Man never is, but always to be, blessed — and hope springs eternal in the human breast, you know."

"Is a fortune of a hundred millions practically greater than a fortune of one million?" I inquired.

"Yes," he said, "it requires more care and tires a man more to keep hold of it; but it will not buy any more of the things a man wants. Whether it brings any greater enjoyment — well, probably not. Riches do not confer happiness, or even comfort necessarily. It depends on what a man does with his money. I know a man who has an income of just about $100,000 a year and gets a heap of satisfaction out of it. He spends it all. On others, of course, most of it. Enlightened self-interest.    He gets his pleasure from making others happy, as Colonel Ingersoll says.    But if he avoids doing mischief, it must require a great deal of time and talent.    To know how to give money away wisely a man needs to be inspired.    It is about the most difficult trade there is — that of philanthropy.    A great many more people would work at it if they were certain that their money would do good."

Cyrus W. Field's immense fortune was squandered by his son, and the fortunes of several of his near relatives engulfed also, immediately after the death of the two who were dearest to him in life.    Ten years before, he was considered worth eight or ten million dollars.    It was about that time that I asked him the question that I had asked Mr. Depew.

"The value of money can easily be exaggerated," said Mr. Field.    "It is really worth only what it will fetch in the things we want, and for that purpose twenty dollars a day is worth just about as much as one thousand dollars a day.    In addition, there is only the gratified pride which arises from having made what men generally call a great success.    No doubt Mr. Gould has just about the same sort of satisfaction that his neighbor General Grant had — the satisfaction of having beaten; the satisfaction that the boy has who swims the farthest, or pitches the ball farthest, or the girl who stands at the head of her class."

Mr. Field was cheerful then, and even jovial.    He lounged upon the leathern sofa in his office and chatted and laughed, and certainly thought less of money than of the plaudits of the world which were showered on him in 1858, when the first Atlantic cable hiccuped its feeble but significant benediction.

I called on Russell Sage within ten years of his life's end and propounded the conundrum to him.    It was no more difficult to get at him than it was before the dynamite crank sought to effect a loan without security.  He was rich; probably he could foot up fifty or sixty millions — it is n't worth while to be too exact.  It was understood in Wall Street that he kept twenty millions in bank constantly on call.  He was frugal in all ways, taking no pleasure in anything not required by comfort.

It was a very warm day when I called and he had his coat off, — a coat that cost ten or fifteen dollars, — and wiped the high retreating front of his business occiput with a red silk handkerchief as he handled the marked envelopes of puts and calls on a little table before him and answered, "Yes," "No," to the clerk who came in every minute or so and asked him a question in figures and symbols which were all Greek to me.

"You seem to work hard to keep ahead of the boys, Mr. Sage," I said.  "There is a prevalent idea that millionaires don't have to work at all."

He uttered a significant but inarticulate sound of disapproval from the upper part of his larynx — a kind of chuckle strangled in its birth — and added, "They have to work, I guess, if they keep anything.  Everybody clutching to get it!"

"It is generally believed that you have enough money," I said; "as much as you can use."

"Yes, as much as I can use," he answered, turning toward me; "yes — I have as much as I can use, advantageously, I suppose."

"I have often wondered why you don't stop work," I boldly continued.  "You have n't a child in the world; you are seventy-five years old; you are worth, they say, $75,000,000, one million for every — "

He interrupted me once more with the same old sound of gratified dissent, and repeated ironically, "They say!"

After a minute or two he added: "You ask me why I don't

stop work. I 'll do it if you will answer me one question: What else can I go at that will do as much good and give as much satisfaction? Well, you can't answer it. Nobody can. I have thought it over. This is my trade. Another thing: every man likes to excel. He likes to prove to be worth as much as folks say he is worth. Hardly any man sold out suddenly would measure up to his reputation. Men take the same pleasure in accumulating that boys do in climbing trees, or winning a wrestling match."

I was struck with the coincidence that he had employed almost the very same figure of speech that Mr. Field had to explain the desire for riches. He turned to the table and sold an "option" or bought a "privilege," and then he added, "I should n't be happy at all if I left the Street. And there are two thousand men in sight of this window depending on me for work — what would they do?

"Wealth is traveling under false pretenses. It confers no such advantages and brings no such gratification as those who don't possess it imagine. Men who are making money keep at it because they like to have credit for sagacity, — for guessing right, — but there is nothing in money itself worth struggling for. They say that no man ever had enough money. It is not true. I have enough — more probably than I can ever use to advantage. The greatest satisfaction I ever got was from the service of others — in the good laws I got enacted when I sat near Lincoln in the Congress of '55, and when I made the first speech in favor of the bill for the purchase of Mount Vernon by the Government."

I talked with Peter Cooper during his very last days on the relation of a millionaire to the public. "I have been luckier than most of 'em," he chuckled, "for I have been the executor of my own will. I have seen the Institute finished and at work for good, but there are so many other things I want to do for the relief of wage earners" — and he gave me a great bundle of his printed schemes for bettering the condition of the poor.

William H. Vanderbilt was worth about five hundred tons of solid gold when he died. But he never handled the money; never saw it; never saw a tenth of the interest of it; never was in its presence in his life. It is difficult to see how he could have got pleasure from it. He dressed no better than his clerks, and ate less than his coachman. He drank chiefly milk. He slept in only one bed. An enormous fortune is a heavy burden to carry and brings annoyances from which there is no protection.

Among the millionaires of New York City, Daniel Drew presented a most remarkable personality. He never went to school a day in his life, but became one of the most illiterate and ignorant and wealthy of men. Lack of school training did not keep him from making money. Perhaps it even increased his sagacity. He made a million dollars in four years in steamboating and gave half of it to the Methodist Church. He was a man of low cunning, avaricious, superstitious, unscrupulous, and tricky. He never swore, but his hybrid English was not much inferior to profanity. He alluded to the "Allbunny and Squee-harry road," to "the Waybosh stiffkits," and to "them-air Erie Sheers" in his ordinary conversation; and when the Chamber of Commerce asked him to put up a fraction of his $18,000,000 to sustain the market in a panic he responded: "Gents, I'd luff to du it, but I've sporn as much money as I kin." He was then a railroad king — high among the magnates, and a rival of Vanderbilt's. After the great Erie fight was settled he testified before the court: "The Com'dore he telled me I had n't never ought to gone over to Jersey, and I telled him how mebby it did circumstance me kind of ockard." Perhaps good grammatical profanity would not have been an improvement on that pigeon English, but I respectfully leave it to the reader's judgment.

What happened? Is it to be supposed that the angel who presides over pure syntax took no revenge on this desolater of speech and insulter of the human ear-pan? Yes, indeed; he did: he took Uncle Daniel confidentially by the collar and led him quietly into Jay Gould's office and filled his soul with an ambition to call often. He did so. The old man died in time, and when the parson who had married his daughter because her father was a millionaire looked around, he could n't find a particle of money, stocks, bonds, deeds, or possessions. He called on Jay Gould and inquired about the financial remains of the deceased. "I do not know," remarked Nemesis sympathetically, "that Mr. Drew possessed one dollar when he died."

I once interviewed Henry Clews. He said: "The men who do the most good in the world are not the professional philanthropists, but the great capitalists who keep their money busy in processes of reproduction. The man who equips and keeps going a great factory does more good than he who builds an almshouse; and he who launches a steamship or establishes a railroad confers more benefit on the world than he who endows an asylum. The man who teaches men to help themselves — he is the real benefactor of his kind."

After Senator Stanford went to Washington to represent California under the Capitol dome, I called on him and asked what were the pleasures conferred by wealth.

"It is pleasant to be rich," he frankly said; "to feel that you are beyond the reach of want and can actually do something to relieve the needs of others when you are certain of the case; but the advantages of wealth are greatly overestimated. I am not comparing it with pauperism. The millionaire is infinitely better off than the penniless; but so is the man who is worth ten thousand dollars above his debts. I do not clearly see that a man who can buy anything that he fancies is any better off than a man who can buy what he actually needs. He can more easily gratify his whimsies, to be sure; but there are some positive disadvantages. In the first place, the life he was compelled to lead in order to accumulate wealth has probably prevented that cultivation of taste for art, music, and letters which is essential to the highest enjoyment; and, in the second place, his life is an incessant struggle to keep what he has got and to fight off the competitors who are clutching for it. No man can keep a fortune under his hat or in his pocket; in order to keep it at all it must be scattered here and there widely in business, and he must protect it at arm's length. Probably the man worth one hundred thousand dollars or even fifty thousand enjoys just as much as a millionaire. For my wife and I are worried almost to death by beggars, between whom it is very difficult to discriminate. Most of them are regular 'rounders,' who solicit, implore, entreat, and command that there shall be given to them or sent to them at once a certain stipulated sum of money. Of course there is no pleasure in being thus tormented, and the man of moderate income escapes it. A man's annoyances increase with his wealth."

Probably, if the exact truth were known, "magnates" do not really enjoy life any better than other people; but, as nobody declines the Presidency of the United States, when offered by a majority of the electoral college, so the man possessing the strength of mind to refuse a million dollars in order to avoid worry has yet to be born.

I could easily write fifty interesting pages about Jay Gould. There is a sort of dignity in mere bigness which small men sometimes sorely feel the want of, as Alexander Pope did when he was on his knees before that brilliant coquette, Lady Mary Wortley Montagu. To the rule that master minds inhabit stout bodies Jay Gould was a noted exception. But there are much more striking exceptions. On Wall Street any day one could meet a sturdy Irishman hurrying around — into banks and out again; in among famous stockbrokers; into the mining exchange; into the stock exchange; everywhere busy among the busiest. He wasn't much of an Irishman either; he was notable only for what he carried on his left shoulder — a dwarf with a big head, fine face, sparkling eyes, and no legs to speak of. This burden could not walk or stand, yet he was one of the most successful speculators in Wall Street, and occupied one of the handsomest suites of offices, where several clerks were always busy. He had an accurate judgment, and was a bold dealer, taking large risks every day and keeping afloat on the swirling maelstrom of the Street.

What were we talking of? Oh, yes; Jay Gould. He was no cripple, but he made a host of cripples in his time. And, truly, he was about the thinnest man I ever met. I saw him take the plunge in the Turkish bath at Saratoga. His arms were small, his chest was hollow, his face was tawny and sallow, and his legs! Well, I never before saw such a prominent "bull" that had such insignificant calves. Perhaps — perhaps you could not put a napkin ring over his foot and push it up to his knee; I am not certain. As to his chest, he once told me when I induced him to speak that his mother had a time of it raising him. This was the little man who took the big world by the collar and filled it with terror many a time; whose name was as familiar in Lombard Street as in Wall Street; and who seriously modified for good or evil the fortunes of thousands who never heard his name.

Jay Gould was one of the daintiest eaters I ever saw. He

was often seen at Delmonico's opposite his office, and if he could get a piece of steak as big as his finger — his finger, mind you! — and half a cup of black coffee he was satisfied. If, in addition, he ate a stick of celery and two slices of broiled potato, he called it gorging. His stomach was in a state of semi-rebellion always. It is astonishing how a man, with the very citadel of life occupied by the enemy, could possess such overmastering power. I don't know where Selover went after he had indignantly flung Jay Gould over the railing in Wall Street, but if he had any manliness in him he was thoroughly ashamed of it.

Gould was lucky at the very start — in being born poor. Few Americans are rich at forty unless they had an inheritance of poverty. His great thirst for knowledge developed early, and he took to books as a duck to water. I could n't induce Mr. Gould to tell me much about this period of his life — or, in fact, any other. "I have nothing to say," he protested. "Why should I talk about myself? It does n't seem to me necessary or proper. I am talked about now ten times as much as I want to be or ought to be. I prefer to remain a strictly private citizen."

"You can hardly be that," I took the liberty of suggesting, "unless you go out of Wall Street, out of speculation, and out of business, and put your money into government bonds and live on the interest of it. At present, the public has a right to feel an interest in you."

"Very well, then," he reluctantly conceded, "my boyhood in Roxbury, New York, was about the same as that of other boys round about. I worked on a farm planting and hoeing, going to district school some, doing chores and milking cows. I wanted to go to the academy and, finding that I could do enough odd jobs to pay my own expenses, I asked Father's permission. 'Of course you can go if you want to,' was the natural reply; 'you ain't good for much here.' It was the solemn truth. I was very fond of mathematics and had already discovered that I was not born to be a farmer."

He started for the academy with fifty cents in his pocket. Thirty-two years later, being charged with treacherously selling out his associates, he called them together and laid upon the table stocks and bonds of his own to the value of $35,000-000, as an evidence of solvency and good faith.

The youth became a professional surveyor and civil engineer in his teens, mapped seven New York counties, surveyed a railroad, published a history, started a tannery, in which he employed two hundred and fifty men, built a town, and established a bank and carried it through the panic of 1857 before he was twenty-one.

Mr. Gould was a natural student, and always aspired to be a scholar. Before he had reached middle life he had become by far the best-informed among the wealthy men of the metropolis. His conservatory was stocked with the rare plants of every zone and meridian, for he made a close study of botany and could call most of his plants by name. In conversation he never spoke a word more than was necessary, but was an excellent listener. He seldom went to balls; early saw the emptiness of miscellaneous society; avoided display; never read novels; spent most of his spare time in the large library walled up with five thousand volumes of standard literature of a solid sort.

## XXI

## P. T. BARNUM AT HOME

PHINEAS TAYLOR BARNUM, probably the most famous showman the world has produced, was born at Bethel, Connecticut, and in a farmhouse near by was born my father and, later, myself. Barnum and my father were playfellows throughout their childhood and schoolfellows during their insignificant schooling. In early manhood they were the closest of friends, and for a time their ambitions developed side by side. Hence my acquaintance with the great showman.

If Barnum had been caught up and sent to school by some philanthropic old maid, he would have expanded into an able lawyer and probably a United States Senator from the state. In his teens he exhibited a fierce controversial spirit, and, starting a little newspaper called the Herald of Freedom, was in jail for libel before he was of age. He had already learned the value of appearances, however, and, on the day of his release, was taken from the prison door in a magnificent chariot drawn by six white horses, to the great chagrin of his persecutors. The vehicle was a precursor of the gorgeous bandwagon ultimately provided for "The Greatest Show on Earth."

He started his paper again defiantly; spoke no less disrespectfully of local grandees; dealt in lottery tickets too extensively; discovered the astounding antique, Joice Heth, 161 years old; found and curled the Woolly Horse; manufactured the Feejee Mermaid from a salt codfish and a dead monkey;

and set up in the show business. Extensive advertising made him rich. He made three or four abundant fortunes, and lost them, though managing to preserve one to the last. He always confessed that he dealt in some humbugs and frauds to attract the public to see the genuine and important curiosities, and there is no doubt that he conducted the best museum ever seen — with a highly moral but not very artistic theatre in the attic, where, to an audience of deacons and Sunday-school scholars, the drama was caricatured. He brought Jenny Lind to entrance us, and she sang his pockets full of dollars. He astonished and amused the world with Tom Thumb, and brought home from the royal palaces of Europe more gold than he had ever had visions of in his wildest dreams.

In later years, when he had filled out the Psalmist's allotted span, he developed an ambition to represent the Third District of Connecticut in Congress, and I became his private secretary while he was trying to corner the necessary votes. In that position I made something of a study of his character, ambitions, and environment, and heard with great delight the numerous stories and practical jokes which he always told with equal gusto whether they were in his favor or at his expense. There is little room here for these reminiscences.

In advertising, Barnum's methods were unique. The advent of King Kalakaua in his voyage round the world was synchronous with the annual advent of the Hippodrome in New York City. The great showman, desiring to extend proper hospitality to the ruler of the Sandwich Islands, called on him at the Fifth Avenue Hotel and sent up his card. Fearing that it might be obstructed in its passage, he followed it immediately to the parlor where the King was surrounded by his court. To the illustrious visitor he spoke as follows: "Your Majesty! Welcome, sir, to the magnificent metropolis of America.   By a singular and most fortunate coincidence my splendid Roman Hippodrome will make its first appearance of the season to-morrow afternoon.   I have called to extend to Your Majesty and your suite an invitation to be present at the inauguration exercises."

After some further explanations, the King said he and his friends would be very glad of the opportunity to attend the world-renowned exhibition of the illustrious Mr. Barnum. He asked where the Hippodrome might be found.

"I shall be delighted to have the privilege and the honor of escorting you to the magnificent aggregation," said the audacious Yankee. "You need not order carriages, for I will bring my own, quite sufficient for all." The King thanked him cordially for his attention, and he withdrew.

On the next day, at the unseemly hour of eleven o'clock, Mr. Barnum made his reappearance. With all necessary ceremony he escorted his royal guest down to the private entrance. Emerging to the sidewalk the visitors were astounded to see a gorgeous golden chariot looming high above the pavement and drawn by six superb cream-white steeds. Without hesitation they climbed up the great vehicle and the three other golden chariots that followed, and the curious cortège moved slowly up Fifth Avenue. For two hours it wound through the streets and avenues, for miles, and great was the amusement of the multitudes who read, fastened to the sides of the chariot, immense banners with the words, "His Majesty the King visits Barnum's Hippodrome." The procession arrived at its destination early in the afternoon, where, after a sumptuous breakfast, the illustrious guests were led through the cheering multitudes to the proscenium boxes, the central one of which had been rebuilt for the occasion. It was a lofty and spacious dais, projected towards the centre of the Hippodrome, embowered in vines and roses and surrounded with the interwoven flags of America and Hawaii.  The applause was continuous and tumultuous.  The rest of the entertainment is briefly described by Barnum himself, in his Autobiography, and I quote it thus: —

Some twelve thousand persons were present, and when the exhibitions were about half finished they called loudly, "The King! The King!"  Turning to me, His Majesty inquired the meaning of this.  I replied: "Your Majesty, this vast audience undoubtedly wishes to give you an ovation.  This building is so large that they cannot distinctly see Your Majesty from every part, and are anxious that you should ride round the circle, in order that they may greet you."  The King looked surprised, and presently the audience commenced calling, "The King! Barnum! Barnum! The King!"  At that moment my open barouche was driven into the circle and approached where we were sitting.  "No doubt Your Majesty would greatly gratify my countrymen," I remarked, "if you would kindly step into this carriage with me and ride round the circle."  The King immediately arose, and, amid tremendous cheering, he stepped into the carriage.  I took a seat by his side and he, smiling, remarked sotto voce, "We are all actors."  The audience rose to their feet and cheered and waved their handkerchiefs as the King rode round the circle, raising his hat and bowing.  The excitement was indeed tremendous.  The King remained till all the performances were finished, and expressed himself as greatly pleased with the whole entertainment.

For this remarkable achievement in advertising, the New York Tribune hailed him as "The Cheekiest Living American," and Mr. Barnum at once inserted the compliment in all the handbills and posters.

While living in his Oriental palace, Iranistan, Mr. Barnum and his nearest neighbor, Mr. James D. Johnson, had considerable fun with each other.  Mr. Barnum built a high fence around ten acres near his homestead and introduced to the park a large number of Rocky Mountain elk, moose, reindeer, and the like, converting it into a deer preserve. Strangers generally supposed that it belonged to Johnson, for it was nearest to his house, and to confirm the impression Johnson had a sign painted and nailed over the gate reading, "All persons are forbid trespassing on these grounds or disturbing the deer. J. D. Johnson." The warning remained undisturbed for a week and Barnum's friends joked him about it severely. One day a party of Johnson's friends came from New York to dinner, and he volunteered to show them his deer park. He led them out into the street and down to the gate, where, to his dismay, he discovered that directly under his name the words had been added, "Gamekeeper to P. T. Barnum." Johnson became facetiously known among his friends as Barnum's gamekeeper. Some weeks afterwards Barnum, as president of the Pequonnock Bank, gave his annual dinner to the directors. It was to be a great occasion, and the host had a month before sent West for prairie chickens and venison. As the time for the banquet approached, the box came, marked "P. T. Barnum, Game." And Johnson, seeing it, remarked to the express agent, "Look here! I am Barnum's gamekeeper, and I'll take charge of this box." He did. He had it carried to his house, and notified Barnum that he had it and would release it when he received an invitation to the dinner and an order for a new hat. Barnum was chagrined and hesitated, till Johnson notified him that he himself was about to give a game dinner. Then the showman "came down" as gracefully as he could, and his humorous neighbor, with a new hat, accepted the invitation and dined with the bankers.

I investigated spiritualism, and, taking a deep interest in all occult phenomena and psychic reports, I once asked my

employer why he did not send to Hindostan and get a yogi
or two for exhibition in the United States.

"Yogi?" he repeated, giving the vowels the broad sound,
as I had done. "Oh, you mean the yogee, as they are called"
— pronouncing the word to rhyme with "bogy," as it probably
ought, both in verse and in reason. "Because," he continued,
"there ain't any yogi."

"Do you really mean that, Mr. Barnum?" I asked. "If
you do, and if you are correct, there must be heaps of people
mistaken."

"There are," he replied. "Most everybody is mistaken.
Almost all of the people of the United States think there are
wonderful magicians in India — so much more skillful and
expert than any we can produce as to be virtually miracle
workers.  One of these fellows can call a boy from the audience in an open field, invert a clothes basket over him, plunge
his sword through and through the basket, drenching the
ground with blood within five feet of the horrified and bewildered spectators, then lift the basket, disclosing nothing,
while the uninjured boy leaps to him from an adjoining field!
Oh, he's a great fellow, the yogi is!  He can throw a rope
up into the air, holding it by one end, and climb it till he
disappears in the sky!  He can plant a little seed in a flower-
pot and cause it to spring into a tree in five minutes or less!
This is the way the newspapers describe the feats of a yogi."

"And you think he is a myth, Mr. Barnum?"

"No, I don't think he is; I know he is.  And I'll tell you
how I know.  Five years ago, though I suspected the yarns
about him, I thought they were important enough to investi-
gate.  To track and catch a live yogi seemed to me to require
altogether a different kind of talent from that possessed by the
agent who brought the sacred white elephant from Burmah, or
by Grizzly Adams or Herr Driesbach, my animal catchers

and tamers, so I hired two shrewd and learned Yankees who were also Oriental travelers, and acquainted with the geography and people of India. I gave them all the money they needed to make a comprehensive tour of discovery, instructed them to bring me an assortment of yogis, and authorized them to make contracts to pay fifty dollars a night for each yogi for one year. Some marvelous stories had just been published and I wanted a yogi the worst way.

"Well, my exhibition of yogis has not yet begun. My two agents returned to me with the report that there were no yogis alive in Hindostan and probably never had been. They heard much of yogis, but no money would ever enable them to see one. They chased rumors from Bengal to Calcutta, to Burmah, to Bombay, to Rangoon, to the Ganges, and up the great river through the Punjab, to the Himalayas.

"They advertised that they would pay yogis ten thousand dollars a year salary. They found no yogi anywhere, although they found sleight-of-hand performers somewhat inferior to our own, and large numbers of mahatmas — the Hindoo priests. The Americans and English in the great peninsula informed my agents on the sly that these were all the yogis in existence. They laughed when told of the report that the yogi was a highly sensitive and deeply devout person, — a kind of priest or cardinal of the local church, — who would consider it horrible sacrilege to exhibit himself for money, and I laughed too at the wanderings of my committee, disappointed of finding a genuine yogi in good working order. Yes, it cost me some thousands of dollars — no matter how many — to prove the wonderful miracle-working yogi a myth. The reason I do not exhibit a yogi is the same as the reason I don't exhibit Santy Claus. I can't catch him!"

One day I received a dispatch from Mr. Barnum asking me

to come up to Waldemere, the third of his spacious palaces which he had built in Bridgeport for his home.

I went and found the old showman fierce to enlist once more in the active vocation of his life. About the first words he uttered were "See here! I want you to go and see what I can buy the Eden Musée for."

He alluded to the pretentious stone sepulchre on the north side of Twenty-third Street, near Sixth Avenue, which advertised itself as the magnificent American copy of the great London Waxworks of Madame Tussaud. It was about as much like that really interesting establishment

> As is moonlight unto sunlight
> Or as water unto wine,

and I never knew anything more depressing than a walk through its dismal chambers. It was disorderly, inartistic, and almost totally without interest.

"I don't know who the managers are," said Barnum, "but they seem to be confounded fools. They ought to turn it into an undertaker's establishment. I could double the attractiveness of that place in a week, quadruple it in a month, and in three months make it a collection of curiosities that everybody that comes to New York would have to visit. You know I could. Come! Don't you know it?"

I really had n't a doubt of it, and I told him so.

"I want you to help me about it," he went on. "I would n't give a tinker's damn for it unless it can be a good deal enlarged. It ought to have four or five stories and three times the ground area that it has now. I don't want to be seen poking round there, but I want you to go quietly and secretly and see just how many square feet of real estate there is and what the buildings on both sides and in the rear can be bought for, and if the supporting walls are thick enough to bear being extended a couple of stories higher.   If expansion can be made at a decent cost, the venture will pay big."

That was the substance of his commission, and pretty nearly the language.   I immediately went and inspected the Eden Musée, visited the adjoining stores and property, measured the walls, and made such investigations as I prudently could of the possibilities of enlargement.   Just as I was ready to report progress I got a wire from Waldemere: "All up!  Suspend operations.  Will see you to-morrow." The next day Barnum came down to the Tribune office and explained.  "My hopes are dashed," he said.  "Can't go ahead.  What's the use of having ambition?   Just because I have celebrated my seventieth birthday, my daughters and their husbands think I am a used-up man.   They tell me to my face that this Eden Musée move is wholly speculative and doubtful, and that I am too old to try any new project.   New project!  It ain't a new project.  It's the same old business I've always been in.   I know every twist of it.   I can see my clear path to success in a very short time by renovating that miserable and offensive old rookery.  But I really suppose on figuring it up that I have money enough if I never make another dollar.  And I don't know but I shall let my folks have their own way.  You needn't bother any more unless you hear from me."

That was the end of it.   If it had not been for the protests of his young wife and the rest of his family I think the old man would have renewed his youth on Twenty-third Street and builded there a Museum Eden equal to the Curiosity Paradise of his dreams.

He was not yet quite through active business.   But the only conspicuous act of his remaining years was peculiarly credi-table and characteristic.  When General Grant was robbed by his partners and compelled to go into bankruptcy for all

he possessed, Mr. Barnum called upon him and offered him
a hundred thousand dollars down and another hundred
thousand in commissions to be permitted to exhibit to the
people of the United States "the unique and valuable trophies"
which had been presented to him by all the nations he had
visited in his tour of the globe. He offered to give bonds of
half a million dollars for their safe-keeping and return, and
reminded the General that, though safe deposit for them
might be found in Washington, a traveling exhibition of them
was the only way in which the great mass of the people in the
United States could ever see them. The proposition was
honorable, but other means were found to recoup the General for his losses. Vanderbilt lent him $150,000 and he
pushed his Memoirs to rapid completion, by which his widow
received checks for $400,000.

Barnum was one of the most entertaining humbugs that
ever bewitched a free people. He imposed on the public
with delightful frankness, holding the article up and exclaiming, "Now I'm fooling you; look out!" But he gave his
patrons thrice the worth of their money. In certain matters
he was a genuine reformer, knowing more about farming
than Horace Greeley, more about "no hell" than Reverend
E. H. Chapin, his minister, did, and more about temperance,
or even intemperance, than Gough. And if he attempted to
exaggerate the bulk of his elephants, the agility of his
monkeys, the amity of his "Happy Family," the moral
tendency of his ballet, and the deadly nature of his anacondas,
he was only vividly illustrating the characteristics of the age
and the land that produced him.

## XXII

### INVENTORS

I AM doubtful about the month, and not quite certain whether the year was 1881 or 1882, but it was sometime while I was still in the service of the Tribune that Mr. Reid said to me one morning, "You are fond of exploiting novelties and there is one up at the Union League Club that is worth some attention. A man named Muybridge of San Francisco has turned a trick that seems rather curious. He has demonstrated by photography that the movements of a horse, especially the movements of a horse going at full speed, are altogether different from what they have generally been supposed to be."

I asked Mr. Reid if we did n't know what we saw with our own eyes. "No," he answered, "that is just what Muybridge says, and apparently proves — that the human eye is very fallible and, in noting moving objects, is generally mistaken."

The assignment puzzled me, but I was still more puzzled when I reached the rooms of the Union League. There, against a wall, was arranged a large canvas showing a horse of life size in postures so conspicuously awkward that it seemed as if no horse ever seen could have stood for such a photograph. Mr. Muybridge explained that this was an exact reproduction of the attitudes of a race horse in full action, and that the attitudes presented in pictures of the Derby, in equestrian statues, and in the races in the Roman amphitheatre, were really caricatures of the actual movements of a horse. He continued to explain that the photograph before us was obtained by stretching a cord across the track which, when touched by the running horse, released the shutter of the camera, cutting the picture off at the instant of exposure. The exposure was for about the thirtieth part of a second, and the result was a picture due to what is scientifically called "persistence of vision." That is, the object was exposed before the camera just exactly long enough to present it in full, but to avoid mixing the attitudes.

This was very strange to me, and when I went back to the office with my short narrative it seemed quite as incomprehensible to Mr. Reid. Indeed, to him it seemed little short of incredible, and he said, "Had n't you better run over and see Edison?"

I was over at the magician's "den" early the next morning and told him of the problem that confronted us.

"Oh, yes," he said. "I have heard of Muybridge and the curious results he has obtained. It is due to the power of the retina to retain a picture for an infinitesimal portion of a second before it is overlaid and wiped out by the succeeding impression. We all know of instances of this. Go and look at my flywheel yonder and you will see that it moves faster than the eye can follow. When viewed from a distance at the side the space where the spokes fly seems to be merely an unbroken disk, but wink your eyes as rapidly as possible, and you will cut that disk up into segments and get a picture of individual spokes, seen as if they were standing still. The same phenomenon can be seen on any rapidly moving wagon wheel. You might have obtained the same impression also from the cars while coming out here — that is, a picture on the retina resulting from persistence of vision. The fence enclosing that large open field is of upright slats six inches wide with an inch or so between them. While you are standing still that fence seems about as solid as a dead wall, but seen from the window of a flying train, the retina receives a multitude of pictures and carries them from one opening in the fence to another till the fence itself almost seems to be translucent or to vanish, plainly revealing the objects in the background. Persistence of vision retains an impression the one-twentieth or one-thirtieth part of a second, so that by cutting off preceding and succeeding impressions, Muybridge succeeds in giving us the picture of an actual horse instead of the imaginary horse that artists have accustomed us to observe. Muybridge's horse seems a crippled and distorted creature, but it is the real thing. Whirling a red-hot stick in a dark room shows that sight lasts after the mechanical action which produced it has ceased. The familiar toy, the zootrope, shows the same thing."

Before I left the building, Mr. Edison added, "I have been thinking of a way in which Muybridge's experiments could be utilized. By making the pictures succeed each other in the camera with sufficient rapidity, there is no reason in the world why a succession of moving pictures could not be thrown upon a canvas by means of a lantern so as to appear absolutely lifelike."

The suggestion seemed full of splendid possibilities, and I asked the inventor to tackle it.

"I am too busy," he said. "It would require a heap of money and time to develop it. I am full of other projects. I know it can be done, but I could not at this moment indicate the details of the device. Receptive cameras would have to be whirled before the moving objects with tremendous rapidity, perhaps fastened on the periphery of a wheel twelve or twenty feet in diameter — or more or less. I can forecast the result with approximate accuracy, but how it would be done can be told only by experiment. It is a grand

idea, though," he added, "and somebody will make it practicable."

"It certainly would be magnificent," I ventured to say, "to
have a moving scene between the acts of a theatre — Niagara
Falls, for instance, falling through the proscenium arch above
the footlights."

I carried dazzling dreams from Edison's laboratory that
night, and though possessing no mechanical ingenuity myself, I felt that somehow, sometime, by somebody, persistence
of vision was destined to become one of the world's popular
entertainers.

For thirty years I have had the privilege of a rather intimate
acquaintance with Thomas A. Edison, and have been greatly
interested in the development of his genius.   I first met him in
the '70s in his laboratory at Menlo Park.   His constant
handling of tools and manipulation of machinery had made
him necessarily careless of his personal appearance, and when
I first saw him he was robed in a striped bed ticking from
neck to heels and looked very much like an overgrown farm
boy dressed for a sack race at an agricultural fair.

He has been so closely confined in the shop that his health
has suffered somewhat at times, but he is stronger than the
average man.   The report going the rounds that "Edison is
dying" is true only in the sense in which it applies to all living
things.   He never was more alive.   He used to be as thin as
an April shad or an evening shadow, dreadfully sallow, and
wearing considerable lampblack or other pigment on his
face, but in time he became solid and plump, weighed nearly
two hundred pounds, was rosy, and looked as if he might
live a century.   Some twenty years ago he had a superfluous
hole in his head somewhere over the ear, but it grew up for
lack of function.   He may have lost a handful of brains, but

he would n't miss them, for he still wears a seven-and-a-half hat.

"I shall die sometime," he said cheerfully, when I last saw him; "that is, I suppose I shall, for people have got into that pernicious habit; but I mean to have a good slice of the twentieth century. If I depart soon, it will be through inadvertence. I am of tough stock. My father was ninety-five; my grandfather was one hundred and three, and my great-grandfather was one hundred and seven when they shuffled off." I asked Mr. Edison what was the present tendency of invention.

"The next great invention, I think," he said, "is likely to be the turning of coal into motive power without the mediation of steam. I am now at work on a machine called the pyro-magnetic dynamo for this purpose — to get electricity directly from coal. Almost all of our available energy is in wood and coal. We get it out at a terrible waste. As four-fifths of the heat in a fireplace goes up the chimney, so about three-fourths of the energy in coal is lost in getting at the other fourth. Coal can be turned immediately into electricity — I have demonstrated that — and I shall know shortly whether it can be done commercially — that is, without costing more than it comes to. If this can be realized, a steamer that now burns five hundred tons of coal a day will burn fifty instead. But perhaps by that time we shall coax electricity out of the air instead of out of the earth, and that will be cheaper still."

"When motive power gets to be four times as cheap as it is, Mr. Edison, what will become of the laboring man?"

"He will be enriched by it, of course. Machinery will be his slave, instead of his associate and assistant. Workmen now get double the wages they did forty years ago, and the necessities of life cost less than half as much. A hand-worker can to-day buy four times as much with ten hours of labor as his father could forty years ago. For the first time in the world's history a skilled mechanic can buy a barrel of flour with a single day's work. The machinery in the United States represents the labor of a thousand million men — or fifty times as much power as all the men in the country. It is terrible stupidity that leads laboring men to suppose that machinery is their foe. It is the only thing which gives them independence or even freedom. Without machinery, society would drift into the condition of master and slave, as it was formerly; the multiplication of machinery means for every worker more food, better clothes, better schooling, better shelter, more leisure. Machinery is to solve the labor question."

"What I want to find out, Mr. Edison, is what sort of new contraption to invest in to make some money."

"That is easily answered," said the inventor. "Invest in anything that is new and mysterious and excites attention on that account, and sell out as soon as it begins to drop. I could make a diagram of the lines which a new and mysterious invention generally follows. To make money, buy a little in the stock of new inventions and schemes that excite surprise, and are not understood. Such stock will climb up the line — gradually, to begin with, then rising with a jump towards the top. The top is reached when it is ascertained by actual experiment just how much a thing is actually worth as an investment. Then the imagination loses its grip and the thing falls. The price always rises as long as it is thought that the investor may possibly get fifty dollars for one dollar. When it is found that he will get only five dollars for one dollar, it drops — drops below what it is actually worth, probably. Sell when it wiggles and starts to go down; buy again when it stops. That's the idea."

"Are people fools, Mr. Edison?" I asked.

"What people? It depends on which people you mean. A good many folks — you'd be astonished at the number — will pay five dollars for one chance in a thousand to win one hundred dollars. In Wall Street it is easier to sell stock in a gold mine in Borneo or Kamschatka than in New Jersey, because one has unknown possibilities, and those of the other are easily ascertained. Most people don't like to buy certainties. They prefer castles in Spain to cabins in Staten Island."

"Probably the experience of loss teaches them at last," I suggested.

"A little. Yes, it teaches individuals, but not the human race. The trouble is — and it complicates everything — that there are young men coming to maturity every minute who want to see the folly of it, just as their fathers did, and a complete new set supersedes the old set every thirty years and imitates it very closely indeed. So human nature is a calculable quantity. This gives liars an enormous advantage. If a mountebank should come forth to-morrow with a secret and mysterious machine for making food from air, or gold from water, I have no doubt that he would sell any quantity of stock. This sets the alchemist up in business."

The inventor kindly showed me his outfit — the most complete laboratory in the world. Any experiment relating to anything of which we have any knowledge can be tried here speedily, for Mr. Edison has ordered a supply of every known substance in the world. In his book containing orders there are indicated 14,000 kinds of chemicals; every variety of nail and screw made, every sized needle and pin, every kind of cord and wire made, hair of humans, horses, hogs, cows, goats, rabbits, minks, buffalo, camels; all skins that are ever removed from animals and used; silk of every texture; cocoons, all kinds of hoofs, sharks' teeth, deer horns, tortoise shell, cork, resin, glass, varnish, oils, ostrich feathers, a peacock's tail, jet, amber, coral, rubber, paper, meerschaum, all ores and metals, a fair epitome of the material world.

One morning in 1878 when I arrived at Mr. Edison's laboratory, on what I had come to consider my occasional tours of inspection, I was surprised to find a crowd of twenty or thirty men in a waiting attitude, discussing some interesting event about to take place. They were mostly civil, mechanical, and electrical engineers, and the event to witness which they were assembled was, as Edison had called it in the few invitations sent out, "an experiment in telegraphing without a wire."

An engine hauling three cars was standing on an adjacent track, and the visitors were invited to "get aboard." The train looked like any other train, except that along the summit of the roof of each car was set a running board a foot wide standing on its edge, and coated with tin foil. Along the side of the track, twenty or thirty feet from the train, were the usual poles carrying the usual telegraphic wire. There was no visible connection between the wire and our train.

Presently we started. Mr. Edison came through the cars and announced that the train was now by induction in communication with the world, and all of his guests were invited to send dispatches to their homes or elsewhere by availing themselves of the operator sitting at a keyboard in each car where the battery was connected with the running tin foil on the roof. The invitation was generally accepted, the inventor walking through the car and explaining in some detail the *modus operandi.* Without resorting to the terminology of electrical science, it may be said that messages hopped as if by magic from the car roof to the distant telegraphic wire, and the answers leaped back through the air to the train; and it was afterwards learned that some of the messages were received in New York before the train reached its destination.

I do not know whether this was actually the first wireless telegraph ever constructed; but I do know that Edison holds the patent for it, that it was a tremendous surprise to all who witnessed its performances that day, and that the Wizard of Menlo Park was widely and warmly congratulated on confuting the allegation of Solomon that "there is no new thing under the sun."

Before his guests left the laboratory the inventor invited them to "come up Wednesday morning" and take a ride on his "electric wagon." This had a novel sound and the response was unanimous and hearty. The thing we found awaiting us was a nondescript vehicle — merely an old engine drawing a railroad truck rudely equipped with uprights for passengers to hold on by. The track consisted of two iron rails laid over the undulations of Menlo Park without the least grading, and as it jolted, jerked, and careened up hill and down, almost without a break, the tumbling together of the passengers produced an effect the reverse of reassuring. Our host was perfectly composed and enthusiastic. He stood on the bow of the queer cart, holding on to a stick which he called a brake, and cried, "Now we're going to start!" "Now look out!" "Lean to the right!" "Now hang on!" "Lean to the left!" And up hill and down dale, plunging and pitching, we went whirling, obeying the injunction, "Hold on tight!" We went fast. It seemed perilous. It was not a very easy or comfortable ride, and as Edison jerked at the emergency brake he shouted to the passengers and seemed like a boy with a new toy. Nobody was killed by the skidding and jouncing, and only one man was thrown off, being picked up again uninjured. The two parallel rails, spiked to the soft and uneven ground, made probably the worst track that ever carried wheels. As the exhibitor brought the strange vehicle again to rest at the laboratory door there was universal acclaim that in 1878 we had ridden on the first electric car, doubtless the forerunner of myriads.

Sitting Bull and his chiefs went over to Edison's laboratory one Sunday. He put electricity through its paces for their benefit. The old theory that savages are never astonished at anything will have to be abandoned, or at least modified. Nothing astonishes them as long as they suppose it to be supernatural; only when they are told that men produce the results without aid from any spirit do they begin to show surprise. Lightning never surprises an Indian as long as he supposes that it is only the flight of the angry thunder bird swooping down for a victim; but when told that it is only a force that man can capture and tame and bottle up and turn on his wires, then he shows astonishment. Tribes that attribute everything to miracle are, of course, never surprised, for nothing can happen that is wholly unexpected. Sitting Bull was shown the enormous dynamo and told that it was the thunder bird. He was shown the incandescent bulb, but would not believe that it would glow in the water till he had actually taken it out and put it in the vessel himself, and then tasted of the water, when he expressed the opinion that Edison was the greatest man in the world. "Damn big!" remarked Spotted Horn in good commercial English. He asked Edison to let him test the battery, "like a white man." A good charge was turned on, and when the thunder bird got hold of the simple infant of the forest, he refused to let go. When the red man was at last released he violently expectorated the bitterness out of his mouth and yelled, "Yeouch!" so that he could be heard a mile.

## XXIII

## A MAN OF CONFIDENCE: JAMES WATSON WEBB

I CALLED upon General James Watson Webb during the last
year of his life, 1884. I knew him as the only survivor of the
great New York editors whose careers began about the time
that the telegraph was added to news facilities, — Bennett,
Greeley, Webb, Weed, Bryant, Brooks, and Raymond. He
was famous also, not only as the owner and editor of the great
Whig newspaper, the Courier and Enquirer, but as the man
who established a daily horse express between New York
and Washington that cost him $7,500 a month, and enabled
him to beat his rivals. Like most old men, he delighted to
talk about the distant past — the events of his boyhood and
youth. It was not the first time I had dropped in to inquire
about his health. He and Mrs. Webb were playing whist
with double dummies. I apologized for intruding on the
finest game in the world, and inquired how they managed
to make two dummies behave.

"It is exasperating," the old gentleman laughed, "but we
keep their faces down so that we are all blind together and it
is amusing to see how much intelligence dummies can show.
The calm impudence with which they trump your ace when
you know perfectly well that they have in hand three or four
cards of the suit, is irritating, especially if the rebellious
dummy happens to be your own partner. And Sarah Battle
gives us no rules for managing him."

General Webb was easily led to talk about the past.

"I was just turned seventeen," he said, "when the first important event in my active life happened. I had been sent away from home to work in my uncle's store; but I did n't like it. I had dreams of glory. One of my old cronies had got into the army, and it stirred my father's blood in me. I went home and told my folks. They violently opposed the fancy, said it was madness in me to think of such a thing, and, anyhow, nobody could get into the army except graduates of West Point. I must stick right to my work, they said, if I ever expected to amount to anything. A rolling stone would gather no moss. I listened, but did n't give up. I went back to my uncle's next day, packed a few things in a handkerchief, and left without saying good-bye. I hurried to Albany and called at once on Governor De Witt Clinton, whom I had often seen at my father's.

"He looked surprised to see me, for it was something for a boy to get to Albany in those days. He was very cordial to me, though, I remember, and took me by the hand and asked how my mother was and the folks at home. I didn't want him to think me the runaway that I was, so I answered glibly that they were well and wished to be remembered. Doubtless the recording angel's tear has long since blotted out that lie. He asked what he could do for me, and I replied that he could get me an appointment as lieutenant in the United States army. He looked at me very gravely and said, 'Young man, do you know what you have asked for? Such places are not to be had. You had better go right home again, quick!'

"I told the Governor that I would not do that, and he finally found out the truth — that I had run away. I had just money enough to go to Washington, I told him, if he would give me a letter to John C. Calhoun, President Monroe's Secretary of War.

"'Calhoun!' he cried out: 'why, Calhoun and I have had a quarrel. We are not on speaking terms. I could n't possibly ask a favor of him. I'll give you a general letter, though, saying that you are a son of my old friend, General Samuel R. Webb, Washington's aide de camp, but I can ask nothing of Calhoun.'

"So it was agreed; and I started off for Washington by stagecoach with a throbbing heart, a thin pocket-book, and a letter of introduction to whom it might concern.

"Reaching the capital I sent in my letter to Secretary Calhoun and waited. No reply. I waited and waited. At last, after several days, I got into his room and made myself known. He asked what I wanted. 'A commission in the army, if you please,' I said.

"He answered bluntly but kindly that such a thing was impossible; that I was not in the line of appointment; that the school at West Point had been established for the very purpose of preparing young men for the army; that there were no vacant commissions to be had anyway, and that when there were any the West Point cadets had the first claim.

"I told Mr. Calhoun that it seemed to me that was not the correct view to take of it; that the government educated these young men at its own expense; that the government was under no conceivable obligation to them, but they were under the deepest obligation to it for their education and support; that they owed a duty to the government, but could have no claim on it, because they had done nothing for it, and that, if anybody could be said to have a 'claim', it was the sons of Revolutionary soldiers, like myself, whose fathers had given years to the service of the country and who had been educated up to the required West Point standard without costing the national treasury a cent.

"This view seemed to set **Mr. Calhoun** thinking; perhaps

it was novel to him. He asked me a good many questions about myself and catechized me about my education, but ended by saying that the appointment I asked for was out of the question.

"I asked him if he would hold the matter in suspension till I could lay my views before him in writing. He said he would. I went back to my hotel, where I had spent about my last dollar, and committed to writing my idea of the nation's 'obligations' to the youth at West Point. Next morning I called again and handed it personally to Secretary Calhoun.

"I waited two days — two endless, interminable days — for a summons — and at last it came. The Secretary asked me some more questions, gave me a lot of good advice, and ended by appointing me second lieutenant in the United States army if I could pass the requisite examination. You may guess how pleased I was. My feet were light as feathers when I walked out.

"I passed that examination, and that's the way I got into the army. There was, of course, no precedent for such an appointment, and perhaps no other boy has ever got into the army without an introduction and a voucher.

"The country was at peace, but the young officers offset this by plenty of personal quarrels. I was known as 'Calhouns' scrub lieutenant', and during seven years I fought two duels and narrowly escaped two more."

I asked General Webb about his service in the army, whether it was agreeable and how he came to resign.

"I was at Detroit, when there were four thousand inhabitants; at Saint Louis when there were a thousand or two, and at Chicago when there was not a white resident, nor one within a hundred miles. In January, 1822 — why, that's some time ago, is n't it? — a friendly Pottawottamie chief brought into camp a piece of tobacco sent to him by the

Sioux chief, with an invitation to his tribe to join in cutting off the Fifth Regiment of Infantry, then stationed at Fort Snelling. This was at Detroit, and I was adjutant of the post. I was ordered to find somebody to carry a letter to Fort Armstrong on the Mississippi, and get relief sent to Colonel Snelling, with whose command there were many women and children. There were no white inhabitants within 180 miles of us, and the friendly Indians declined to go. Colonel Mc-Neil, in charge, said he did n't want to detail anybody for such a dangerous mission, so I resigned my adjutancy and volunteered to go. I left within four days, accompanied only by a sergeant and an Indian guide. The fourth day out we got to Rock River ford, and here, lying in the bushes, we overheard the Winnebagoes planning an attack on Fort Armstrong, to which we were bound. We eluded them and, though my guide deserted us, I pressed on with the sergeant. It was 27° below zero at Fort Armstrong. The Winnebagoes gave chase and even surrounded the fort before we could get there, but we crept through their lines and joined our friends in safety. Our guide, who went back, reported that we were ambushed, and I was lamented as killed by the Indians."

Webb remained in the army eight years, having a rather monotonous service. In 1827 he resigned his commission, went to New York and plunged into the newspaper business. The transfer at that time was scarcely a change of occupation, for the Indians were hardly more ferocious than the New York editors of that decade. To my question about these gentlemen General Webb said, "Yes, it was pretty rough sometimes. Bennett was on my paper. He wrote short, jerky exclamations rather than sentences, and I always had to amend his copy. Henry J. Raymond was the most useful man I ever had. A friend came to me and said, 'There's a very bright, smart young fellow up in the Tribune office working for twelve dollars a week, and he wants to get married and can't afford it. Why don't you get him?' I hired Raymond and a most capable and accomplished man I found him. He could do anything on a newspaper, and do it to perfection. Greeley was much more grieved than I was when Thurlow Weed and some other conservatives established the Times for Raymond. He probably felt like Byron's eagle — something about Kirke White, was n't it?

> 'Keen were his pangs, but keener far to feel
> He nursed the pinion that impelled the steel;
> Viewed his own feather on the fatal dart,
> And winged the shaft that quivered in his heart.'"

I bade the old gentleman good night, apologized to the lady, for the interruption, and by the time I was on the pavement both the dummies were doubtless up and at it again.

A large part of the secret of Webb's success was his magnificent reliance upon himself. He treated his own conclusions on all subjects as if they were infallible. It was said in England that Lord John Russell held so high an opinion of his own talents that "he would accept command of the Channel fleet at ten minutes' notice." General Webb could have given Lord John odds. There was no station that he thought too difficult for himself. The same audacity which led him to ask Calhoun to make him an army officer in defiance of all precedent, led him in 1861 to ask Lincoln to make him a major-general. The President was not willing to take such chances and appointed him brigadier-general. Webb indorsed the commission "Respectfully declined," and sent it back. Mr. Seward sent him his appointment as Minister to Constantinople. It was declined with the same indorsement.

He finally accepted an appointment to Rio Janeiro. Here

again he relied supremely on his intuitions. Though he had never been in the diplomatic service and had never traveled in South America, he made no inquiries of an ex-Minister or any consul; he studied no manual; he did not even examine the laws he was expected to execute. Instead of collecting the monster tomes of Grotius, Puffendorf, and Vatel, he did not carry with him a single page relating to the difficult technique of his duties, but he took one hundred and fifty volumes of select novels.

He felt himself fully equipped for every emergency that could possibly arise in life. When he started off he said to a friend: "Mr. Lincoln would have done a wise thing for himself and a good thing for the country if he had made me a major-general. Having originated the theory of the conduct of the war which the government has accepted and on which the armies are now acting, it would be absurd for me to be in a subordinate position. I would have divided the forces of the United States into three columns, to move southward simultaneously — one via Richmond, one via the Mississippi, and one through Atlanta. This very plan is now being executed, and there is not the slightest doubt that in four months at farthest the rebellion will have been terminated and the leading insurgents will have expiated their crimes on the gallows!"

With this impression he sailed away to Brazil. He went to his post of duty preferably by way of Europe, and Mr. Seward made him useful on the way. When Louis Napoleon was exiled by King Louis Philippe in 1836, he sought and found refuge in New York City. General Webb told me about meeting him:

"Yes, sir; I was at dinner at Delmonico's, opposite Stewart's down town store on City Hall Park," he said, "when the fugitive, Mr. Napoleon, sent up his card with a letter of introduction. I received him, and insisted on his staying to dinner, considerably against his inclination. I suppose he felt he was intruding. After that he was often at our house and we got well acquainted. He was phlegmatic and a little stolid and even sleepy, but when roused he was full of fancies, not exactly visionary, perhaps, but an eccentric philosopher. I didn't suppose he would really ever mount the throne. While he was here he was never the roué he was afterwards said to be and I have always defended him from such slanders.

"On my way to Brazil I called on Louis Napoleon at President Lincoln's request, and urged him not to interfere with our blockade of the southern ports. We met at Fontainebleau and had a most satisfactory interview. It was said that the purpose of the Emperor was changed during that conversation; at any rate, he promised not to interfere to aid the rebellion, at the very time, too, when Americans were filled with apprehension and the French cotton mills were suffering. 'Tell the President,' said the Emperor, 'that France will recognize the blockade.'

"It was in 1863 that the Mexican trouble became annoying. The French troops had overrun the country and offered the crown to Maximilian. I wrote to the Emperor, respectfully protesting against his conduct. I told him he had made a serious mistake, that the United States would never consent to his plans, and that he would be defeated. As a friend I urged him to withdraw. Two months later I got from him a long and courteous letter, explaining just how he got into the scrape and promising to withdraw his troops as soon as practicable. This I sent to Mr. Lincoln.

"When I returned from Rio I received at Lisbon a dispatch from the Emperor urging me to visit Paris. I did so, and there was met with a command to breakfast with him at Saint Cloud. I went; and after breakfast a long conference was had, the result of which was a specific agreement to get out of Mexico at a particular date named. That agreement was exactly executed."

During his diplomatic career he never allowed anybody to say a single word in a slighting tone of the United States. The British minister, Mr. Christie, said something at a card table in a tone which Webb objected to, at which a blow and a challenge passed and Mr. Christie had to apologize or fight. He chose the former alternative. Webb's distinguishing characteristic as a minister was great courtliness and stateliness of bearing. This was so marked that it would have seemed in some men an affectation, but it suited his manner and he was always something of a formalist. I learned to look upon him as one of "the last of the Barons." He was a great reader. He told me he would give $100 if he had not read one of Bulwer's novels. Why? So that he could again have the delight of reading it afresh! There was one saying of his which had a formative influence on me: "All facts," he said, "are valuable. Do not lose one, however apparently trivial. Somewhere, sometime, it will find its place."

I asked him about his duels — those in the army, that with Tom Marshall in which he was shot in the knee, that between Graves and Cilley, in which Cilley was killed, and other affairs to which he was a party.

"The killing of Cilley," he answered, "was a horrible affair — a deplorable mistake — and the men engaged in it ought to have prevented it. They eluded me, or I would have stopped it. I took my rifle and scoured the woods around Bladensburg for them and if I had found them, the meeting — at least that meeting — would not have taken place. I have changed my mind about duelling, and do not now regard it as a personal right. I believe it should be resorted to only in behalf of an insulted country or an afflicted people."

On whichever side he enlisted General Webb was a red-hot adversary. For many years he hated the abolitionists intensely and when Wendell Phillips went to New York to speak Webb shouted in every column and paragraph, as the law-abiding incendiary did in London, "Don't nail his ears to the pump." When the war broke out at last he was just as dogmatic on the antislavery side. Yet this man was not Bombastes Furioso. He not only talked, threatened, and promised, but he did things. He secured the settlement of long standing claims against Brazil, and was one of the principal agents in inducing the French emperor to withdraw his army from Mexico.

That evening with the double dummies was the last time I ever saw General Webb. He was a very distinguished looking man. He was more than six feet tall. His hair, thin at the apex, blossomed out upon each side of his head into a lily-white chrysanthemum, and a mass of English whiskers, white as snow, flanked his pink face, illumined by a pair of blue eyes under heavy black eyebrows at the base of a forehead as majestic as Walter Scott's.

# XXIV

## TRIALS OF A BIOGRAPHER AND EDITOR

In December of 1885 William H. Vanderbilt died. I was not a little surprised one morning shortly afterward to receive the following dispatch from Chicago: —

Will you write a history of the Vanderbilt family for $———, manuscript to be delivered in six weeks?

Belford, Clarke, & Co.

Being a newspaper man in active service, and accustomed to hurry orders, I, of course, answered at once, "Yes."

Then I went and found out who Belford, Clarke & Company were. Publishers. Successful. Large business. In good standing.

The next mail brought from them a letter confirming the liberal offer, but it scarcely increased my knowledge of what was wanted. It repeated the general proposition and added as a specific condition, "The biography must be written for the public and not for the Vanderbilts." Beyond that one proviso the entire family history seemed to be left to my discretion.

An hour later found me at the portal of the great offices of the New York Central Railroad, where I sent my card to Mr. Cornelius Vanderbilt, the head of the family since the death of his father a fortnight before, intimating my business. The card was intercepted by Mr. Depew, to whom I was slightly known, and into whose presence I was now ushered.

"I don't know as the publication of such a book is worth while," he said. "But I see no objection if you make yourself certain of your facts."

"That 's what I am here for," I rejoined; "to get a verification of facts."

He laughed and said, "You 've taken an immense contract. There is nobody here who knows enough of either the Commodore or his son to produce such a work."

I was somewhat taken aback, but rallied and remarked, "I can certainly get the framework of such a biography as the public wants from magazines and from newspapers of dates concurrent with the most famous financial and industrial achievements of the great Commodore. What I especially need is an opportunity to verify this and something of the harmless private and personal chronicle — the obscure incidents — the amusing trivialities — the dialogue, if may be, which eludes the casual search and is generally perhaps known only to the participants."

"Yes," said the new President of the Central, "if you could get enough of that sort of thing it would make an interesting book, sure!" and he laughed vociferously.

To encourage his facetious mood I added, "I can put my finger on enough of such matter already to ensure success, and I hope the volume may owe some of its excellencies to the Commodore's old friend and attorney."

"Meaning me?" he asked, lifting his shaggy brows.

I acquiesced.

"If I had time," he answered, "and a taste for that sort of thing — which I have n't. But I tell you what I will do. I 'll take you in and see what Mr. Cornelius Vanderbilt says about it."

A colored servitor pulled open a door and I followed the new President into a snug back room where I was presented to the head of the Vanderbilt family. To him Mr. Depew briefly explained my errand. Mr. Vanderbilt surprised me and disappointed me by saying, "You will certainly have to seek elsewhere for information. I really know little of my father and almost nothing of my grandfather, and I doubt if my brother William K. knows much more than I. You see we have never worked in the same office or in the same business till lately, and most of our knowledge and impressions have been obtained from others. Mr. Depew will no doubt help you all he can." And with a bow he turned to his desk.

"I 'll tell you what we 'll do," said Mr. Depew. "Go ahead with your book. When a chapter is in type, send me the galley proof and we will immediately revise it and return it to you. As to fundamental facts and statistics, our Mr. Rossiter will be able to help you."

This seemed a workable proposition. An hour later found me at the Astor Library deeply immersed in magazine indexes and the files of the Tribune, Herald, Sun, Evening Post, and Times for twenty years. There for a month I spent a part of almost every day. My pockets were plethoric with memorandum books, and these I crowded with data. Wherever I found the name of Vanderbilt or the roads that a Vanderbilt had created, my pencil spiked the recorded fact.

In a few days after my call at the Vanderbilt offices the first chapter was in type and a galley proof of it was sent up to Mr. Depew. The next day it was returned to me with no changes whatever made or suggested. This looked very hopeful, and I submitted a second chapter, trusting that it might prove as acceptable. It proved too much to expect. The work of elision had promptly begun. There were not only questions and suggestions, but important erasures. The blue pencil had gone relentlessly through an entire paragraph concerning the genealogy, manners, and vigorous — perhaps too vigorous — speech of the old Commodore. If he had been living, I am sure that the frank if not pleasant picture of him would not have been effaced. He would have let it stand, for he would have seen that it was just and accurate, and he had not a particle of the vanity of little men. "Here," he once cried to a photographer, "don't you rub out the wrinkles and paint me up that way! I ain't particularly pretty, as I know of, but I'm damned if I'll travel in disguise."

Nor was his less vigorous son, the farmer of New Dorp, Staten Island, by any means a dilettante or prude. I do not believe that William H., if living, would have insisted on endowing his rugged father with a fanciful character or the family with romantic virtues which they never claimed to possess. But the virile creators of the vast fortune were dead, and "the boys" who had come lately into the inheritance insisted that the family chariot should thenceforth travel in the ruts of conventionality.

I revised the galleys liberally in accordance with slight suggestions indicated in the margins, but restored the unwelcome paragraph. I then returned the proof to Mr. Depew with the explanation that the volume was to be published wholly for the public and not for any private individual; that if the expunged paragraph was untruthful, it would be canceled or amended on its inaccuracy being shown; that nothing offensive would be admitted to the pages, and that the subjects of the biography would be treated with respect, even should it sometimes be necessary to criticize their methods of dealing with the public. I then asked that I be furnished with reasons why the deleted paragraph should be omitted. I waited, — waited long, — but received no answer. Our collaboration was at an end. My galley proof was destroyed or thrown away. I made no further effort to secure the coöperation I had sought. The volume was not only written but printed wholly in the interest of the public, without partiality or prejudice and uninfluenced by rich or poor; and whatever errors crept into the volume of 310 pages — *The Vanderbilts and the Story of Their Fortune* — are not chargeable to the sensitiveness of its subjects.

I never held the duel in high esteem as a wise method of settling controversies, and I had even less confidence in it after it was offered to me. I had been sitting in the editorial chair of the Washington Post for six or eight months when the opportunity occurred. The owner of the paper, Mr. Stilson Hutchins, was in Europe, but I was well acquainted with the convolutions of his remarkable brain, and I well knew that he would kick an intruder downstairs or fling him out of the window rather than do so idiotic a thing as to fight a duel.

A Culpeper politician, Colonel Barker, who had just done time as Governor of Virginia, now aspired to a seat in Congress, from the Eighth District, just across the Potomac from Washington. While making a very fervent and feverish canvass, and having some breath still left, he stepped over into his country's capital and advertised a meeting where he could pour out his woes and wants to a Washington audience. It promised to be rather a spectacular and preposterous affair, as nobody in Washington had a ballot of any kind to cast, and even if they were permitted to vote they would not have voted in Virginia. I assigned to the meeting a young reporter bubbling over with merriment, named Boyle, merely remarking to him incidentally, "You may get some fun out of it." The hint was sufficient. He did. Indeed I was astonished at the amount of fun which he managed to extract, and I laughed over it when it appeared in the morning. It was a half column of political banter, persiflage, and good-natured satire — ironical, but without a particle of bitterness in it. When Boyle came in to get his assignment for the day, I congratulated him on the performance.

Shortly after he left, two strangers appeared and walked straight to my desk. Without any ceremony the foremost said, "We are from Virginia. P'raps you can guess what we came fer."

I answered that I had not the slightest idea, and motioned them to be seated. They declined.

"Ye 're the editor, we 're told," the spokesman said.

"I am officiating just now."

"Did yese write that article?" inquired he, laying the offending print under my nose.

I replied that his right to ask such a question was not admitted, but to relieve his mind I was willing to say that I did not write it.

"Are yese any way at all responsible for it?" persisted the speaker, evidently a citizen imported from the evergreen isle.

"Yes, I suppose I am," I answered; "that is, I sent the reporter to write it."

"You did, did you?" said my interlocutor in a quarrelsome tone and attitude. "Well, did you know that yese have insulted and vilely slandered one of the finest men on God's footstool — the late Governor of Virginia?"

I answered that I was not aware of it: that the article he had indicated with his finger was a playful and facetious expression, but quite harmless — not at all intended to skin Governor Barker, but only to promote the gayety of nations. He picked up the article and pointed to some amusing sentences, sarcastically adding, "Oh, yes, certain! Damn funny, ain't it?"

I insisted that it was, and called his attention to the fact that there was not an epithet or a syllable of invective in it, though we always kept some in the refrigerator for emergencies.

"Look here!" he exclaimed, standing off and scowling at me under his shaggy brows. "We ain't come here to argy the case or to play marbles. See? We come here from Governor Barker to demand satisfaction and get it." And he told me the names of himself and his companion, adding, "We 're his ex'lency's friends."

"Very well, gentlemen," I said. "What can I do for you to-day?"

"Give us satisfaction," he said curtly.

"All right; I will do it," I responded. "Take the article over to that desk by the window and pick out the errors of fact in it and then let Governor Barker point out those errors and sign it. We will print it to-morrow morning."

"Print be damned!" he angrily exclaimed. "You 've got to fight him or us. See? That 's the only satisfaction that 'll wipe out the insult. Aint that aisy to understand?"

"I don't care about fighting," I explained. "I hardly ever fight except in self-defense, and have n't had a fight in a month. I don't believe I want to accept a challenge. I never saw the Governor in my life, and have nothing whatever against him. I don't want to get hurt and don't want to kill him."

"If you refuse to fight, he 'll post you."

"How will he do that?"

"He 'll stick up posters and handbills all over the city calling you a coward and liar and poltroon — everything he can think of to insult you."

"How much will it cost?" I asked.

"Cost? It don't make no difference. It 'll be done — and done to the queen's taste! Don't you worry about the cost."

"It only occurred to me," I said, "that I could perhaps save you some expense, while making the posting much more effective."

"What do you mean?"

"Just this. I can do the posting cheaper and better than you can. For instance, I am willing to give Governor Barker half a column in the Post to-morrow morning and permit him to say in it anything he pleases about me. He can call me a coward, poltroon, or anything that he can think of that would relieve his mind. He must sign his name to it, and I will merely introduce it with the line, 'The Governor Airs His Grievances.'"

"What? You will let his ex'lency call you a coward in your own paper?"

"Why, certainly, if it will give him any comfort. I have great confidence in our readers."

"Holy Moses! And you would n't feel insulted?"

"Not at all. Why should I? The Governor is well known."

"What the divil!" exclaimed the hitherto silent man.

"You see, in the first place," I continued, "it would not cost the Governor a cent. It would give him an immense audience in which to express his opinions."

"What the divil kind of man is this?" repeated the taciturn one.

They put their heads together a moment at the window, then faced me again, saying, "This propisition of yours is new and damn curious. We must consult the Governor and we 'll see yese towards evening."

They sidled out, looking considerably embarrassed.

They did not see me towards evening.

At any rate, I did not see them. And I have not seen them yet.